Sustainability and University Life

Environmental Education, Communication and Sustainability

edited by Walter Leal Filho

Vol. 5

PETER LANG

Frankfurt am Main · Berlin · Bern · Bruxelles · New York · Wien

Walter Leal Filho (ed.)

Sustainability
and University Life

PETER LANG
Europäischer Verlag der Wissenschaften

Die Deutsche Bibliothek - CIP-Einheitsaufnahme

Sustainability and university life / Walter Leal Filho (ed.). -
Frankfurt am Main ; Berlin ; Bern ; Bruxelles ; New York ;
Wien : Lang, 1999
    (Environmental education, communication and
    sustainability ; Vol. 5)
    ISBN 3-631-35297-2

ISSN 1434-3819
ISBN 3-631-35297-2
US-ISBN 0-8204-4367-0

© Peter Lang GmbH
Europäischer Verlag der Wissenschaften
Frankfurt am Main 1999
All rights reserved.

Printed in Germany 1 2 3 4 6 7

Titles of chapters

Preface

Sustainability, acknowledged as one of today's most discussed issues, has many implications in many contexts, including in the routine of universities. It is widely accepted that the debate on the principles and theory of sustainability needs to be complemented by concrete examples and concrete initiatives, so as to illustrate how feasible it is. This book is an attempt to illustrate some ways whereby sustainability may be put into practice in universities.

Like its predecessors, namely "Implementing Sustainable Development at University Level" (1996) and "Environmental Conservation and Sustainablity at Universities" (1998), this book tries to contribute to the state-of-the-art debate on sustainability by going over and above the traditional theoretical discussions and focusing more on its practicalities. To this purpose, a wide range of perspectives from Europe and North America is presented, being complemented by case studies showing some of the initiatives on the ground. The aim here, is to place beyond any doubt that there are merits in pursuing sustainability at universities and that universities themselves have much to gain by integrating sustainability as part of their activities.

The elements of sustainability discussed here are manifold. They vary from institutional approaches in which goals set by some institutions are outlined, to specific measures undertaken by some universities in areas as varied as energy, waste management or transport. Components related to teaching, research and extension, the basic activities of any institution of higher education, are also found in this book. Very often, authors have referred to some historical landmarks such as the World Commission on Environment's report "Our Common Future", to the UN Conference on Environment and Development (UNCED) and to documents such as the Talloires Declaration and the Copernicus Charter. This trend should not be seen as a mere repetition, but as further evidence of the impact such documents have had on the process of evolution of sustainability in various countries and in various geographical regions today. Modern sustainability owes much to the process set in motion at Talloires and at Rio, to the point that the understanding of today's trends needs to be substantiated by information on what has happened in the past.

In preparing this book, thanks are due to the various authors -among whom some Senior colleagues and some bright students from European, North American and African universities- for their time and efforts in documenting their experiences and views. We are particularly pleased to have been able to reflect the views of people involved with university administration, teaching and research and to have successfully gathered the views of some students, a vital group in any university, but a group to which relatively little attention is usually paid. There is by now a wide degree of consensus in relation to the fact that students' involvement in efforts towards sustainability is vital if long-term results are to be expected. It is thus encouraging to see that, parallel to attempts to promote sustainability on an institutional level, teaching and research programs are increasingly taking it on board.

Thanks are also due to the Association of University Leaders for a Sustainable Future (ULSF) for the support provided to the production of this book and to Olaf Gramkow, a tireless assistant, without whose help this project could not have been brought to fruition. I hope this book will inspire more and more universities to take advantage of the benefits the various approaches to sustainability may bring to their institutional lives.

Walter Leal Filho, Ph.D., DSc
Hamburg, Summer 1999

Introduction

Richard M. Clugston, Ph.D.
Executive Director, University Leaders for a Sustainable Future

Institutions of higher education serve three missions: teaching, research and service. In addition, each campus functions as a formative community. Students develop as persons in an academic "village" that expresses its values not just in its lecture halls and laboratories, but in its architecture, sports programs, public relations and full range of student activities. Colleges and universities are vested by society with the task of discerning truth, imparting values, and socializing students to contribute to social progress and the advancement of knowledge. They have a major responsibility to impart the moral vision and technical knowledge needed to ensure a high quality of life for future generations.

Yet, as educator David Orr points out, universities often emphasize "... theories, not values, abstractions rather than consciousness, neat answers instead of questions, and technical efficiency over conscience" (Orr, 1994). Many academic disciplines as well as institutions are struggling with the limits of their current paradigms in responding to the environmental challenge. They are recognizing that the basic assumptions that organize academic disciplines are fundamentally flawed and that many practices exacerbate the problems that need to be solved. For example, in reflecting on the changes that need to take place in management theory, Thomas Gladwin, in the October 1998 issue of The Academy of Management Journal, asserts:

> Organizational science has evolved within a constricted or fractured epistemology, such that it embraces only a portion of reality. The organic, biotic and intersubjective moral bases of organizational existence, we submit, have been neglected or repressed in the greater portion of modern management theory. This has resulted in theory which is at best limited, and at worst pathological. By disassociating human organization from the biosphere and the full human community, it is possible that our theories have tacitly encouraged organizations to behave in ways that ultimately destroy their natural and social life support systems.

> The task ahead for management theorists is one of reintegration. Will management scholars reconceive their domain as one of organization-in-full community, both social and ecological? (Gladwin, 1998)

Perhaps in the past, higher education itself contributed unwittingly to the exploitation of the Earth through the development of technology for technology's sake, with too little consideration of its implications for the human and natural environments. However, educators increasingly recognize the need to provide a foundation that engenders an understanding of sustainability, not just the technical skills and credentials necessary for career development.

Steve Breyman introduces the case of campus greening at Rensselaer Polytechnic Institute by observing that it is difficult to build a sustainable university in an unsustainable economy. Yet, he observes, "individual sustainable institutions...are most important as signals to society that alternatives to waste and excess, to myopia and disregard for the future are not only desirable and urgently necessary, but possible" (see chapter 5).

The chapters in this book provide many perspectives on the nature of sustainability in higher education. Many are instances of "picking the low hanging fruit," i.e. institutions which increase cost savings through ecoefficiency or respond to student demand by assembling an environmental program from existing courses. But some colleges and universities seek to dramatically overhaul their institutions to fully embody sustainability in their research, teaching, operations and outreach to the community.

What is Sustainability?
For nearly thirty years, academics, policy-makers and civil society organizations have wrestled with the nature of sustainability and its implications for the economy and education. Efforts to develop a set of principles for ecological security began at the United Nations Stockholm Conference on the Human Environment in 1972. Since then, many groups and coalitions have made valuable contributions to the articulation of principles and values that define sustainable development. In 1987, The Brundtland Commission called for a new charter "to consolidate and extend relevant legal principles to guide State behavior in the transition to sustainable development" (World Commission on Environment and Development, 1987).

The Earth Charter, begun in 1989, attempted to synthesize the emerging consensus on the key dimensions of sustainability. It was to have framed the ethical foundation for Agenda 21 and other outcomes of the Earth Summit, held in Rio de Janeiro in 1992. During the two years prior to the Earth Summit, NGOs and government delegations from around the world worked on various drafts of the Charter. However, governments did not achieve any agreement on principles for an Earth Charter and instead adopted the Rio Declaration on Environment and Development (Rockefeller, 1997).

After the Earth Summit, two international NGOs, the Earth Council and Green Cross International, with the support of the Dutch Government and the United Nations Economic, Social and Cultural Organization (UNESCO), joined forces with others to continue the development of an Earth Charter. In early 1997, the Earth Charter Commission, composed of 23 distinguished individuals from every continent, was formed to oversee the drafting and consultation process. This Commission has released a "Benchmark Earth Charter Draft II" in April of 1999. The Earth Charter contains a preamble, sixteen major principles, forty-seven subprinciples and a conclusion (Earth Council, 1999). Five central themes are emphasized in this landmark document:

1. The Earth Charter recognizes that existence is a living community of diverse subjects who deserve our respect and care. The preamble and the principles of the Earth Charter affirm a

sensibility about existence that includes an appreciation of the beauty, integrity, and interconnectedness of natural systems and the recognition of the intrinsic value of nature. The Earth Charter reflects a shift in our basic understanding of reality away from the anthropocentrism and mechanistic reductionism that has dominated the modern age to an appreciation of the life and feeling that flows through all things.

2. Diversity is lifted up as a central value. Protecting the diversity of life forms, cultures and languages, as well as rights and opportunities for each individual, is fundamental. When we lose these different expressions of life, we lose sources of essential knowledge, wisdom, and technologies. We also lose the richness of our souls, for at some deep level our ecological and ethical selves require the enhancement of diversity against both the violence of exploitation and the efficiency of monoculture.

3. The Earth Charter demands the creation of open, participatory processes that empower people to contribute at all levels of decision-making. Despite the fact that many societies are filled with coercive violence and restrictions of basic freedoms, a global ethical consensus is emerging on human rights in general, with particular emphasis on the needs and rights of women and indigenous peoples. Also, nonhuman nature deserves more standing. The criteria and processes of decision-making must be transparent with individuals having real influence over decisions affecting their lives.

4. It recognizes that humans must accept a world of material limits. This new world view demands that we humans accept a set of restraints on our exploitation of the natural world, based on respect for the integrity of the life community, as well as healthy skepticism about human ability to control and manage extraordinary complex natural systems benignly. We must live within a frame of ecological laws—exercising caution and preventing harm. Human humility is essential.

5. The principles of the Earth Charter demand a "new bottom line." The U.N.-sponsored conferences have made significant progress in recognizing the interconnections among problems of population, consumption, and environment. But the world is not yet on a path toward just and sustainable development. Governments still gauge the success of development mainly by the amount of economic growth and profit it produces. Godfrey Gunatilleke of Sri Lanka's Centre for Development Studies laments, "In development strategies it is always the pursuit of material well-being, the socioeconomic component of development, which has primacy. Underlying this bias are the Western ideologies of social change and the cognitive systems which grew out of the industrial revolution, enthroning the economist view of society and human existence" (Clugston, 1995). The dominant economic indicators of "successful" development fail to distinguish between constructive and destructive activities. The new bottom line must be able to discern the difference between healthy and cancerous growth in the economic and social order, valuing both natural and social "capital."

The Earth Charter articulates general commitments to sustainability. Statements such as the Talloires Declaration of University Leaders for a Sustainable Future and the CRE Copernicus University Charter for Sustainable Development (see chapter 2) spell out in more specific ways those commitments colleges and universities must make to be on the path to sustainability. Alan

Atkisson provides a useful concluding definition on sustainability in "The Compass of Sustainability: Framework for a Comprehensive Information System:"

> "Sustainability is an ideal end-state. Like democracy, it is a lofty goal whose perfect realization eludes us. For this reason, there will always be competing definitions of sustainability. We know these definitions will always include the well being of people, nature, our economy, and our social institutions, working together effectively over the long term. But as the process of attempting to achieve sustainability will continuously reveal new challenges and questions—pushing back the horizon, as it were—a definitive definition is an impossibility. Any indicator framework, therefore, needs to be flexible and adaptable to these changing definitions. It needs to grow as our understanding grows, while continuing to serve its purpose as a simplifier and guide to complexity. It needs to maintain a trail of continuity from year to year and decade to decade. Most important, it needs to speak to people in ways understandable both to the rational mind, and to the intuition" (Atkisson, 1998).

Critical Next Steps to Promote Sustainability Through Higher Education

As Walter Leal Filho points out in chapter one, institutions in different countries approach sustainability in different ways. Some emphasize technical greening of operations. Some are more philosophical in orientation, debating the meaning of sustainability and, at times, redesigning curricula. While sustainability varies widely from institution to institution, there are some foundational commitments that must be achieved for an institution to be on the path to sustainability. These include:

1. The written statements of the mission and purpose of the academic institution and its various units express an explicit commitment to sustainability.
2. The college or university appropriately incorporates the concepts of sustainability into all academic disciplines, including liberal arts and professional education requirements.
3. Students learn about the values and practices of the institution by reflecting on the school's role in its social and ecological systems.
4. Knowledge of sustainability is a critical concern in the hiring, tenure and promotion of faculty members and is a central concern of faculty development.
5. The institution seeks to reduce its "ecological footprint" through sustainable practices and policies (e.g. CO_2 reduction practices, sustainable building construction, local food purchasing program, etc.).
6. Student support services and the structure of campus life emphasize sustainability (e.g. green committees, audits and celebrations are visibly present).
7. The institution is engaged in outreach and forming partnerships locally and globally to enhance sustainability (See chapter 2).

While there are many hopeful signs that some academic disciplines and institutions are responding to the environmental challenge, a commitment to sustainability - in academic programs, operations and outreach - is not present in most academic settings. Certain initiatives will help accelerate the transition to sustainability through higher education. In the present climate, we believe these are the critical leverage points for greening colleges and universities. Unless we, and many others, move forward on these fronts, higher education will change too little and too late. Major priorities include:

1. Develop sustainability indicators for higher education. Many academic institutions have focused on greening their campus operations. A few have positioned themselves as the leading "sustainable universities." Yet, when a critical champion leaves, when major external funding dries up, or when staff seek to move from rhetoric to reality, these initiatives often reveal their lack of real support in the institution. The Association of University Leaders for a Sustainable Future is developing a sustainability assessment questionnaire that identifies the critical dimensions of sustainability in higher education and assists university faculty members, administrators and others in assessing where their institution is on the path toward sustainability (University Leaders for a Sustainable Future, 1999).

2. Conduct in-depth research and evaluation of sustainability in higher education. We have reached the state where there are many sustainability initiatives under way. However, the information we have on these is mostly anecdotal; we do not really know how well these initiatives are working, or what makes them work. Therefore, we need:

- To develop a clear analytic framework on what sustainability in higher education is (based, for example, on the questionnaire described above).
- To develop comprehensive case studies on the range of sustainability initiatives in higher education (both in the disciplines and professions and in various institutions). These would be both cross-sectional—looking at all the functions of an institution—as well as longitudinal, and would describe: a) the scope of initiatives in curriculum, operations, outreach; and b) the unfolding of the initiatives over time (e.g. how they originate, who was (is) involved, what actually was institutionalized, and which efforts came to naught).
- To analyze and assess the extent to which these cases are implementing the various dimensions of sustainability.
- To analyze cases for critical conditions that determine the success or failure of initiatives and their various aspects. Various factors (e.g. the competence of sustainability advocates, the mission of the institution) determine if sustainability initiatives will succeed (see chapter 2).
- To develop a formative evaluation system that can assist institutions and disciplines in moving down the path toward sustainability.

3. Identify and support lead institutions. These are institutions of higher education (colleges, universities, seminaries, schools of theology) in which a "critical mass" of stakeholders (faculty, administrators, staff, students, community, trustees) take the "environmental challenge" seriously and are changing academic programs and institutional operations to foster a humane and sustainable future. David Orr suggests that lead institutions would:

- Set standards for ecological literacy for students, faculty, trustees, etc.;
- Power campus by current sunlight plus efficiency;
- Eliminate waste in all forms: they would be zero discharge campuses;
- Adopt green standards for architecture and landscaping;

- Conduct research to support sustainable livelihoods, sustainable communities and ecological economics; and
- Link research and service to wider community efforts to establish just and sustainable cities, bioregions and global economies (Clugston, 1998).

Increase demand for sustainability in higher education from key opinion leaders, employers and funding sources. As Anthony Cortese observes:

> "Higher education is not likely to change in its direction far enough or fast enough without strong outside influence. Strong, rapid and largely unprecedented efforts by all of higher education's stakeholders are necessary to motivate the system on a path to sustainability. Students, parents, prospective employers, organizations funding research and education (government, industry and foundations) and the public are all consumers of higher education's services. If we are to encourage the educational system to produce the environmentally aware professionals and specialists needed to lead us on a sustainable path, the stakeholders must work with the higher education system in creative ways to encourage environmental education and research ".

5. Establish regional centers for faculty development to accelerate this transition. Those locations that embody sustainability most fully can provide education, demonstration and research services to higher education. The functions of these regional centers could be to provide models of ecologically sound living, emphasizing renewable energy, sustainable agriculture and forestry, and sustainable community analysis and work; research on ecological design and on learning experience; sabbatical leave opportunities; integration of learning, living and operation; and training grounds for university change specialists.

6. Develop new modes of collaboration and information sharing. In the United States, the major organizations promoting sustainability through higher education have formed an organizational alliance to better coordinate initiatives. A Higher Education Network for Sustainability and the Environment has recently been launched, providing a broad organizational base to pursue these six objectives (HENSE, 1999).

The South Carolina Sustainable Universities Initiative represents an intellectual community committed to the advancement of theoretical and practical knowledge, as well as a collection of physical operations rivaling small towns in size and scope of impact on the environment. Recognizing their role as a positive force in the state's economic and social advancement, those participating in the initiative believe it is incumbent upon them to cooperate in leading the way toward a more sustainable future through teaching, research, community service and facilities management (Sustainable Universities Initiative, 1998). It states:

(...) "We therefore singly and collectively commit to:

1) Fostering in our students, faculty and staff an understanding of the relationships among the natural and man-made environment, economics and society as a whole.

2) Encouraging students, faculty and staff to accept individual and collective responsibility for the environment in which they live and work.
3) Serving as a center of information exchange for other institutions within the state.
4) Operating existing facilities and constructing new facilities to maximize efficiency and minimize waste, thereby protecting the environment and conserving resources."

(Sustainable Universities Initiative, 1998)

The statement above by the presidents of Clemson University, Medical University of South Carolina and University of South Carolina points to the type of commitment needed by the major academic institutions of one U.S. state to change course toward a sustainable future. This book provides a wealth of case studies and analytical frameworks to assist colleges and universities in making this change. The dissemination of information through publications such as this will help ensure a more rapid transformation to a sustainable world.

References

Atkisson, A. (1998)   *The Compass of Sustainability: Framework for a Comprehensive Information System*. Version 1.0.

Clugston, R. (1998)   A Strategy to Accelerate the Shift to Sustainability through Higher Education. In *The Declaration* 2 (2), pp. 1-3.

Clugston, R. (1995) Money, Ecology and Spirituality: Toward a Holistic Framework for Social Development. In *Earth Ethics* 6 (3), pp. 4.

Earth Council, The (1999) Introduction to the Earth Charter Initiative and Benchmark. Draft II.

Gladwin, T. (1995) *The Academy of Management Journal*, October.

Higher Education Network for Sustainability and the Environment (HENSE) (1999)   (draft paper).

Orr, D. (1994)   *Earth in Mind: on Education, Environment, and the Human Prospect*. Washington, DC: Island Press, p. 8.

Rockefeller, S. (1997) The Earth Charter Process. In *Earth Ethics* 8 (2 & 3), pp. 3-8.

Sustainable Universities Initiatives. (1998) Statement of College Presidents. (unpublished paper).

University Leaders for a Sustainable Future. (1999) Sustainability Assessment Questionnaire. (questionnaire).

World Commission on Environment and Development. (1987) *Our Common Future*. Oxford, NY: Oxford University Press.

Chapter 1

Sustainability and University Life: some European Perspectives

Walter Leal Filho

Abstract

This chapter outlines some developments related to sustainability and describes some of the trends seen in relation to sustainable development at European universities. It also outlines some of the misconceptions related to the topic "sustainability" seen among many institutions of higher education, and the role of institutional policies as tools towards facilitating the implementation of sustainability in a given institution.

Introduction

The goal of sustainable development, as proposed by the Brundtland Commission (WCED 1987) and operationalized in the action plan "Agenda 21" (UNCED, 1992) agreed at the UN Conference on Environment and Development (UNCED), has proven more difficult to realise than earlier expected. The integration of political, economic and social considerations (PESC) into the environmental decision-making process is now seen as a challenge far more complex than one would normally expect. In pursuing sustainability, therefore, it is important that key words such as policy-making, coordination, networking and evaluation are incorporated as part of the PESC discourse.

This line of thinking also applies to initiatives aimed at promoting sustainability at university level. Similarly to what is seen at the macro (i.e. country) level, pursuing the goal of sustainable development is also a complex task at the micro (i.e. local) level. There are no exceptions to this, and the context seen at universities and other institutions of higher education supports the view that PESC needs to be enhanced by the above listed keywords, which need themselves to be translated into practice.

In a continent so vast and diverse as Europe, the task of overseeing and monitoring sustainable development initiatives at universities is a complex one. One of the reasons for this is the different levels of emphasis given to sustainability and the varied attention given to aspects related to it.

As seen in Table 1, the emphasis on sustainability varies significantly among countries, where some conspicuous focal areas may be identified.

Country	Emphasis
Sweden	institutional (all-house) approaches
Germany	technical „environmental conservation"
UK	curricular matters (curriculum greening)
Spain, Italy	specific matters (e.g. recycling, transport)
France	philosophical (e.g. what should be done)

Table 1: Different levels of emphasis given to sustainability among universities in some European countries

Although there are, no doubt, organisations within the above countries also looking at other issues, Table 1 offers a rough profile of the state of affairs today. Roughly speaking, the emphasis given to sustainability by European universities in various countries looks like this:

* *technical emphasis*: refers to those institutions which look at technical issues, such as mechanisms to reduce energy use or improve the efficiency of heaters; this is predominantly the case in Germany, it is seen to some extent in the Netherlands and Austria and, thanks to the success of some pilot projects, is likely to be favoured by universities seeking quick results.

* *curricular emphasis*: here, institutions tend to look at the issue of sustainability via curricular provisions and staff training; often seen in the UK and observed in many universities across Scandinavia.

* *strategic emphasis*: exemplified by institutions which deal with sustainability via holistic approaches (i.e. as an all-inclusive concept); especially favoured in Sweden and adopted by some universities in Germany and the Netherlands.

* *specific emphasis*: those institutions which tackle the matter from specific angles, such as via litter reduction or energy-saving programs; widely disseminated in Spain and Italy. Here, the emphasis is often given to the involvement of students and staff alike.

* *philosophical emphasis*: refers to the approach used by some institutions which often discuss the problematic of sustainability and its merits under a philosophical perspective. This is sometimes followed by concrete projects, but this is by no means always the case. Philosophical discussions are seen in many French universities as well as in universities in emerging countries such as Poland and Hungary, which are now looking at the issue of sustainability more closely.

Due to the fact that universities tend to follow a certain pattern of behavior in relation to sustainability and since such a pattern may suddenly change for political or administrative reasons, it is difficult to establish a system of values as to whether one of the above approaches is better or more efficient than another or, indeed, better than the rest. This is, in any case, not the point. The fact that universities in a given country are inclined to follow a certain path, is closely related to the local circumstances and the local context. The main point here is to acknowledge that such patterns of behavior do exist and they need to be identified before any further action may be taken. Let us see some further examples of what universities are doing to pursue the goal of sustainability, taken from "Implementing Sustainable Development at University Level" (Leal Filho, MacDermott and Padgham 1996):

University of Uppsala (Sweden): via the Baltic University Programme (BUP), Uppsala has created one of Europe's largest networks of universities, whose main concern is the environment and the environmental, social and economic issues in the Baltic region. BUP offers a good example of what can be achieved via networking.

University Autonoma of Barcelona (Spain): the nomination of a Vice-Rector with responsibility for environmental and sustainable development issues was seen as an innovative approach in the early 1990s, which has proven successful. The message here, is that having someone at the senior level helps to get things moving.

University of Hertfordshire (UK): the execution of a specific staff training program on the environment was seen as a generator of further interest and concern for environmental matters. Nowadays, an office oversees the university's environmental programmes and tries to link up the various initiatives happening in this field via an environnment coordinator.

University of Utrecht (Netherlands): thanks to the personal commitment of the Rector, Utrecht University has shown how much can be reached by the integration of a well-elaborated sustainability initiative and its spin-offs in different parts of the university.

A further example that might be added comes from the University of Lüneburg (Germany), where the creation of a Senate Commission on Agenda 21 and Sustainability, has ensured that the issue has the full attention of the administration. Such an approach also means that the successes of the Commission's work will find broad dissemination at the University.

These case studies, complemented by various others seen throughout this book, show what can be achieved. The successes should, nonetheless, be seen on their own merits since trends and contexts do differ. Although there is a certain degree of preparedness among universities in Sweden - for example- to adopt whole approaches to sustainability, which go as far as to include the appointment of staff in charge of overseeing such work, other universities in other countries may not yet be ready to go all the way. As a result, they favour a certain approach, i.e. the focus on an initiative such as a waste reduction project, as a way to keep the ball rolling and to, later on, attempt other, more complex and demanding tasks. It should not be forgotten that, within any university, administrators always try to make decisions based on consensus and until a consensus is reached (in this case, that sustainable development-related initiatives are worth pursuing), such initiatives are not likely to be implemented, nor will resources be allocated to them.

A further example of what can be done if the will is strong enough, can be taken from Britain. A report commissioned by the universities´ funding body, the Higher Education Funding Council for England (HEFCE) in partnership with the Committee of Vice-Chancellors and Principals (CVCP) and the Standing Conference of Principals (SCOP), shows the results of pilot reviews at six higher education institutions. Performed at the Falmouth College of Arts, Surrey Institute of Arts and Design, University of Bath, University of Cambridge, University of Sunderland and University of Essex, the "Environmental Report" (HEFCE 1998) provides evidence that universities and colleges can indeed "green" themselves and even save money by conducting environmental reviews which can benefit an institution by:

• reducing waste
• reducing the risk of penalties for breaches of regulations
• involving staff and students
• dealing with practical issues such as waste, emissions, traffic and transport
• improving the external perceptions of the organization

The rationale of the whole scheme is that carrying out reviews may enable institutions to develop an environment policy, identify an action plan and implement it.

Some misconceptions related to sustainability and university life

Even though the goal of sustainability at universities is generally accepted as being worthy of pursuing, there are still some people who doubt whether it should be pursued at all. During a national conference on environmental conservation and sustainable development at universities, for example, held at the University of Lüneburg, Germany in February 1997, a sceptical participant asked: "So if the introduction of the so-called sustainable development perspective at universities is such a positive thing, why is it then, that not all universities follow it on?"

The answer then, and indeed now, is amazingly simple: because there are so many misconceptions of what the process of sustainable development is, and what sustainability represents to an institution. Such misconceptions are usually translated into a negative view, which in its turn usually reflects on an institution´s lack of willingness to join in efforts towards making their activities more environmentally-friendly and their business more sustainable. Some of the most frequently seen misconceptions, documented by Leal Filho (1999) in the book "The Concept of Sustainability in Higher Education" (Bor, Hole, Wals 1999) are:

i. *sustainability is too abstract*: partly because of the scope of the theme and partly because of lack of information (how many heads of universities are able to define sustainability correctly?), there are people who see the theme as too abstract and as too distant from reality. The truth is, that if carefully looked at and properly inferred to, in the activities of higher education institutions such as teaching, research, extension or even purchasing and electricity use, sustainability is very close to their lives.

ii. *sustainability is too broad*: second to "abstract", the adjective "broad" is also often used, as an argument against the undertaking of sustainable measures. Once again, a mistake is being made, since the fact that you can apply the principles of sustainable development to different parts of university life means that a lot of room for maneuvre exists. Those who name sustainability as too broad are usually those who would also consider it "too narrow" if only one area of action were chosen.

iii. *we have no personnel to look after it*: such a misconception is based on the fact that, traditionally, a job at a university (e.g. tutoring, counselling) is performed by someone formally qualified. This is especially the case in countries which attach a great value to formal education, such as Germany, where practical and operational skills (also greatly valued elsewhere) usually come second place. The reality is that anyone familiar with the principles and practices of sustainable development and sensitive to the impact university activities have on the environment, is in a position to do a good job in this area. It is often a question of having someone sufficiently motivated to do the job and to undertake the necessary consultations and liaisons needed to do it effectively.

iv. *the resources needed do not justify the trouble*: again, a misconception not based on facts. Although financial considerations do not always come at the top of the list of what higher education institutions expect from the application of the principles of sustainability to their work -and some of us believe that this is rightly so- they do play an important role. As exemplified by the pilot project "50-50" now widely spread in Germany, savings in areas such as energy consumption can be translated into immediate financial benefits, which institutions can then use to purchase goods or services, or re-invest in infra-structure.

v. *the theme has no scientific basis*: this is seldom but -unfortunately- still mentioned by those ill-informed. The view that sustainable development is a fashion which derived from the UN Conference on Environment and Development in Rio de Janeiro in 1992, has hopefully by now been changed, but there are still people who refer to it as a temporary field. Wrong. The fact that sustainable development is an area officially listed in scientific programs across Europe such as the EU's 5th Framework Programme, means that the contestation of its scientific basis is futile. As a result, institutions of higher education may not only run pilot projects and programs, but also include various aspects of sustainability as part of their research and teaching agenda.

An underlying feature of the examples of misconceptions here listed, to which many more could be added, is that no matter which misconception (or sets of misconceptions) an institution has, these are invariably translated into a lack of willingness to act.

There would thus seem to be a substantial need for information, education and awareness-raising initiatives at the top level, so as to persuade university administrators that the whole thing makes sense. Such a difficult job is usually left to one or two enthusiastic members of staff, who often try to persuade sceptical colleagues and sceptical administrators by inviting outside speakers to come and talk about their experiences and about what their universities have achieved. Another commonly used venue for changing the attitudes of reluctant administrators is by attending events with them, where speakers describe their successes. Although this is not always easy to achieve, having a university Rector or Vice-Rector for a day or so in a meeting, means that the necessary persuasive work can take place without distractions and that, upon returning to their routine work, there will be one more voice to speak for such important work.

Ironically, one of the main arguments for sustainable development approaches at universities is not environmental, but financial. Show the administration of any higher education institution that the change of certain patters of behavior or consumption can lead to financial benefits, in addition to environmental ones, and you are more likely to be taken seriously. For many organisations, especially at a time of shrinking budgets, financial arguments speak louder than any other line of discourse and, in some cases, this can and should, with a little bit of creativity, be done.

Sustainability in European universities: quo vadis?

The previous sections of this chapter have provided a rough view of current patterns in Europe today. But perhaps more interesting than seeing what is going on today, is to check what is likely to happen in the future. The past gives reasons for cautious hope. An analysis of the previous works aimed at pursuing sustainable development at universities in Europe inevitably leads to the **Copernicus** programme. Initiated by the Association of European Universities (CRE) in 1994, **Copernicus** was a concrete and successful attempt to deal with the situation by networking universities and supporting a wide range of initiatives, varying from training programs to the production of publications dealing with various environmental issues.

Unfortunately, the scheme has suffered some setbacks over the past three years, especially with respect to its funding and administration, but it is progressively getting back on track. It is hoped that it will recover its previous ability to undertake projects, mobilise personnel and play a meaningful coordinating role in fostering the cause of sustainability at university level in Europe today. In particular, there are hopes that the programme will be re-structured in a way that its international nature and interdisciplinary focus may be re-established.

More recently, in September 1998, a UNESCO Conference on Higher Education was held in Paris. The meeting outlined the need to enhance sustainability programs at universities and the need to disseminate such initiatives more widely, so as to motivate more universities to act.

But despite the progress outlined above, there is a need to –in the future- address the lack of coordination at the European level and a need to change the misconceptions earlier referred to. Moreover, there are three further problems preventing the wider dissemination of sustainable initiatives at European universities and which deserve attention in the future:

i. the first is that most staff, at a disappointingly high number of universities, see sustainability as an abstract issue, not connected to reality. Also, administrators at many universities feel that they can get away with doing nothing in this area -which they in fact do- so why bother to have extra work and engage yet again in more challenging initiatives? Although meant to be ironic, these comments are as close to the truth as they can be. Whoever has tried, from the bottom, to set initiatives related to sustainability in motion, will have met some degree of resistance, if not active discouragement. Such a perspective is reflected in the lack of financial provisions for activities in this field, which helps to consolidate the problem even more.

ii. a second problem seen is that many European universities see the undertaking of concrete steps towards sustainability as matters which are "complicated", "too costly" or "irrelevant"; often, a combination of all these arguments. The lack of familiarity with the theme and its scope have the unusual effect of driving many people away from it. The number of institutions whose staff have given careful consideration to sustainability - and what it may mean to them - is very limited.

iii. the third problem is that most of the good initiatives which are happening on the ground, are not sufficiently documented. This is a shame since documentation of initiatives may not only assist staff at any given institution to compare progress made over the years, but also help to show others how effective such initiatives have indeed been. Examples of "good practice" have an enormous persuasive value. Unfortunately, documentation of experiences in individual European countries and in Europe as a whole is not widely practised. The publication "Implementing Sustainable Development at University Level" (Leal Filho, McDermott and Padgham, 1996), which is one of the few attempts to document and disseminate such experiences, has not been followed up by more recent works. An exception is the book "Environmental Conservation and Sustainability at Universities", written in German (Leal Filho 1998), which looks at the situation at German universities and resulted from one of the few seminars held in Germany on the topic.

So how can European universities move on? Can the listed problems ever be overcome, and if so, how? Three action points may guide further action in the future.

Point 1. More integration

Since the setbacks involving the **Copernicus** program, there have been no European-wide mechanisms which may enable universities to integrate their work or to offer mutual support in a systematic way. Since more integration and more coordination are helpful in moving things forward, it would be desirable to set in motion mechanisms for the further development of these areas. The key question is: who would assume such a role? In order to succeed, attempts to foster more integration in this area would require:

- the input from a well-established institution prepared to take on the challenge;
- the involvement of a personality well-known and respected in this sector to oversee the work;
- the institutional ability to work in at least three languages;
- the provision of the basic secretarial and logistical resources needed to perform the various tasks.

In addition, the relevant organisation willing to take on the coordination/integration job would need to be willing to make a long-term commitment to the demanding tasks a coordinating role entails.

Point 2. Improved communication and networking

Closely related to point 1, point 2 refers to the well-documented advantages of improved communication and networking. Fortunately, there are some electronic lists which mediate information exchange and facilitate networking, such as the "The Greening of Campus" list based at Lund University in Sweden (address: greencampus@lu-imi.envecon.lu.se), with around 300 members from Europe and the United States. More such communication mechanisms are needed, and interested colleagues should always note that, in addition to the need to nourish their own information needs via networks, information exchange needs to be a two-way process if it is to succeed. Most list owners feel frustrated to see that the majority of their members are silent listeners who are happy to be informed but not always willing to take an active part in the communication process itself. As a matter of fairness, all of us concerned with information exchange need to ensure that we too are truly involved.

Point 3. Increased financial support

Attempts to promote sustainability at universities should be awarded as much support as other areas of university life, such as teaching and research. In this context, it is important that budget lines are allocated to such works. A good example is seen in Hamburg, Germany, where the City-State´s six institutions of higher education (Universities and Fachhochschulen) can apply for funds allocated via a "green budget line". With resources of around DM 5 million over five years (1998-2002), the universities in Hamburg know that they can count on a source of funding for their work in this otherwise financially fragile sector. Institutions interested in acquiring funds for sustainability-related projects may do so by means of the submission of their projects, with no complicated forms. Proposals are reviewed via a panel of independent experts and, if accepted, funds are then passed on to the recipient university for perusal.

An interesting feature of the Hamburg example is that the Presidents (Rectors) of the universities have to countersign the applications, so as to ensure that they are fully behind the proposed projects. This good example ought to be repeated in other European regions.

Some readers may be wondering why such a list of points is so short. After all, three points of action may not be so difficult to follow, one might say. The answer to this is simple: since the nature of the problems is well-known and since these barriers have been consistently referred to as the greatest ones, it would seem sensible to focus attention on them as a means of enabling long-term results to be seen. There are certainly many other points that might be added and which might contribute to the cause of developing sustainability at European universities further, but this cause will be better served by addressing the most basic problems first.

Towards sustainability policies?

Based on the difficulties inherent in the implementation of European-wide sustainablity programs, one tends to wonder whether a "micro" approach, i.e. the focus on the institutional level, may be used as a complement to broader, international initiatives. Surely, European-wide initiatives need to be backed up by similar ones at the regional and local level. In this context, institutional policies on sustainability may provide an important help, and this section will devote some attention to the elements that need consideration in institutional, policy-oriented approaches to sustainability.

At the outset, some critical guiding questions in the preparation of sustainability policies at universities need to be asked. Some of these are:

i.   what purpose can a policy serve?
ii.   what can a policy achieve, which may not be achieved through present arrangements or structures?
iii.   which institutions/ agencies should coordinate a policy and which ones should participate in the preparation process?
iv.   which items, themes or measures should a policy entail?
v.   how will a policy be implemented and under what conditions?
vi.   what is the most adequate time-table for policy implementation?
vii.   how will funding be provided?

The answer to the above questions, especially the last one, is important, for the decision to go ahead with the preparation of a sustainability policy should not be based on the assumption that it is an easy job that can be completed from a desk. Studies by MacDermott (1995) on environmental education policies in Europe, have shown that such documents need to be handled with great care if they are to be authoritative. The amount of time, effort and negotiations involved should therefore not be underestimated, for, if not duly taken into account, the final document (i.e. the policy) which needs to be authoritative and involving, will become another worthless piece of paper whose likelihood of being successfully implemented becomes compromised.

A combination of commitment, wide support, discipline and effective management are pre-conditions for their success. Also, as shown in other areas (Elliot 1992, Johnson 1991, Nash 1991, Norton 1994 and Partidge 1981), a sense of ethics and responsibility towards future generations is equally important.

In a report outlining environmental education policies in Europe (Leal Filho 1997), it was seen that such documents need to pay due attention to the wide range of themes that integrate the universe of sustainability and which will inevitably influence their implementation, such as staff training, availability of resources, advice and institutional support, among many others.

Despite their complexity, university-wide sustainability policies have the advantage of potentially facilitating the coordination of the ways sustainability measures are implemented through the so-called "policy impact" (Lazin, Aroni and Gradua 1988) and may help to deal with the problem of communication (Hollingsworth 1988), one of the major factors behind failures. In addition, a policy may provide in some cases some badly needed guidance in relation to the priority areas and the outline of areas where action is needed at the institutional level. Moreover, sustainability policies, at least in principle, may facilitate a dialogue between all of those who have a stake in the area (e.g. funding agencies, staff, students, professors, suppliers) since no single individual can take on the job of performing such comprehensive work on his/her own.

But perhaps one of the main benefits to be gained from the preparation of a university-wide sustainability policy is the *preparation process* itself. In the universities which have followed such a path, the preparation of policies involved an intensive dialogue with the stakeholders and has enabled a profile of the situation in each institution to be built. Not only that, the process of preparation, which involves so many actors, will no doubt establish constructive dialogues which may have led to an increased understanding of the nature of the work performed by the various people, and this can only be good news.

The fact that so many people may be invited to take part and influence the preparation of the policy document may also indicate that the final text will have found a broader ownership, as opposed to being a document 'imposed' on people, as is sometimes the case. This is why such policies are difficult to prepare, but this is, at the same time, the reason why well-prepared policies survive the usual storms and small crises seen at universities: their sound basis is a guarantee of stability.

```
1. Political support

    2. Economical basis

        3. Participation

            4. Commitment

                5. Coordination

                    6. Networking

                        7. Debate

                            8. Monitoring

                                9. Evaluation

                                    10. The sustainability
                                        component itself

                                        11. Other requesits
```

Figure 1: Factors that integrate the preparation of sustainability policies*
(*) Modified from Leal Filho 1997

An aspect which nonetheless needs attention in planning an institutional policy on sustainability, is the tendency to 'centralise' the tasks of implementing it to a single person within the university or to a couple of people. In such cases, wide, grass-root based support becomes difficult, since many people may feel reluctant to be part of a process which they see as not fully open and transparent.

But perhaps the strongest argument used by universities against the implementation of institutional policies on sustainability is the fact that some Rectors, Presidents or Vice-Chancellors may see it as a 'declaration of commitment' and shy away from subscribing to it. This sometimes happens on the basis of the reluctance that can be caused by stating that a university is committed to do 'this and that', when in fact there is no readiness to perform the work envisaged. In such cases, however, the gap between 'intention' and 'action' is wide and the whole work may lose its purpose.

Having given due consideration to the "pros" and "cons" of policies, one will hopefully reach the conclusion that it is worth the trouble.

An institutional policy can, in most cases, be a useful tool towards systematising the implementation of sustainable development at a university and in providing guidance in relation to what a institution can realistically achieve. They can, therefore, be helpful tools in moving forward the cause of sustainability in a university and concretely contribute towards a broader sense of environmental awareness among its students and staff alike.

Conclusions

This chapter has attempted to provide an overview of trends related to sustainability and university life in Europe today, with some examples illustrating the extent to which action is happening where it matters most: on the ground. There are many problems which prevent progress or which slow it down, but these may be overcome provided care is taken and provided goodwill is there. The many examples showing what universities can achieve, no matter how big or how small they are, indicate that the integration of sustainable approaches to university programmes is indeed possible. A list of key points to help to break down the inertia seen at European level, is provided as an indication of what needs to be done. For those organisations seriously considering following their own path, an internal policy on sustainability can be a valuable ally and here the factors that need to be considered in following up such a route were listed.

The advantages of systematic approaches to sustainability at European level are many and it is hoped that, sooner or later, mechanisms may be put in motion to fill in the gap left by **Copernicus**. Until then, it is the responsibility of each university to make sure that sustainability is part of their routine and that it is part of their institutional lives.

References

Barrett, C.B. (1996) Fairness, stewardship, and sustainable development. *Ecological Economics* 19(1): 11-17.

Bor, W. van den, Holen, P. and Wals, A. (eds) (1999) *The Concept of Sustainability in Higher Education*. Rome: FAO.

Elliot, R. (1992) Intrinsic value, environmental obligation and naturalness. *Monist* 75: 138-160.

Higher Education Funding Council (1998) *Environmental Report*. Bristol: HEFC.

Hollingsworth, J. R. (1988) Specialisation and the Problem of Communication Within and Across Academic Disciplines. In Lazin, F., Aroni, S. and Gradus, Y. (eds) (1988) *The Policy Impact of Universities in Developing Regions*. London: MacMillan Press.

Johnson, L.E. (1991) *A Morally Deep World: An Essay on Moral Significance and Environmental Ethics*. Cambridge, MA: Cambridge University Press.

Lazin, F., Aroni, S. and Gradus, Y. (eds) (1988) *The Policy Impact of Universities in Developing Regions*. London: MacMillan Press.

Leal Filho, W. D. S., MacDermott, F. & Padgham, J. (eds) (1996) *Implementing Sustainable Development at University Level*. Geneva: Association of European Universities/CRE.

Leal Filho, W. D. S. (1997) Policies in Environmental Education in Europe. *Proceedings of the Seminar held in Lüneburg, Germany, February 1997*. Brussels: Commission of the European Communities/University of Lüneburg.

Leal Filho, W. D. S. (1998) (ed) *Umweltschutz und Nachhaltigkeit an Hochschulen* („Environmental Conservation and Sustainability at Universities"). Frankfurt: Verlag Peter Lang.

Leal Filho W. D. S. (1999) Recognising and Addressing Misconceptions on the Concept of Sustainability at University Level. In Bor, W. van den, Holen, P. and Wals, A. (eds) (1999) *The Concept of Sustainability in Higher Education*. Rome: FAO.

MacDermott, F. D. J. (1995) *Environmental Education Policies in the European Union*. Unpublished MPhil thesis. Bradford: University of Bradford.

Nash, S. (1991) What price nature? *BioScience* 41: 677-680.

Norton, B. G. (1994) On what we should save: The role of culture in determining conservation targets. In *Systematics and Conservation Evaluation*, P.L. Forey, C.J. Humphries, and R.I. Vane-Wright (eds.). Systematics Association Special Volume 50. Oxford: Oxford University Press.

Partidge, E. (ed.) (1981) *Responsibility to Future Generations: Environmental Ethics*. Buffalo, NY: Prometheus Books.

UNCED (United Nations Conference on Environment and Development) (1992) *Agenda 21, the United Nations Programme of Action from Rio*. New York: UN Department of Public Information.

WCED (World Commission on Environment and Development) (1987) *Our Common Future*, Oxford: Oxford University Press.

Chapter 2

Critical Dimensions of Sustainability in Higher Education

Richard M. Clugston and Wynn Calder

Abstract

This chapter explores the evolution of the concern for sustainability in higher education. It describes the origin of the Talloires Declaration as a guiding set of commitments for colleges and universities pursuing sustainability. Critical dimensions of sustainability in higher education are presented as a result of the Association of University Leaders for a Sustainable Future's (ULSF) Sustainability Indicators Project. Critical conditions determining the success of sustainability initiatives are then discussed. Two case studies of university efforts to "green" their institutions are described in light of these dimensions and conditions for success.

Sustainability and Ecojustice

A concern for sustainability arose in the early seventies as growing numbers of people realized that the degradation of the environment would seriously undermine our ability to ensure expanding prosperity and economic justice. The most frequently cited definition of sustainability came from the report of the World Commission on Environment and Development, in its description of new directions for "our common future." Sustainable development is "development that meets the needs of the present without compromising the ability of future generations to meet their own needs" (World Commission on Environment and Development, 1987).

Note: The Association of University Leaders for a Sustainable Future (ULSF), located in Washington, D.C., is an international membership organization of academic leaders and institutions committed to the advancement of global environmental literacy and sustainability. ULSF helps colleges and universities build and strengthen institutional capacity to make sustainability a major focus of academic disciplines, research initiatives, operations and outreach. The ULSF Secretariat promotes the 1990 Talloires Declaration and maintains an international network of signatories, facilitating information exchange, providing technical support, and sponsoring conferences that foster organizational and individual capacity to develop sustainable policies and practices. ULSF is an affiliate of the Center for Respect of Life and Environment (CRLE). The Center, founded in 1986, promotes the greening of higher education and fosters earth ethics to guide sustainable development.

A series of United Nations' conferences and NGO (Non-Governmental Organizations) meetings in the 1990s have provided a major framework in which the meaning and implications of sustainability have been clarified. In these major international events, representatives of governments, business and civil society have met to wrestle with the direction of development. They produced a series of international agreements, including: Agenda 21 from the United Nations Conference on Environment and Development in Rio; the Vienna Conference Tribunal on Violations of Women's Human Rights; the Cairo Consensus and Action Plan of the International Conference on Population and Development; the Copenhagen Social Summit discussions of equitable, "people-centered" development; the Beijing Commitments regarding Rights and Roles of Women in Development; the Habitat II agenda concerned with sustainable human settlements; and the Rome World Food Summit. These international agreements, developed with U.S. government participation, set promising policy directions for a sustainable future (Clugston, 1996).

Agenda 21, adopted by the 1992 Earth Summit, emphasizes that human population, consumption, and technology are the primary driving forces of environmental change. This document outlines steps to reduce wasteful and inefficient consumption patterns in some parts of the world while encouraging increased but sustainable development in others. *Agenda 21* also states that "education is critical for promoting sustainable development and improving the capacity of all people to address environment and development issues" (*Agenda 21*, 1994).

Analysts increasingly recognize that poverty, unemployment, community disintegration, and ecological abuse have accelerated globally, despite a seven-fold increase in global GNP since 1950. A major reason is that we have defined our goals in terms of growing economies to provide jobs—a means—rather than developing healthy sustainable human societies that provide people with secure and satisfying livelihoods—an end. David Korten claims that a new agenda must be designed „*to support the right of all people to a place in society and on the earth with access to the resources required to create a secure and fulfilling life for themselves at peace with their neighbors and in balance with the earth's natural systems; to build complementary to the money economy strong gender-balanced, non-monetized household and community economies able to replenish the social capital that is essential to healthy societies; and create a global system of localized economies that root economic power and environmental responsibility in people and communities of place*" (Korten, 1994).

Definitions of and approaches to sustainability vary depending on the view and interest of the definer, but each emphasizes that activities are ecologically sound, socially just, economically viable and humane, and that they will continue to be so for future generations. Historically, the term "sustainable" arose among those with environmental concerns, and most definitions reflect this emphasis. It is critical, however, to address social justice issues and to know that there can be no sustainable communities and institutions without social justice. So, too, is humane consideration toward the whole community of life an essential part of true sustainability. Fundamentally, a commitment to sustainability implies recognition that the social and environmental challenges of the 21st century are real and they require that the global economic and political order be grounded in different values and practices.

A Movement to Promote Sustainability in Higher Education

A significant attempt to define the sustainable university was made in 1990 with the Talloires Declaration. Jean Mayer, the President of Tufts, convened twenty-two university leaders in Talloires, France, to voice their concerns about the state of the world and create a document that spelled out key actions universities must take to create a sustainable future. Recognizing the shortage of specialists in environmental management and related fields, as well as the lack of comprehension by professionals in all fields of their effect on the environment and public health, this gathering defined the role of the university in the following way: "Universities educate most of the people who develop and manage society's institutions. For this reason, universities bear profound responsibilities to increase the awareness, knowledge, technologies, and tools to create an environmentally sustainable future" (Report and Declaration of The Presidents Conference, 1990).

The following excerpts from the Talloires Declaration describe critical aspects of the presidents' vision of sustainability through higher education:

> We the presidents, rectors, and vice chancellors of universities from all regions of the world, are deeply concerned about the unprecedented scale and speed of environmental pollution and degradation and the depletion of natural resources. Pollution, toxic wastes, and depletion of the ozone layer threaten the survival of humans and thousands of other living species, the integrity of the earth and its biodiversity, the security of nations, and the heritage of future generations.

> We believe that urgent actions are needed to address these fundamental problems and reverse the trends. University heads must provide the leadership, so that their institutions respond to this urgent challenge.

> We, therefore, agree to take the following actions...

> • Encourage all universities to engage in education, research, policy formation, and information exchange on population, environment, and development to move toward a sustainable future.

> • Establish programs to produce expertise in environmental management, sustainable economic development, population, and related fields to ensure that all university graduates are environmentally literate and responsible citizens.

> • Set an example of environmental responsibility by establishing programs of resource conservation, recycling, and waste reduction at the universities. (ULSF, 1990)

The Talloires Declaration has been signed by more than 265 university presidents and chancellors at institutions in over 40 countries across five continents. This suggests a growing recognition that academic research, teaching, and service must address the sustainability challenge. Undoubtedly, signing the Talloires Declaration for some institutions constituted a symbolic act in the moment. For others, however, the document continues to be an impetus and framework for steady progress toward sustainability.

With or without the Talloires Declaration as a guiding set of commitments, the obstacles to transforming higher education are daunting. The modern university is the embodiment of the mechanistic, utilitarian worldview that shaped the scientific and industrial revolutions. Cartesian dualism (separating pure from applied, objective from subjective); Baconian method (emphasizing manipulation, control, and quantitative measurement); and utilitarian philosophy shape academic functioning. The academy is also deeply involved in providing expertise for an "unsustainable" world economy.

Academic work -research, teaching and service - is organized in disciplines such as psychology, engineering, and theology. It is the responsibility of eminent scholars in each of the disciplines to define what is understood and appropriate to pursue within them. The department is the local, campus-based manifestation of the discipline. The current body of fact and theory accepted by the disciplines largely determines what is taught in these local places. Academics move from campus to campus but remain in their disciplinary fields. Promoting sustainability in higher education depends significantly on the active engagement of disciplinary leaders in promoting ecologically sensitive theory and sustainable practices as central to the scope and mission of their fields (e.g. in peer-review criteria for journal articles and in the themes and organization of professional associations).

Fortunately, many are engaged in transforming their disciplines at both the national and local (campus) levels. Members of various professional associations have started special interest groups, divisions, or sections focused on environment and sustainability. For example, the American Institute of Architects provides an environmental education program for teachers called "Learning by Design." The American Planning Association and the American Management Association both have formed special interest groups. The American Academy of Religion has an ecology and religion section. Professional journals are emerging, such as the *Journal of Interdisciplinary Studies in Literature and Environment*. This publication provides a forum for critical studies of the literary and performing arts proceeding from or addressing environmental considerations, including ecological theory, conceptions of nature and their depictions, the human/nature dichotomy, and related concerns (Clugston, 1995).

Critical Dimensions of Sustainability in Higher Education

What would a sustainable college or university look like? An academic institution committed to sustainability would help students understand the roots of environmental degradation and motivate them to seek environmentally sustainable practices while also teaching the roots of today's injustices in full integration with modeling justice and humaneness.

While the manner in which academic institutions and programs define and approach sustainability varies, we would expect a genuine commitment to creating a sustainable future to be evidenced in the critical dimensions of institutional life (e.g. in its written statements of mission and purpose; academic programs; energy and purchasing practices; outreach; faculty hiring and development, etc.). ULSF's on-going Sustainability Indicators Project has revealed a set of orientations and activities found in colleges and universities fully committed to sustainability. Though approaches to "greening" higher education vary considerably, the institution must be implementing practices in these seven areas to be very far along the path to sustainability:

1. The written statements of the mission and purpose of the institution and its various units express their philosophies and commitments. The descriptions of learning objectives and public relations materials of the various schools, departments, programs or offices thus would express prominent and explicit concern for sustainability.

2. The college or university appropriately incorporates the concepts of sustainability into all academic disciplines and in liberal arts and professional education requirements, as well as into faculty and student research. Likewise, a firm grounding in basic disciplines and critical thinking skills is essential to pursuing a sustainable future. Institutions committed to sustainability prominently feature certain topics in their course offerings, e.g. Globalization and Sustainable Development; Environmental Philosophy; Nature Writing; Land Ethics and Sustainable Agriculture; Urban Ecology and Social Justice; Population, Women and Development; Sustainable Production and Consumption; and many others.

3. A major shift from the current academic paradigm lies in a conscious reflection of the role of the institution in its social and ecological systems. Students learn about the institutional values and practices in this context. For example, all students would understand:
   a. how the campus functions in the ecosystem (e.g. its sources of food, water, energy, endpoint of waste and garbage) and its contribution to a sustainable economy.
   b. how the institution views and treats its employees (such as student, staff, faculty involvement in decision-making, their status and benefits, etc.).
   c. the basic values and core assumptions present in the content and methods of the academic disciplines.

4. Since research and teaching are the fundamental purposes of academic institutions, knowledge of sustainability is a critical concern in the hiring, tenure and promotion systems. We would expect the institution to.
   a. reward faculty members' contributions to sustainability in scholarship, teaching, or campus and community activities.
   b. provide significant staff and faculty development opportunities to enhance understanding, teaching and research in sustainability.

5. The institution has an "ecological footprint." In its production and consumption the institution follows sustainable policies and practices. for example, CO_2 reduction practices and the use of emission control devices; sustainable building construction and renovation; energy conservation practices; local food purchasing program; purchasing and investment in environmentally and socially responsible products; and many others. Furthermore, these operational practices are integrated into the educational and scholarly activities of the school.

6. Institutional support and campus student life services that emphasize certain practices, such as:
   a. new student orientation, scholarships, internships and job placement counseling related to community service, sustainability and/or justice issues;
   b. an Environmental or Sustainability Council or Task Force, an Environmental Coordinator or Curriculum Greening Officer;
   c. regularly conducted environmental audits;
   d. prominent public, student and staff celebrations of sustainability on campus (for example, lectures, conferences, Earth Day celebrations, etc).

7. The institution is engaged in outreach and forming partnerships both locally and globally to enhance sustainability. The college or university supports sustainable communities in the surrounding region and relationships with local businesses that foster sustainable practices. The institution seeks international cooperation in solving global environmental justice and sustainability problems through conferences, and student/faculty exchanges, among others. This list is an abbreviated version of the questions found in ULSF's Sustainability Assessment Questionnaire, 1999.

Critical Conditions Determining the Success of Sustainability Initiatives

Sustainability initiatives meet with various degrees of success. In some institutions, seemingly broad-based and strong initiatives have faded away. In others, significant academic programs and operations policies have been institutionalized. A variety of factors determine the success of sustainability initiatives at colleges and universities. Seven critical conditions are noted below.

1. How are the "champions" of sustainability initiatives perceived by others in the institution? Do they have the credibility and the personality needed to promote the initiative or are they marginal institutional actors complaining and promoting their narrow self-interest? Do they persist in the face of resistance, with adaptability and grace, or do they give up or become frustrated?

2. Do the initiatives have the endorsement of key administrative leaders at the institution? Is a commitment to sustainability supported by the President or Chancellor (e.g. by signing the Talloires Declaration), or by other high level and influential figures (e.g. senior managers)?

3. Who benefits from the initiative? Which departments and programs will the faculty and administration perceive the initiative to be strengthening, and which will it threaten? If it is perceived to be the imposition of a special interest group demanding that all faculty understand "Earth Sciences" or embrace a new counter culture or "politically correct" movement, then it is doomed. However, if it promises to empower and strengthen many programs, it will be supported.

4. Does the initiative fit with the institution's ethos, its saga, and its organizational culture? Each college and university has a particular story that it tells about itself and a particular

"niche" that it fills in the ecology of higher education. How well does the initiative conform to this institutional identity?

5. Does the initiative elicit the engagement of the college or university community? Is there sufficient publicity (through awareness events, press releases, articles, etc.) for new policies and initiatives? Is there regular disclosure of progress, successes and failures? Is information made available to ensure accountability on the part of those managing and carrying out the initiative? Finally, is the process for critique of current sustainability programs and determining next steps broadly participatory across the school community?

6. Is the initiative academically legitimate? Is it perceived to be grounded in a recognized body of knowledge: of sound theory and scholarly backing? Can it claim an academic rigor and validity? If it lacks this basic sine qua non of academic credibility, it will be rejected.

7. How successful is the initiative in bringing in critical resources (e.g. grants and contracts, state funding, student demand, recognition and support from key stakeholders such as the media or trustees, and state, national and international leaders)? Does the initiative produce cost savings over time (e.g., energy conservation)?

Two Case Studies

The two case studies in this section demonstrate different strengths according to the "critical dimensions" of sustainability and "critical conditions" for success. In its mission to become a "green university," Liverpool John Moores University exemplifies strong environmental practices in operations, and is moving forward in curricular reform and other areas. Santa Clara University shows advancement and innovation in its academic programs, while making genuine progress in its operations.

Liverpool John Moores University (JMU)

For Liverpool John Moores University (JMU), in Liverpool, England, the last decade has been one of considerable accomplishment in sustainable operations. As a city-based institution, JMU comprises approximately 45 buildings spread over three main campuses. Over 20,000 students work with a staff of nearly 3,000. The organization is typical of a 'new' university with fifteen schools in three Academic Divisions (Engineering and Science; Education, Health and Social Science; Arts and Professional Studies).

In 1994, the University's Executive Management Team stated its commitment to:

1. Developing a range of academic programs, from general environmental literacy to specific professional preparation.
2. Ensuring that appropriate environmental content is present throughout its academic programs.
3. The rationalizing and improvement of the physical and working environment and the effective, efficient and sustainable use of all resources.

4. Enabling all members of its community to develop healthy and ecologically sound lifestyles and to protect and improve the physical and social environment in which it is situated. (Liverpool John Moores University's Executive Management Team, 1994)

The following is a list of milestones in JMU's environmental progress over the last decade:

- "Toyne Report on Environmental Responsibility" published, 1993.
- Environmental Policy and Action Plan (EPAP) was approved by the Executive Management Team in response to Toyne's recommendations, October 1994.
- Three new undergraduate degree programs with an environmental theme were approved, 1994.
- Environmental purchasing policy implemented, 1995.
- In response to "Toyne II," funding was secured for a full-time Environment Coordinator to steer the University's environmental program, 1996.
- Energy efficiency awards received in 1994, 1995 and 1997.
- Vice-Chancellor signed the Talloires Declaration, October 1996.
- Environment Officer position made permanent. Curriculum Greening Officer appointed, 1997.
- Environmental awareness training introduced as a core requirement for new staff induction program, 1997.
- Publication of first Environmental Performance Report (EPR) stating clear and achievable objectives and targets for continual performance improvement (supervised by an Environmental Review Team), 1997.
- Health, Safety and Environment Unit (HS&E Unit) established, born out of the existing Health and Safety Unit and Environmental Management Unit to allow the integration of evolving management responsibilities and operational systems, 1997.
- Appointment and introduction of School/Service Environment Officers across the University to champion the new HS&E Policy, 1998.
- Environment Officer position made permanent. Curriculum Greening Officer appointed, 1997.
- Environmental awareness training introduced as a core requirement for new staff induction program, 1997.
- Publication of first Environmental Performance Report (EPR) stating clear and achievable objectives and targets for continual performance improvement (supervised by an Environmental Review Team), 1997.
- Health, Safety and Environment Unit (HS&E Unit) established, born out of the existing Health and Safety Unit and Environmental Management Unit to allow the integration of evolving management responsibilities and operational systems, 1997.
- Appointment and introduction of School/Service Environment Officers across the University to champion the new HS&E Policy, 1998.

The university's first serious excursion into the sphere of environmental responsibility and sustainable practice was formalized following the first "Toyne Report on Environmental Responsibility" in 1993. Professor Toyne, Vice-Chancellor and Chief Executive of JMU, wrote the report after chairing a Committee established by the Government Department of Education to investigate the potential for greening higher education. The Environmental Policy and Action

Plan (EPAP), which was established in 1994 to fulfil the recommendations of Toyne I, became the stimulus for a number of critical decisions made by the Executive in the years that followed.

A full-time Environment Officer was appointed to spearhead the remaining implementation of the EPAP as it became clear that projects required coordination on a regular basis. The Officer also established an Environmental Management Unit (EMU) to carry out the recommendations of Toyne II, published in 1996.

In January 1997, the EMU brought together a small in-house group of Senior Managers to form an Environmental Review Team (ERT) and oversee a comprehensive review process. This resulted in the inaugural Environmental Performance Report (EPR) 1997, which represents the University's commitment to accountability through the disclosure of actual performance against stated policy objectives.[1] Moreover, it establishes the University's intentions for continual performance improvement and describes how this is to be achieved.

Highlights from the Environmental Performance Report

JMU is fulfilling many of its policy goals in all areas of campus operations. In Energy Conservation, the University has established an ongoing energy management program which has performed an energy audit for all University buildings; completed ten specified energy conservation projects; conducted a University-wide energy awareness campaign including good practice publications and training seminars; developed and promoted Energy Conservation Task Groups; and re-negotiated utility contracts. JMU has earned three energy efficiency awards from utility companies since 1994.

In the area of Waste Management and Reduction, a Waste Management Steering Group was established in 1997 to reduce waste bound for landfill and begin comprehensive recycling programs. With the transfer of various institutional publications, such as the staff and student handbooks, to the Campus Wide Information System (CWIS), paper use has dropped significantly. Many University handbooks and other procedural documents are now only available on the CWIS. A recycling scheme to collect computer consumables such as ink and toner cartridges has been introduced into all University learning resource centers and Information Technology suites. The use of the double-sided printers has been encouraged and they have started to replace old printers. A strict policy of double-sided printing and copying was then introduced within the Print Office. A Waste Audit and Review occurred in early 1999.

The JMU Food Policy includes the following goals: to make healthy, nutritious and ethnically sensitive food generally available at all University catering outlets; to purchase foodstuffs from local suppliers wherever possible; to maximize use of organically grown foodstuff; to minimize energy usage in the preparation and cooking of food; and to minimize the packaging of foods at catering outlets. JMU is making significant progress in meeting these goals. Recent changes

[1] The EPR 1997 was put on the university website and distributed to a wide audience. The new Health, Safety and Environment Report 1998, replacing the EPR, was due to be released at the time of this writing.

include in-house production of refectory sandwiches which had previously been brought in, and an increase in vegetarian options at food services.

JMU's policy on Purchasing states: "In purchasing its services, materials, equipment and consumable items, the University will give preference to products which do least harm to the environment, which are not supplied with excessive packaging, and which are benign or at least harmless in their effect on the environment. Where possible, preference will be given to local or regional suppliers to maximize the University's input to the local community." Currently, JMU requires suppliers of furniture and computer hardware (over ten units) to take away packaging after delivery and installation. Cleaning solution containers are also disposed of or refilled by suppliers. JMU held an awareness event to teach product awareness among purchasers in early 1999.

JMU's policy on Transport and Commuting includes a commitment to purchasing fuel efficient University vehicles and minimizing damaging emissions; encouraging walking, bicycle use and public transport among the University community and between campuses; and a campaign for cycling paths linking campuses and other student facilities. In July 1997 a Transport and Commuting Steering Group was established to address these issues. The Steering Group helped introduce a shuttle bus service linking the main University campuses and buildings. JMU also contributed to the Liverpool City Council's cycling strategy in 1997 and then established a University strategy to complement the local plan which includes improved bicycle parking facilities and interest-free loans for staff to purchase bicycles. A University Travel Survey was conducted in February 1999.

The production of an EPR has provided an opportunity to promote positive and practical solutions to environmental concerns; acknowledges the vital contribution made by a number of key 'champions' within the organization; allows the assessment of performance against a set of target indicators; and highlights the need for sustained efforts to raise awareness and encourage cooperation across the organization if policy statements are to be transformed into reality. (excerpts taken from Blyth et al., 1999)

Also in force at JMU is a plan for "greening" the curriculum. The Curriculum Greening Officer, a member of the faculty, is coordinating this effort. As stated in a "Curriculum Greening" summary by a JMU Environmental Policy Officer, "Our students need the means to: develop their own sense of environmental responsibility; understand the principles of sustainability; fully participate as global citizens; and contribute to the efforts of employers to meet their environmental obligations." An initiative in Education for Citizenship is underway and a recent review of curriculum offerings identified "16 degree programs with a major environmental component" (Small, 1998).

Santa Clara University (SCU)

Santa Clara University (SCU), in Santa Clara, California, founded by Jesuits in 1851, is a Catholic institution with an academic organization of five units, including arts and sciences, business, law, engineering, and counseling psychology and education. Enrollment includes just under 2,000 undergraduates and about 4,000 graduates. SCU's undergraduate school has shown considerable motivation and progress on the part of the faculty and administration in "greening" their academic programs. An Environmental Studies Program was founded in 1992 which supports the largest minor on campus in Environmental Studies. A Campus Environmental Assessment (CEA) was conducted in 1995 which spawned debate and environmental action in many other areas on campus.

The strategic plan of the university sets as a primary goal the development of "integrated education" in a "community of scholars," which includes faculty, students and staff. Many courses in the undergraduate school are interdisciplinary in content and some are team- taught. There is even an interest in hiring professors with interdisciplinary backgrounds. For example, the school is in the process of hiring a tenure track ecological archaeologist to work half-time in Environmental Studies and half-time in Anthropology, and a tenure track political ecologist to divide her time between Environmental Studies and Political Science. As a Jesuit school, Santa Clara's teaching and public debate are attentive to social justice issues. Course offerings of this nature include African Economic Development, Environmental Activism, and Environmental Politics in Less Developed Countries.

An Environmental Coordinating Committee (ECC) was formed in 1997 to promote and administer environmental efforts on campus with a particular concern for the ecology and social heritage of Santa Clara. The ECC, which includes a student, staff members and faculty, is currently working on an environmental decision-making procedure to guide all decisions in terms of impact on the community, the physical campus and the region. Recent ECC issues have included the plight of a small burrowing owl population on campus that could be displaced by new construction.

On the operations side, the university is making progress in numerous areas. There is a long-range plan to replace most campus vehicles with electric; two electric vehicles are now in use for waste removal and recycling. SCU is currently improving the energy efficiency of its mechanical systems, in particular heating and air conditioning. In landscaping, the school has recently connected to a local reclaimed water system and will soon use this water to irrigate the grounds. SCU's recycling program compares with the best programs in the country in approaching a 50% recycled solid waste level. Facilities is working to eliminate all hazardous waste products from housekeeping and building and grounds work.

A strong driving force for "greening" of the campus has been student and faculty interest manifested primarily as course-based campus projects at the undergraduate school. Campus environmental research related to the CEA has been conducted in several departments including Chemistry, Biology and Anthropology, with interdisciplinary collaboration in numerous cases. Many of these projects are subsidized by a very supportive administration. Since 1995, specific projects have included:

In Biology:
- survey of campus bird populations especially focusing on their relationship to specific plants and gardens.

- development of a Native Species Garden and of educational materials describing the natural and cultural history of native Californian plants.
- development of a Community Garden utilizing composting techniques for yard waste and yielding produce for donation to local community centers.

In Chemistry:
- evaluation of indoor air quality involving testing for pollutants in areas near copy machines or where complaints of poor air quality had originated.
- investigation of the efficacy of solar energy and of options for incorporating passive solar systems in new campus buildings.
- investigation of handling of hazardous materials in the sciences including an evaluation of spill preparedness, radioactive isotope storage, and inventory methods.
- investigation of electricity deregulation and future "green power" choices.

In Anthropology:
- student/faculty research into SCU's history as a former Franciscan mission site and the environmental impact of early mission activities.
- student/faculty research for the *Research Manuscript Series on the Cultural and Natural History of Santa Clara.*[2]

Off Campus:
SCU has also supported student research beyond the campus. In 1998, twelve natural and social science students learned basic interdisciplinary, environmental research skills in a quarter-long seminar course during the academic year and then participated in a summer research program in Trinidad and Tobago. Research included:

- assessment of local villagers' environmental knowledge for development of an environmental education program on Trinidad.
- testing methods for surveying biodiversity for comprehensive biodiversity census on the island of Tobago.
- bird and ethnobotany survey at a site soon to be developed for ecotourists on Trinidad.
- study of social concerns facing members of the rainforest community as they confront the new industry of tourism on Trinidad.

The Trinidad and Tobago research program has become a paradigm of environmental studies and community outreach. In the near future, students will help the Trinidadian non-profit environmental group, Paria Springs Trust, establish a model of permaculture and sustainable development in the rainforest. SCU's International Programs and Environmental Studies Program sponsored the Trinidad and Tobago program.

---

[2] Begun in 1994, the series has focused primarily on the cultural ecology of the region, including topics such as the oak woodlands, the riparian zone, medicinal plants and how different cultures have viewed their environment. Nine series have been published to date.

Outcomes: Quantitative and Qualitative

Through their research experience, students gain some level of mastery regarding specific content and learn basic methods. They review previous work on campus, obtain information on similar issues at other campuses, gather information through interviews and available documents, and analyze and interpret results. For group projects, leadership and group dynamics skills begin to emerge. Furthermore, students must learn how to present results in various types of written reports and in poster presentations.

Although many projects begin as scientific research, due to the complexity of environmental issues, students learn that ethical, social, and economic relationships are often key to the success of their project. Students doing research on campus must develop relationships with staff and administrators to obtain information and gain an understanding of how the university operates. In establishing those connections, students learn the complexities of operations and develop sensitivity to the roles staff and administrators play in defining daily campus functions. Finally, students gain a sense of ownership and a connectedness to the campus. Participating in campus-based projects forces students to realize that they are stakeholders, along with the faculty and staff, in the "greening of the campus." Ultimately, it is hoped that students recognize they are environmental stakeholders in any place they choose to live.

Enhancing Research Experience

Faculty can use the environmental studies curriculum (multidisciplinary by its nature) as a template for developing a program of instruction for conducting research. Clearly, guidance from colleagues in diverse fields is required for faculty to become more effective mentors for the environmental studies students. Workshops focused on the ethical dimensions of multi-disciplinary research, such as those offered by SCU's Markkula Center of Applied Ethics, have been helpful. In these workshops, students and faculty address questions concerning interpersonal relationships before and concurrent with their research.

Implementing Change

Disseminating the results and recommendations of course-based projects is considered as important as conducting the research. Several avenues for publicly presenting research results have been adopted at SCU: campus-wide symposia and poster sessions, and student-authored articles for an environmental newsletter and the student newspaper. Implementing a set of recommendations for "greening the campus" has proven to be one of the more difficult and most rewarding aspects of conducting environmental research.
(excerpts taken from Edgerly-Rooks et al., 1999).

Reflections on JMU and SCU in Terms of Critical "Dimensions" and "Conditions"

The following comments make specific reference to critical "dimensions" and "conditions" of sustainability (using "D" for dimensions and "C" for conditions in parentheses). According to the seven "critical dimensions" of sustainability, Liverpool John Moores University is clearly strongest in its comprehensive approach to reducing its ecological footprint in terms of waste reduction, transportation and so on. (D5). This has been possible, in part, because of significant accomplishments in other dimensions. For example, JMU's mission statements are evolving to reflect a commitment to sustainability (e.g. written statements by the Executive Management Team and by Vice-Chancellor Toyne) (D1). Significant efforts are underway to incorporate sustainability into the philosophy and content of academic programs (e.g. statements by Environmental Policy Officer, hiring of Curriculum Greening Officer) (D2). JMU is increasingly reflecting on the role of the institution in its social and ecological systems (e.g. new Health, Safety and Environment Unit and the Education for Citizenship initiative) (D3). Numerous student support mechanisms and institutional practices are in place (e.g., awareness events, steering committees and task groups, environmental performance reports, etc.) (D6).

In terms of the "critical conditions" necessary for long-term success, JMU appears to have respected and credible "champions" (C1). Its environmental initiatives are endorsed by the Vice-Chancellor and Chief Executive (e.g. the Toyne Report) (C2). The university's initiatives conform to the new culture and direction of the institution, especially as defined by Vice-Chancellor Toyne, though it is unclear to what extent some university constituencies hold on to the old ethos (C4). JMU's commitment to accountability and disclosure of information is clear from its publication and distribution of the Environmental Performance Report 1997 and its determination to continue this practice (C5). In the area of "greening the curriculum," it is not clear at this point whether the faculty consider this reform process academically legitimate (C6).

The Santa Clara University undergraduate school shows greatest progress in its academic programs and has the backing of administrative leaders in this arena. In terms of "critical dimensions," SCU's curriculum and student research activities are broad in scope and encompass environmental as well as social justice issues (e.g. research in anthropology and off campus on Trinidad and Tobago; courses listed include Environmental Politics in Less Developed Countries) (D2). There is some degree of reflection on the role of the institution in both its social and ecological systems (e.g., coursework and fora stemming from the university's Jesuit tradition, student interaction with staff and understanding of campus operations through research) (D3). There is recent interest in hiring faculty in Environmental Studies who demonstrate an interdisciplinary expertise, and faculty development is emphasized through workshops at the Markkula Center of Applied Ethics (D4). SCU is clearly attempting to minimize its environmental impact through energy efficiency initiatives, recycling of solid waste, etc. (D5). In the area of student support services and campus life, SCU has an established Environmental Coordinating Committee. The university also holds events such as campus-wide symposia to present student research, an example of campus life activities intersecting with academic work (D6). The Trinidad and Tobago research program is a good demonstration of student research functioning as community outreach for sustainability (D7).

In terms of "critical conditions" for success of sustainability initiatives, the faculty at SCU's undergraduate school who are leading the way in reforming academic programs appear to be highly motivated and well respected by their colleagues (C1). They also enjoy the support of their administrators in their endeavor to enhance environmental studies and interdisciplinary research (C2). Furthermore, there is strong belief on the part of numerous faculty in the academic legitimacy of these recent academic initiatives (C6). Finally, efforts to inform the school community of student academic work have been very successful (e.g. sharing of results is a priority in research, campus presentations and poster sessions, environmental newsletter and student newspaper) (C5).

Both institutions are addressing key areas in their progress toward sustainability, though with different emphases. These examples show that the stated "critical dimensions" are interrelated, that it is unlikely to have success in one area and not in others. However, it is also evident that the task of achieving comprehensive change across all dimensions is immense, can only happen slowly, and, depending on the institution, will occur more quickly in some areas than others. A key indicator of long-term success for any sustainability initiative is the extent to which it has been institutionalized, whether through official policy, budgeting, or permanent staff positions. JMU is particularly strong in this area, having created positions and offices for forwarding the sustainability agenda.

Conclusions

Every institution committed to sustainability will find its own way of defining sustainability for itself. Few, if any, institutions have achieved transformation across all the "critical dimensions" outlined, while many have succeeded in a few areas. Most of the efforts to date, including those discussed in this chapter, are heavily oriented toward environmental initiatives. The emphasis is not on sustainability broadly defined, even while the term "sustainability" is often used in the rhetoric of reform.

Even if all the "critical conditions" are present, sustainability initiatives do not necessarily succeed, except in a few market niches. The two major factors controlling the structure and functioning of academia—disciplinary structure and economic forces—have moved very little toward sustainability. Academic disciplines continue to fragment and specialize, and faculty usually owe their allegiance to their subdisciplines, not their institutions.

Perhaps no obstacle is so great as the overpowering disincentives to sustainability built into the economy: both perverse subsidies and pricing that fails to distinguish between healthy (sustainable) and destructive economic activities. Many cost savings can be (and should be) achieved with eco-efficiency through conservation and sound ecological design (see the Campus Ecology study, Green Investment, Green Return, 1998). As long as sustainability confines itself to eco-efficiency and its appropriate market niche, it can meet with significant success. But an authentic reframing of the institution is difficult. To build a sustainable future the economy must change. Many academics are laying the groundwork for this needed "paradigm shift." At some point, the capacity to shift will intersect with the necessity to shift, and the new sustainability paradigm will crystallize as the dominant metaphor of higher education.

References

Blythe, J., Calder, W. (1999) Going Green at Liverpool John Moores University. In *The Declaration* 3 (1).

Clugston, R.M. (1995) CRLE Report: Greening Higher Education. In *Earth Ethics* 6 (2), pp. 11-12.

Clugston, R.M. (1996) Agenda for Action. In *Theology and Public Policy* 8 (1&2), pp. 101-111.

Edgerly-Rooks, J., Shachter, A., Calder, W. (1999) Course-Based Campus Environmental Research Projects. In *The Declaration* 3 (1).

Korten, D. (1994) Sustainable Livelihoods: Redefining The Global Social Crisis. In *Earth Ethics* 6 (1), pp. 11.

Liverpool John Moores University's Executive Management Team (1994) *http://cwis.livjm.ac.uk/hse/environment/performance/pledge.htm*

Liverpool John Moores University's Environmental Performance Report (1997) *http://www.livjm.ac.uk/environment/*

National Wildlife Federation's Campus Ecology Program. (1998) *Green Investment, Green Return.*

Orr, D. (1995) Ecological Design. In *Earth Ethics* 7 (1), pp. 11-12.

Report and Declaration of The Presidents Conference (1990) Tufts University.

Small, R. (1998) Curriculum Greening. At *http://cwis.livjm.ac.uk/hse/*.

Sitarz, D. (ed.) (1994) *Agenda 21: The Earth Summit Strategy to Save Our Planet*. Boulder, CO: Earthpress.

University Leaders for a Sustainable Future. (1990) *The Talloires Declaration*. Washington: ULSF.

University Leaders for a Sustainable Future. (1999) *Sustainability Assessment Questionnaire*. Washington: ULSF.

World Commission on Environment and Development. (1987) *Our Common Future*. Oxford, NY: Oxford University Press.

Chapter 3

Driving Environmental Strategy with Stakeholder Preferences – A Case Study of the University of Surrey

Andy Davey, Graham Earl, and Roland Clift.
Centre for Environmental Strategy, University of Surrey

Abstract

In response to growing demands for more responsible institutional environmental practices, the University of Surrey has adopted an environmental policy statement as a precursor to the development and implementation of a more detailed environmental policy and environmental management system. This ongoing pursuit of improved environmental performance has been influenced by the findings of a stakeholder study which was designed and conducted to support research and practical objectives, and the Local Agenda 21 concept of wide-consultation and participation in decision-making (see UN, 1992). Using a robust methodology for eliciting stakeholder preferences (the MADE model), a wide selection of the University's key stakeholders were interviewed to elicit their preferences for aspects of the University's environmental strategy. This chapter describes the approach employed and discusses both the experimental and experiential findings.

Introduction

In 1994 the University of Surrey signed the CRE Copernicus University Charter for Sustainable Development, a European Higher Education sector voluntary code which aims to encourage institutions to embrace the challenge of sustainable development. In the same year, a research project was established at the University with the primary aim of developing an environmental policy. As a consequence of the early findings of this research project, a "bottom-up approach" to policy implementation was pursued (Davey, 1998). This approach is believed to optimize the efficacy and durability of the policy and requires university community involvement from the outset in order to embed a sense of ownership in the policy. At the University of Surrey this was facilitated through the establishment of environmental policy working groups with membership open to any interested member of the University community (i.e. students or employees).

Almost four years after the policy work was first initiated, the University officially established an environmental policy statement with which to guide the future development of a more detailed environmental policy. Prompted by this slow rate of progress and justified by: the Agenda 21 theme of "participatory decision-making"; the rising popularity of the stakeholder concept; and the pursuit of the "bottom-up approach", a stakeholder study was designed to try systematically to involve a wide selection of the University's stakeholders in the development of ist environmental strategy. Specific research objectives of the study included testing the applicability of the stakeholder concept in the UK Higher Education sector and evaluating the utility of stakeholder preferences in developing environmental strategy. In effect, the study was conducted to:

1. fulfill research objectives;
2. systematically involve a wide range of stakeholders that otherwise may not have participated in the development of the University's environmental strategy;
3. disseminate the emergence of the University's environmental activities;
4. stimulate the interest of key stakeholders in the University's environmental endeavors.

The Framework for the Study

The study was designed around two specific areas of research:

Earl et al's (1998) Multi-Attribute Decision Evaluation (MADE) model provided the overall framework and methodology for the study - essentially how stakeholder preferences are elicited; Davey et al's (1997) SMART Approach (a tri-partite environmental management framework which advocates the use of well-defined categories of environmental impact, rather than more protean environmental issues, as the focus for environmental strategies) provided the detailed content - essentially what preferences should be elicited.

Eliciting Stakeholder Preferences – The MADE Model

The Multi Attribute Decision Environment (MADE) model, which is a stand-alone component of Earl et al's Stakeholder Value Analysis (SVA) Toolkit, provides a structured process to support the canvassing, quantification and analysis of stakeholder priorities. It covers four basic steps: (1) stakeholder identification, (2) value tree design, (3) priority quantification and (4) analysis of stakeholder priorities, though only the stakeholder identification stage is discussed in detail here.

Stakeholder Identification

Stakeholder identification is a pivotal process in any stakeholder study and should not, therefore, be considered nugatory. Not only does the term "stakeholder" need to be defined, but the following challenges need also to be resolved:

1. *resolution* - how to define a stakeholder group and which groups to include in the study;
2. *representation* - who should be chosen to represent a group.

What is a stakeholder?

There are many definitions and interpretations of the 'stakeholder' (Cowell et al, 1997; Clift, 1998b; ACBE, 1997; IBM, 1995; SustainAbility/UNEP, 1996a; Wheeler and Sillanpää, 1997). To assist the identification of appropriate stakeholders in the context of the decision to be made, the term "stakeholder" should be defined. For the purposes of this study, a University of Surrey stakeholder was defined as "anyone that can affect, or can be affected by, the University's environmental policy and strategy".

Who are the appropriate stakeholder groups?

Once a "stakeholder" has been defined, the next stage involves identifying what generic groups or individuals should be involved in the process, how tightly to define stakeholders groups (referred to as stakeholder resolution), and which groups (if any) to exclude from the study. There are obvious trade-offs between defining a large number of groups, the manageability of the exercise and its financial cost. In addition, there can also be practical limitations to involving potential stakeholders in the identification/selection process as suggested by Cowell et al (1997).

A common list of stakeholders includes employees, local communities, shareholders, pressure groups, regulators, insurers, investors, media and customers (see, for example, SustainAbility/UNEP, 1996). Some authors have even suggested such groups as the natural environment, non-human species and future generations . The approach recommended here is to start the stakeholder identification process by defining a set of generic 'stakeholder groups', for example as simple and broad as internal and external stakeholders. The next step is to break down these broad groups into their common denominators, which may involve a number of intermediate steps. Thus, for an institution of higher education, internal stakeholders could initially be defined as employees and students. Since these groups are still rather heterogeneous they could be broken down further until it is felt largely homogenous groups have been identified. "Students", for example, could be represented through postgraduates and undergraduates. However, the process does not necessarily end here since undergraduates could be further broken down into their respective departments and then further by their age, gender etc.

Who are appropriate representatives of the groups?

A further challenge is one of representation - how can an identified stakeholder group be appropriately represented? Clearly the "tighter" the group (i.e. more rigidly defined) the easier it is to represent it. It is often necessary to identify individuals from a stakeholder group who, by virtue of their responsibilities, can be considered to represent the views of the group and/or who from an organisational perspective are held accountable for the performance of the group. For example, this might be elected representatives (e.g. local councillors, MPs, Trades Union representatives) or senior managers. The alternative is to engage a representative sample of members of a group which can become quite unwieldy, time-consuming and costly. Whilst it is desirable to limit the number of identified groups and representative individuals from a logistical and practical perspective, this aim has to be reconciled with the very real danger of isolating and/or not accurately representing a potent and influential group. The breadth, types and number of stakeholders to include is therefore very much context-driven.

The University of Surrey Stakeholder Study

To achieve the practical aims of the study in terms of developing a stakeholder-driven environmental strategy for the University of Surrey, the MADE model was employed at two levels:

to elicit the relative importance a selection of the University's stakeholders place on environmental performance in comparison to other major aspects of the University's activities, services and operations, such as financial performance, ethical performance and quality;
to elicit the relative importance stakeholders place on the various ways in which the University may impact on the environment.

The first stage was defined in order to identify from where the greatest pressure and support for the University's improved environmental performance originates and more specifically, to elicit how important environmental performance is to the University's most senior employees (as the traditional key decision-makers). The second stage was designed to provide information with which the University's environmental impacts could be ranked according to their "significance", an exercise required by the two most prominent standards for environmental management systems, the international standard ISO 14001 (BSI, 1996) and the European Eco-Management and Audit Scheme (EC, 1993). It further served as an educational endeavor by introducing and explaining to participants somewhat unfamiliar categories of environmental impacts. These categories of environmental impact were based upon those most popularly used by the Life Cycle Assessment community (see for example, Nordic Council, 1995), as shown in Table 1 below.

	Categories of Environmental Impact
1	Resource Depletion
2	Human Health - Toxicological, non-toxicological, outside the working environment.
3	Global Warming
4	Depletion of Stratospheric Ozone
5	Acidification
6	Eutrophication
7	Photo-oxidant formation
8	Eco-toxicological impacts, habitat alterations & reductions in biological diversity

Table 1: Impact Categories to Describe University of Surrey's Environmental
          Performance

Procedure

The study can be considered to have consisted of three main stages:

1. Preparation or pre-stakeholder engagement;
2. Stakeholder engagement;
3. Post-engagement analysis.

Stage 1 - Pre-stakeholder Engagement

Value Tree Design

A value tree describes the hierarchical structure used to describe and structure the different performance elements which underline and drive a decision or strategy. The major benefit of the value tree is that it pictorially structures the decision context. It is common practice for participating stakeholders to be involved in the process of value tree design to ensure their concerns and/or priorities are accommodated. However, for the University's study it was considered more appropriate to develop the value tree without input from participating stakeholders, for two main reasons:

- the desired outcome was to influence strategy, not to assist with an explicit decision;

- to secure the participation of key stakeholders with notoriously busy schedules, it was deemed necessary to engage stakeholders through structured interviews rather than through a more typical workshop, which obviously requires stakeholders to be available on the same day.

Instead of developing a value tree with the participants, a pilot study was conducted using the views of the members of the Centre for Environmental Strategy (CES), a multidisciplinary research centre in the University's School for Engineering in the Environment.

Members of CES were canvassed for their opinions on any aspects of the University of concern to them. The wide range of issues that resulted were classified into a more manageable set of encompassing and essentially discrete performance categories which included the definition of an overall aim driving the University's existence. These are shown in Figure 1 and Figure 2 as follows.

Figure 2

Overall Aim
The University of Surrey effectively aims to maximise the net benefits to its stakeholders from its activities, services and operations, defined as follows:
Activities: Primarily teaching and research.
Services: Those which underpin the activities, for example - education and information provision, consultancy, policy guidance, catering, conferences, printing, sport, recreation, entertainment, retail, accommodation, library, leaseholds, careers guidance, staff training, employment, career development, hospitality.
Operations: How it carries out its activities and provides its services. For example: it manages resources (human, energy, materials and waste) and finances (sources and spends revenues); it cleans, constructs, maintains, heats and lights buildings; it maintains and develops land; it transports people and goods; it generates documents, waste, pollution, noise and odour; it consumes money, energy, land and food.

Figure 1

Performance Categories
The performance categories which together help to achieve the overall aim or top level goal are:
• Environmental performance - a measure of how well it manages its environmental impacts, or the environmental effects of its activities, operations and services.
• Financial performance - a measure of how well it manages its finances.
• Ethical performance - a measure of how well it manages the ethical implications of its activities, services and operations.
• Comparative performance - how it compares with other FHE Institutes on less tangible but value-laden aspects; e.g. geography, accessibility, reputation, familiarity.
• Health and Safety performance, e.g. health and safety record - number of reportable accidents or near misses, number of prosecutions for non-compliance.
• Quality of services provided (as measured by for example, employment record - number of dismissals; salaries paid; skilled/unskilled; student performance - pass/failure rate; administrative performance; standard of accommodation; graduate recruitment rate; research assessment exercises etc).

With the categories of environmental impact already pre-defined by the existing LCA literature but set in the University context, the resulting value tree for the University of Surrey is shown in Figure 3.

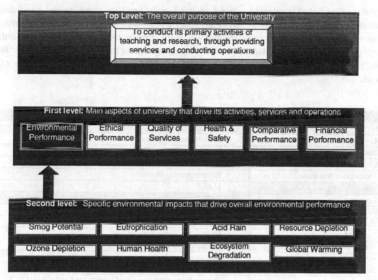

Figure 3: Value Tree for the University of Surrey

Identifying the Stakeholder Groups

Using the basic guidelines outlined above, it was possible to identify several categories of stakeholder for the University. The top-level classification is 'internal' and 'external', i.e. those that are "members" of the organisation and those that are not (as defined by University regulations), also indicating stakeholder groups and sub-groups[3]. The identification procedure resulted in six main stakeholder groups (three internal, three external) with thirty-three representative sub-groups considered sufficiently homogeneous for the study (Table 2). The next steps involved identifying appropriate individuals/organisations for each representative group and inviting their participation.

Identification was facilitated by an internal database containing contact details for individuals and parties with whom the University has had previous contact. Identified individuals were first sent a brief letter/invitation to participate, explaining the objectives of the study and what it would involve on their part. This was then followed by a phone call to enquire whether or not they were prepared to participate and, in the positive case, to organise a time and date for the interview.

---

[3] Other important Higher Education stakeholder groups identified as a consequence of this study include Professional Institutions, Course Validators and Trade Unions.

The majority of those contacted agreed to take part and, in some cases, candidates even recommended and recruited other individuals from within their organisation to also participate in an interview. In total, forty-two interviews were conducted with fifty-seven individuals (reflecting the use of group consensus in some cases) spanning most of the identified stakeholder groups. Table 3 provides a breakdown of the stakeholder interviews and the number of people involved.

INTERNAL	EXTERNAL
Students:	*Regulators:*
Undergraduates	Environment Agency
Postgraduates	Local and County Planners
Continuing Education	Health and Safety Executive
Prospective Students	Environmental Health
Employees:	MAFF
Lecturers	*Financial:*
Research Staff	Companies on the University of Surrey's Research Park
Heads of Schools	Lending Bank
Junior Management	University Insurance Brokers
Senior Management	Industry Representatives
Administrative and Clerical	Collaborative Partners
Technical	Research Councils
Librarians	Higher Education Funding Council for England (HEFCE)
Students Union	*Community:*
Lay-members of University Court	Locally Represented non-governmental organisations (NGO's)
	Elected Representatives
	Schools & Local Residents Group
	Local Forums and Business Groups
	Local Press

Table 2: University of Surrey Identified Stakeholder Groups

Stakeholder Group	No. of sub-groups represented	No. Separate Interviews	Total No. People Interviewed
Students	2	7	8
Regulators	5	5	7
Local Community	6	7	14
Finance	6	6	10
Employees	6	17	17
Total	Total Internal	24	31
	Total External	18	25
	Grand Total	42	56

Table 3: Participating Stakeholders

The most senior employees who participated included the Vice-Chancellor, the Secretary, the Senior Pro-Vice-Chancellor, the Deputy Secretary, the Senior Assistant Secretary and the Director of Estates and Buildings. Due to the failure to secure the participation of a key representative of the students, the "student" group was only represented by a small sample of postgraduate and undergraduate students. This is disappointing because it is acknowledged that the "student" group has not been sufficiently represented in this study. Nevertheless, the views of those that participated have been used as an indication of how, with appropriate representation of the group, student views could be incorporated into the development of an environmental strategy. This disappointing lacuna is considered reflective of environmental apathy amongst the University of Surrey's student elected representatives for the academic year 1997-98. Members of the local community included the local Member of Parliament, local councillors and local community groups, while the finance group included representatives of funding councils and local companies (who recruit the University's graduates and lease its buildings).

Stage 2 - Stakeholder Engagement

The medium for measuring stakeholder priorities was through structured interviews conducted mostly at participants' premises. Following agreement to participate, stakeholders were sent an interview pack approximately one week before the scheduled interview. This contained a briefing sheet indicating the time required (one hour), and a booklet which concisely described/defined the performance and impact categories. Stakeholders were advised to familiarise themselves with the booklet contents to speed up the interview, although this was not a pre-requisite. The interview itself was split into four parts: (1) introduction to the aims of the study; (2) priority measurement of the performance categories; (3) priority measurement of the impact categories; (4) graphical feedback of data.

The priority measurements were conducted through the application of Earl *et al's* MADE Model and its utilisation of the *pairwise comparison technique* developed by Saaty (1980). Pairwise comparisons allow users to methodically and systematically determine their weights for a value tree's performance attributes, simply by comparing pairs of attributes one at a time. The analysis of the pairwise preference data that results from this process produces a distribution of criteria weights which can be analysed in association with the weights of other stakeholders to provide a portfolio of stakeholder preferences with which to guide strategy development. A particular advantage of this approach is that the method has been found to be relatively simple to use, which is an essential ingredient if the weights of lay persons are sought.

To help candidates with the pairwise decisions each was supplied with two sets of laminated cards describing the two-levels of categories as shown in the pre-distributed booklet. These cards were single-sided for the performance categories and double-sided for the impact categories - one side showed a technical description and the reverse showed a summary bulleted list. Working through each set in turn (first the performance categories, then the impact categories), candidates were first asked to rank the cards in order of importance (for the impact categories they were left to choose which side of the double-sided card to use). Once candidates had decided on an overall ranking, they took one pair of categories at a time, and considered which category they considered more important and by how much (on a scale of 1-9), whilst referring to the card in order to help keep track of their overall preferences (although this order could be altered at any time). The data was entered into a spreadsheet and a graphical output of their results displayed, an example of which is shown in Figure 4. Candidates were asked to confirm that the output reflected their preferences and given the opportunity to refine their relative preferences if so desired. The example shown in Figure 4 suggests that the candidate considered quality of services and comparative performance to be significantly more important than the other four, with environmental performance considered more important than health and safety, and so on.

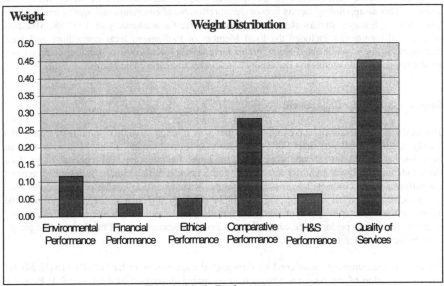

Figure 4: Sample Output of a Stakeholder's Preference

Categories	Weights
Environmental Performance	0.12
Financial Performance	0.04
Ethical Performance	0.05
Comparative Performance	0.28
H&S Performance	0.06
Quality of Services	0.45
	1.00

Stage 3 - Post-Engagement Analysis (i.e. Results)

The methodology employed produced considerable quantitative data which was analysed in depth but which is only summarised here by examining the average data for the performance categories (top-level issues), the average data for the impact categories (bottom-level issues) and the average data for the stakeholder groups.

The Performance Categories (or Top-Level Issues)

Perhaps unsurprisingly, there was not universal agreement on the most and least important performance categories or on an agreed rank order of most important to least important category. However, the methodology employed allows the data to be analysed in a number of ways:

- Averaging the weights of all the participants gives the following rank order (from most important to least important): (1) Health and safety performance; (2) Quality of services; (3) Environmental performance; (4) Financial performance; (5) Ethical Performance; (6) Comparative Performance.

- Totalling the frequency of the ranked positions of each category (i.e. how many times each category was ranked in the top three - "more important", and the bottom three - "less important") reveals the same rank order.

- Analysis of the distribution of ranked positions for each category reveals, for example: environmental performance was ranked across all six positions, with the most popular positions being tied between 2nd most important (i.e. 2nd) and third least important (i.e. 4th); health and safety performance was most frequently ranked as the most important category (i.e. 1st) and no participants considered it the least important category.

The Impact Categories (or bottom-level issues)

An identical analysis to that conducted for the performance categories revealed:

- Averaging the weights of all the participants gives the following rank order (from most important to least important): (1) human health; (2) resource depletion; (3) ecosystem degradation; (4) smog formation; (5) global warming; (6) ozone depletion; (7) eutrophication; (8) acid rain.

- Totalling the frequency of the ranked positions of each category (i.e. how many times each category was ranked in the top four – "more important", and the bottom four – "less important") reveals the same rank order as above except ozone depletion (5) is ranked above global warming (6).

- Analysis of the distribution of ranked positions for each impact category reveals, for example: the most popular ranked position for human health was the most important category (i.e. 1st), yet two participants also considered it the least important category (i.e.8th); all categories were ranked the most important (i.e.1st) by at least one participant.

Stakeholder Group Data

Since participants were identified for participation in the study through their perceived membership of certain stakeholder groups, the data for each group was also examined by considering the average weights and ranked positions attributed by the constituent members. In general, participants allocated to the same group revealed different preferences for both the performance and impact categories, i.e. a consensus was not apparent from the "individuals" who constituted each group (which may not be surprising considering they were not engaged in justifying their preferences to each other and the groups were quite broadly defined). However, even though there is ostensibly little intra-group agreement, in some circumstances it may still be considered appropriate to use this group data as the basis for decision-making. For example, there is scope for weighting a group's contribution to the decision either to increase or decrease its influence.

For this study, the average data for each group for both performance and impact categories is shown in Table 4, where 1st = most important and $6^{th}/8^{th}$ = least important (reiterating that using the average group data effectively disregards any differences that may exist within each group).

Category	Community	Financial	Regulators	Employees	Students
Environmental performance	1st	4th	2nd	4th	6th
Financial performance	5th	3rd	6th	3rd	5th
Ethical performance	3rd	6th	4th	5th	4th
Comparative performance	6th	2nd	5th	6th	3rd
H&S performance	2nd	5th	1st	1st	2nd
Quality of services	4th	1st	3rd	2nd	1st
Resource depletion	3rd	5th	2nd	2nd	2nd
Human health	2nd	1st	1st	1st	1st
Global warming	5th	4th	4th	3rd	7th
Ozone depletion	7th	7th	6th	5th	4th
Acid rain	8th	8th	8th	6th	7th
Eutrophication	6th	6th	6th	8th	6th
Smog formation	1st	3rd	5th	6th	3rd
Ecosystem degradation	3rd	2nd	2nd	3rd	5th

Table 4: Stakeholder Group Data (Average)

From this table, notable observations are:
- there was inter-group "agreement" on the most important performance category between the Employees and Regulators who, on average, considered health and safety performance to be the most important category, and between the Financial group and the Students, who considered the quality of services to be the most important;
- only the Financial group did not, on average, weigh health and safety performance as either 1st or 2nd most important;

- only the Community and Regulators groups weighed environmental performance as a "more important" category (i.e. in the top three positions);
- only in the Community group did the average data not rank "human health" as the most important impact category;
- the average data from each group ranked "human health" as either first or second most important impact category.

When using the data in this manner, there is potential to mis-represent participants' preferences if there is little intra-group agreement. It is therefore advisable to make explicit from the onset whether identifying stakeholder groups is for the sole purpose of ensuring adequate representation in the decision-making process or whether the groups are also instrumental in the outcome of the decision. This can be elucidated by asking: do the groups become irrelevant once participants have been recruited? If the groups are not irrelevant, it is essential that participants are given the opportunity to agree the stakeholder group into which their preferences are essentially immersed (noting that some individuals may be legitimate members of more than one group). Since this observation emerged from this study, the University's stakeholders were not given such an opportunity and the group data has therefore not been used to influence the University's strategy.

The Utility of the Study Data

One of the primary reasons for entering dialogue with stakeholders is to bring a diversity of opinions, beliefs and priorities into the decision-making process. However, it is just as important to attempt to define elements on which stakeholders basically agree and disagree so that this can help to both specify a strategy and to focus its negotiation and refinement. In this respect, the data analysis showed some strong trends running both across all individuals and across the defined stakeholder groups. These trends constitute both agreement and disagreement on strength of preferences (i.e. how much more important one category is than another).

Implications of Data for the Performance Categories
The majority of stakeholders do not regard environmental performance to be of greater importance than health and safety or quality of services. It is therefore unlikely that environmental management will secure sufficient investment or attention as long as it has to compete for resources against the "more important" categories, particularly in the current climate of reduced funding in the sector. To avoid this potential competition for resources, it becomes prudent not to introduce environmental management as an appendage to core activities but to attempt to integrate it as an essential requirement of managing health and safety and delivering quality "services".

A similar argument can also be made for the performance categories considered less important by the University's stakeholders, i.e. comparative, financial and ethical performance. In this respect, the implication is not to justify the need for environmental management solely by making comparisons with the progress made by other universities, by the potential for financial savings, or because of ethical responsibilities and obligations.

Implications of Data for Impact Categories

Although there were significant differences between the preferences of the participants, the results do show some strong trends of use to the University's environmental strategy. Human health consistently arose as a more important category and can therefore, in terms of the standards for environmental management systems, be considered a "significant" environmental impact. This impact can be addressed in the University's environmental strategy by focusing upon hazardous, clinical and radioactive waste management and on the purchase and use of chemicals or hazardous substances. For example, the University could set a priority aim to better manage its use, purchase and disposal of chemicals by setting-up a central database and aiming to reduce both the diversity and volume of hazardous substances. In contrast, acid rain and ozone depletion consistently arose as "less important" which suggests that targets associated with nitrate and sulfate emissions or CFC use, have less utility as an indicator of improved environmental performance, as they do not address the concerns of those stakeholders interviewed.

Perhaps most importantly, it is worth noting that the majority of those categories considered 'more important' are those that are considered local rather than global, which lends support to the "think-local, act-local" adage reiterated by Adams (1995). This finding would not have been so apparent if the study had been based upon more amorphous environmental issues (e.g. waste, transport, energy) as opposed to the specific impact categories. For example, the average of the community group data indicated that smog formation and human health were the most important impact categories whilst global warming and acid rain were considered less important. It was clear from the interviews that transport was a major issue for these stakeholders and if the study had focused upon stakeholder preferences for issues, then it is highly likely that transport would have emerged as an important issue for members of this group. However, it would have been less obvious whether this group were actually concerned with local impacts associated with transport, such as smog or global impacts, such as global warming. Using impacts instead of issues has made this distinction explicit and provides the opportunity for the University's environmental policy to more precisely target areas that are of specific relevance to its environmental performance according to stakeholder preferences.

To summarise, although there was little agreement between stakeholders, this is to a certain extent expected, especially using a pre-defined value tree with unfamiliar categories. However, it is reasonable to expect that any process leading to the development of a strategy incorporating a wide range of views will be iterative. This data should therefore be viewed as an initial step and not a final result. In fact the greatest benefit of a process such as this, is often not the experimental but the experiential findings.

Experiential Findings

Stakeholders

While some proposed participants were not successfully contacted within an appropriate timeframe, only four actually declined to participate. The most popular reason for declining was time constraints while one erudite employee declined because he did not believe he was a stakeholder of the University (even after discussing the definition) and could not see how an environmental policy would affect his activities! In addition, one stakeholder from the employee group was not a solicitous participant, only agreeing to participate following persuasion from an influential source. The same stakeholder demonstrated cynicism about the value of the whole study and the 'stakeholder' concept.

These experiences have significant implications for the theory and definition of "the stakeholder" and lend support to the definition reported by Cowell et al (1997), that there is a distinction between a 'stakeholder' and an 'interested party'. However, while their discussions focused upon the qualification of an interested party as a stakeholder through the legitimacy of the "interest", the findings from this study suggest that not all stakeholders are interested in participating, i.e. they are not interested parties. This raises a significant point that some stakeholders may not be willing to engage in dialogue nor, therefore, fulfil the role which is expected or required of them in today's stakeholder society. This notion, that the relationship between an organisation and its stakeholders is entirely reflective, i.e. that an organisation is also entitled to expect a certain performance from its stakeholders, is implied in a model for social auditing proposed by Jones and Welford (1997). In the Higher Education sector context, this finding is also of particular relevance to the idea of 'responsible global citizenship' - a topical item on the sector's core learning for sustainability agenda (Ali-Khan, 1996).

Impacts versus Issues
Most candidates found the comparison of impact categories quite challenging, some seemingly relishing the challenge, others actively resisting it. The reasons for this may be attributed to: the number of categories to be compared; the unfamiliarity of some of the categories; and/or the lack of relevance of the categories to the candidate. Evidence of these reasons was apparent during many of the interviews where candidates expressed concern about the task ahead of them. The epitome of this discomfort was the candidate who refused to participate in this part of the study despite seeming to enjoy the challenge of the first part. Another candidate who ranked all the categories as equal appeared to genuinely believe that to be the case, and did not appear to be pursuing any other motive.

For many candidates the driving force behind their preferences was the University's perceived greatest contribution. For others, it was the relative contribution of the University's activities in comparison to other organisations or sectors both in the UK and world-wide. For others still, it was the perceived severity of the effects of the impact category, regardless of the University's contribution. Importantly, this implies that for some stakeholders, the scale of the University's contribution to a particular category is irrelevant but what concerns them most, is how (positively or negatively) the University contributes. This suggests that it may be advantageous not to quantify environmental impacts before conducting a study of this nature and that this aspect of the 'value tree' is appropriate - it does not reference the scale of the University's impacts. (Note: the aims of the study did not include identifying what drives the preferences of the University's stakeholders but this evidence arose during the course of the study).

Candidates often interpreted the impact definitions in different ways (as expected) but in some cases inaccurately. For example, many could not make a distinction between resource depletion (the category definition) and resource consumption (more familiar issue). For this category some candidates could not relate to the reduction in the available stock level as the essence of the category but insisted on focusing upon the other categories of impact associated with resource consumption, e.g. extraction, processing, transport etc. In this case there is an unclear distinction between resource depletion as an environmental impact (i.e. 'change to the environment'), and resource consumption as a human activity which drives resource depletion through resource extraction, transportation, use and disposal all of which contribute to various categories of environmental impact. The category of human health also proved to be frequently misinterpreted. However, unlike the confusions with resource depletion which were only revealed as the interviews proceeded, the misinterpretation was anticipated, and candidates were consistently reminded that human health referred only to impacts outside the University workplace (human health inside the workplace is considered to be part of 'health and safety performance' not 'environmental performance'). The other categories did not suffer from the same problems for the majority were familiar to the candidates, except eutrophication which seemed to be satisfactorily defined.

Conclusions of the Study

The Stakeholder Study for the University of Surrey proved a worthwhile endeavor. As a research exercise, it provided a useful insight into the process of stakeholder engagement for a higher education establishment in the UK (an insight that can usefully be adopted by other institutions and adapted by other sectors) and has provided evidence in support of the need to evangelise impact categories as the basis for measuring environmental performance (recent Environmental Reporting research identified a need for greater use of impact categories [Bennett and James, 1998, p.50]).

The time and effort expended in conducting the study perhaps explains why more HE institutions have not widely engaged their stakeholders in such a manner. The interviews were conducted over a period of four months and involved a fair amount of travelling. Printing costs were not insignificant. However, it is not the research value of the exercise alone that has made the expenditure worthwhile. As for all stakeholder engagements, there is considerable unquantifiable value in involving a wide range of individuals in a process that can ultimately affect, or be affected by, those individuals. In particular, the involvement of key and senior University employees and members of the local community was particularly rewarding for a number of reasons. The majority of members of both groups were seen to enjoy participating in the process.

However, some members were particularly cynical regarding the University's use of the findings i.e. whether or not they could actually influence the University's future strategy. This suggests a potential morale/public relations/image problem for the University to address (both internally and externally). At the same time, the expression of disinterest and other opinions concerning the environment by some of the employees has revealed a number of potential friends, foes, advocates and adversaries within the University's internal community, who may resist or assist the pursuit of improved environmental performance. This information (see Figure 5 for an example of some "enlightening" comments!) would certainly not have been gleaned without the personal structured interview approach and has been strategically utilised.

Figure 5: A Selection of Comments from the Interviews

"Global warming isn't happening is it?"

"Acid rain is important but we're not in Scandinavia"

"Global warming, that's if you believe in it"

"They're all very similar" (on impact categories)

"They're not my problem" (on global impact categories)

and

"Nothing left to do" (on ozone depletion)

"People that will die from climate change will not be in the UK"

"The University does not significantly influence or have a role in shaping policy"

"Within the great aggregate of things, the University cannot make much of a difference"

"The University does not have a role in leading by example"

While it is conceded that the performance categories have their flaws, in particular the manner in which they were defined without input from the participants, as a starting point this has been considered an acceptable trade-off. The data implications, that quality of services and health and safety performance are the most important categories, is corroborated to a certain extent by: the teaching quality assurance exercises currently being pursued; by the "value for money" initiative being pushed in the whole of the UK public sector; and by the high profile that health and safety currently enjoys within the university milieu.

The stakeholder study has enabled the relative importance of these issues to be quantified and individuals who do not concur with this perspective to be identified, thereby providing information for a more precise environmental strategy to be developed. The most important conclusion from the data is the postulate that the most efficacious strategy for improving the University's environmental performance is to integrate environmental management into health and safety and quality management. This is an approach frequently employed in industry, whilst an integrated environment, health and safety approach is already employed in the UK HE sector, most notably by Liverpool John Moores University and the University of Sunderland.

The second stage of the study was specifically designed to identify about which categories of environmental impacts the University's stakeholders are most concerned, to enable the environmental policy to prioritise the activities for attention that contribute to such impacts. Within the limitations of the data, the study suggests that human health issues should be prioritised as most important, while acid rain and ozone depletion are less important. A recent decision by the Estates and Buildings Department to pay a premium for ammonia-based refrigeration on environmental grounds, is in direct contravention of this mandate and provides a useful example, where the output of the stakeholder study could have been used to assist the decision-making process or to justify the decision made.

The use of specific impact categories rather than environmental issues proved somewhat controversial. In fact, the categories caused greater difficulties than was envisaged. Perhaps perversely, this actually lends greater evidence to the need for this approach to be more widely employed, through the direct consequence of the University's educational responsibilities. Thus, the fact that on average, participants did not grasp or had difficulty in grasping the concept of impact categories, demonstrates the lack of understanding that currently surrounds environmental degradation. It is a misunderstanding of environmental impacts and issues that can be considered to be contributing to "profligate environmentalism" (Clift, 1995) while the HE sector via its educational responsibilities has long been identified as having a responsibility to contribute towards a greater understanding of environmental degradation. Therefore, while the use of impact categories was not on the whole successful, the study did successfully identify the need for further development of this approach and highlighted its potential as a tool for learning. In addition, lessons can be learnt from the experiences of the University's stakeholders. For example, the experience of the study suggests that the categories need several attributes, including: clear definitions; units of measurement; examples of contributing activities; relevance to contemporary environmental issues.

Quite convincingly, this study has shown that entering dialogue with stakeholders is worthwhile for the HE sector and that a stakeholder driven strategy can be developed. Perhaps less convincingly, the study has also identified where the University's environmental performance ranks in comparison to other performance categories for a selection of stakeholders. For the categories of environmental impact there is even less certainty that a rank order has been obtained. However, the data has revealed that this information can be obtained through engaging stakeholders and that to achieve a satisfactory degree of accuracy, stakeholders need to be carefully chosen, and stakeholder groups need to be carefully identified. There is also an implicit assumption that those who are responsible for implementing the strategy should be the ones to select the participants and the stakeholder groups (for the University, the Environmental Policy Steering Group) and perhaps be advised by an experienced facilitator.

From a practical perspective, the data provided by the study is useful but is not considered sufficiently statistically robust, with some key stakeholder groups notably inadequately represented. It is not, therefore, being used as the sole basis on which to justify critical decisions about the University's pursuit of improved environmental performance though it is still of use to the ongoing development of its environmental policy. While the University is not yet at a stage where it can make use of the information regarding the impact categories, the University's Environmental Policy Steering Group is currently attempting to integrate environmental management into health, safety and quality management at a strategic level. Naturally, it is avoiding the involvement of those who mistakenly believe that "the University does not have a role in leading by example" or that "within the great aggregate of things, the University cannot make much of a difference"!

References

ACBE (1997) *Seventh Progress Report to and Response from the President of the Board of Trade and the Secretary of State for the Environment.* London: DTI.

Adams, J.P., (1995) *The Value of Environmental Action: An Investigation into Environmental Values, Knowledge and Action.* MSc Dissertation in Environmental Psychology, Department of Psychology. Surrey: University of Surrey.

Ali-Khan, S. (1996) *Environmental Responsibility - A Review of the 1993 Toyne Report.* London: HMSO.

Bennett, M., James, P. (1998) "Environment under the Spotlight - Current Practice and Future Trends in Environment-Related Performance Measurement for Business". *ACCA Research Report 66*, pp 50. London: Certified Accountants Educational Trust.

BSI (1996) *Implementation of ISO14001: 1996 Environmental Management Systems - Specifications with guidance for use.* London: British Standards Institution.

Clift, R. (1995) *Rapporteur's Summary "Engineering For Sustainability".* London: Royal Academy of Engineering.

Cowell, S., Hogan, S., Clift, R. (1997) Positioning and Applications of LCA - LCANET Theme Report. *European Network for Strategic Life-Cycle Assessment Research and Development.* Centre for Environmental Strategy. Surrey: University of Surrey.

Davey, A.P. (1998) Engineering Doctorate in Environmental Technology. *Portfolio, Volume 1.* Centre for Environmental Strategy. Surrey:University of Surrey.

Davey, A. P., Hodgson, S., Clift, R. (1997) The SMART Management of Environmental Impacts. In *Business Strategy and Environment Conference*, University of Leeds, 18th-19th September 1997.

Earl, G., Clift, R., Moilanen, T. (1998) Reducing the Uncertainty in Environmental Investments: Integrating Stakeholder Values into Corporate Decisions. In James, P. and Bennett, M. (eds.) *The Green Bottom Line: Environmental Management Accounting - Current Practice and Future Trends.* London: Greenleaf .

EC (1993) *Council Regulation (EEC) No 1836/93 of 29 June 1993.* (allowing voluntary participation by companies in the industrial sector in a Community eco-management and audit scheme). Brussels: Council of European Communities.

IBM, (1995) *Consulting the Stakeholder - A Profile of IBM UK's Environmental Performance.* London: IBM UK Limited.

Jones, D., Welford, R. (1997) Organising for Sustainable Development: Structure, Culture and Social Auditing, Chapter 7, pp157-178. In Welford, R. (ed) (1997) *Hijacking Environmentalism - Corporate Responses to Sustainable Development*. London: Earthscan.

Nordic Council (1995) *Nordic Guidelines on Life-Cycle Assessment*. Nordic Council of Ministers.

Saaty, T. L. (1980) *The Analytic Hierarchy Process*. New York: McGraw Hill.

SustainAbility/UNEP (1996) Engaging Stakeholders Volume 1: The Benchmark Survey, SustainAbility Ltd and United Nations Environment Programme.

SustainAbility/UNEP (1996a) *Engaging Stakeholders Volume 2: The Case Studies*. London: SustainAbility Ltd and United Nations Environment Programme.

UN (1992) *Report of the United Nations Conference on Environment and Development*. Resolutions Adopted by the Conference, 3-14 June. Volume 1, Chapters 23, 27, & 30, New York: United Nations.

WBCSD (1997) *Environmental Performance and Shareholder Value*. World Business Council for Sustainable Development. Conches, Switzerland.

Wheeler, D., Sillanpää, M. (1997) *The Stakeholder Corporation: a blueprint for maximising stakeholder value*. London: Pitman Publishing.

Chapter 4

Technology and Sustainable Development
Sustainability as a challenge for engineers

Karel F. Mulder

Abstract

This chapter describes the experiences of Delft University of Technology in relation to sustainability and some of the approaches used towards it.

Introduction

In the spring of 1998, Delft University of Technology (DUT)[4] adopted a plan to introduce sustainable development in all engineering curricula. This chapter will sketch the main points of this plan. It will start with an overview of the traditions within engineering that shape engineers' attitudes towards sustainable development. It will also outline the social environment of engineering and analyze the problems which result from introducing sustainable development within the various engineering curricula. The paper will conclude with a sketch of a curriculum for aerospace engineering in which several elements of sustainable development have been included. The primary message that DUT wants to convey to engineering students is that *sustainable development is not a burden for the engineer, but a challenge.*

Technology in modern culture

Since the 1960s, many people have been regarding technological change as one of the main reasons for environmental degradation and depletion of natural resources. The same 'progress', that was so overwhelmingly present in the reasoning on technology in the fifties (Atoms for Peace, post WW II reconstruction), was earmarked as a road to collapse in the seventies.

---

[4] DUT was known as Technische Hoogeschool Delft (TH Delft) from 1905 to 1987. Before 1905 it was named the Polytechnische School. To avoid confusion, I will use the name DUT.

The instrumental way in which technologists dealt with nature (Habermas, 1968) was held responsible for environmental exploitation and destruction. Although many technology criticisms left scope for an alternative technology, the alternatives presented were generally too far away or just too weird to be taken seriously by technologists (e.g. Ulrich 1979, Dickson, 1974). Unsurprisingly, engineers often reacted in a rather hostile manner to environmental issues: no matter what engineers did, their work was condemned anyhow. Every solution that was developed by engineers would lead to new problems, and 'technological' solutions of environmental problems were regarded as inferior to 'social' solutions. Although engineers can find many useful lessons in Tenners book Why things bite back (1996), the picture it draws for engineers is rather depressing.

This interpretation of the role of technology and technological change in regard to environmental degradation was based on various, partly contradictory starting points:

- that technological change is unidirectional, i.e. that the history of technology (and its future) is a linear sequence of artefacts, practices and systems, moving away from the natural, 'technologyless' man
- that the rate of change of specific technologies is (except for minor aberrations) determined by the growth rate of the pool of scientific knowledge and technological change of adjacent technologies
- that technology is not influenced by society, or societal change
- that technological change is the driving force of societal change

Although much technology criticism of the sixties and seventies was mixed with various political analyses, these basic statements could be discerned in various criticisms of technology per se. For example, Marxists would generally not agree with the last statement as they assumed class struggle to be the driving force of history. Therefore, the application of technology was in their view determined by the class struggle, not the technology[5] itself. However, if the technology under debate becomes problematic in itself, as many people see, for example, in the case of weapons of mass destruction, nuclear power generation or genetic manipulation, there seemed to be only two alternatives to many people: acquiescing in the fatal destiny of mankind or withdrawal from society. One might question the moral aspects of these options. Apart from that, it would be wrong to accept technological determinism, since it leaves no hope for a humane future. In a more moderate form, some people have argued in favour of a counterbalance of the autonomous technological drive, by social means. In such circumstances, technological change should be curbed in order to solve the world's environmental problems only by social mechanisms (Commissie Lange Termijn Milieubeleid, 1990).

However, there is no reason to give up so easily on technology. Over the last 15 years, there has been a flood of publications that stress the very intimate relations between the social and the technological. Hughes (1986) for example, even used the term 'seamless web' by which he meant the inextricable relations between the various kinds of factors that were involved in technological

---

[5] An exception to this can be seen in the analysis of the Newtonian revolution by Boris Hessen (1931). In this analysis, 17th century navigational technologies were described as resulting from the mercantile society.

change. The vast array of studies, whether they focused on technological artefacts or systems, and whether these technologies were related to political or industrial decision-making, social or cultural change, they all contributed to the basic understanding that technological and social change are deeply intertwined.

It therefore appears to be important not only to push technology in different directions, but also to change the social context of technology. If a technology is unsustainable, it is not only because that is the way such a technology has been made, but also because consumers and producers, technologists or laymen, have consented to that.

Even the fully accepted technologies of today still have great potential to be environmentally improved, as Greenpeace has proven via its projects on cars and refrigerators. However, it takes an outside actor to bring it about. Some other examples:
• In transport, there is a great potential to cut back environmental damage by using plastics or composites instead of metals, even if the problems of material recycling are taken into account.
• Large parts of our fossil fuel consumption might be replaced by more sustainable sources of energy. However, wind energy and solar energy raise a lot of problems that are related to land use, visual hindrance, noise pollution, changing ecosystems, and changing power relations. Sustainable sources of energy will involve a lot of clever technology as well as a lot of clever social thinking.
• Large parts of the world do not possess reliable drinking water. Although purification is generally not terribly expensive, many countries seem unable to deal with this problem. What often seems to be lacking is a 'fit' between the water purification technologies and culture, traditions and geographical circumstances that people are living in.

"Sustainable Development", is therefore, the great new challenge for the engineer of the 21st century. However, we must admit that engineers also created a lot of environmental problems in the past. What engineer do we need to do a better job? How do we train such engineers?

The paradigm of engineers

The profession of scientifically-trained engineer came into existence in the 18th and 19th century. It was in fact a product of the "Enlightenment". As the "Enlightenment" implied re-arranging political and administrative structures in a rationalist way in order to abandon superstition and injustice, it implied for engineers rethinking traditional technologies in order to rationalise and optimise them. The training of engineers therefore had to change from merely apprenticeship (in order to learn the traditional methods) to the teaching of science and mathematics (Lintsen, 1979). In various debates, engineers generally took the view that they had the means to solve a problem best. What they sometimes failed to recognise, was that the real issue at stake was not a scientifically/mathematically solvable optimisation problem, but a choice between irreconcilable norms and values. For example, when engineers were asked in the 1920s about their view regarding the preservation of the Dutch windmills by technological improvements, they generally argued in favour of demolishing them, thereby neglecting the appreciation that many people had for this national heritage (Mulder, 1993). In the debates on (nuclear) energy in the 1970s and 1980s, engineers often failed to recognise that there was far more at stake than (cost-) efficient electricity supply. Even if they took the issue of safety seriously, they often failed to recognise that disasters in the order of magnitude of a nuclear meltdown were just completely unacceptable for many people, no matter how small the chances might be (Schuuring et al. 1983, Nelkin 1992). Enormous efforts to calculate risks, minimise them, control them or play them down appear to be futile.

Developing technology is not a matter of optimising artefacts or systems in regard to a given (set of) demand(s). Demands of society are dynamic, just as technology is itself. Successful technologies generally do more than just fulfilling people's existing demands; they challenge people and show them new possibilities that they had not even thought of before. Developing new and successful technologies can only take place if the technologist has a deep understanding of the motives and desires of people that will be related to the new technology and of the effects of his design on society as a whole and on nature. This problem orientation is hard to achieve within engineering curricula that are generally composed of disciplinary courses (Neef, 1995).

A paradigm shift is therefore required in engineering, and it will profoundly affect engineering curricula.

Engineers have to learn that their technology driven concepts are not the central issues of society, and that people have to adapt to these concepts[6]. The demands of people (especially the weaker, and unborn) are what counts, and technologists have to be challenged to contribute to fulfilling those demands. If engineering students realise that, they can make invaluable contributions to the environment. It is, therefore, natural that problem-oriented forms of training are of growing importance at DUT. For example, the Faculty of Mechanical Engineering is in the middle of a reform process that aims at transforming the entire curriculum into problem-oriented training.

Delft University of Technology and its culture

In 1842, DUT was established in Delft as the first institute of its kind in the Netherlands. It was intended to train civil engineers (as opposed to military engineers who were trained at military academies). The organization flourished as engineers became of key importance for a country that started developing its water, road and rail transport, and mining, metal and electrical industry. Academically, the DUT was also successful as its graduates were allowed to use the title „Ingenieur" („Ir.") and the organization was allowed to grant PhDs. DUT graduates organized themselves in the „Koninklijk Instituut van Ingenieurs (KIvI)"[7]. Before WW II, Delft graduates were often involved in public policy. The rationalistic approach of these engineers often lead to sympathy for socialist planning policies, and several graduates went East to help the development of the Soviet Union.

---

[6] This gap between engineering ideas on 'useful' technologies for society and the ideas of the layman was nicely illustrated by a study of the IEEE (1984). US Engineers rated 12 (electrical) technologies about the same laymen did. However, there was a large gap regarding the usefulness of 'automation' and 'robotics'.

[7] Royal Institute of Engineers.

After WW II, Delft´s engineers became part of the establishment of Dutch society. Technology became overwhelmingly important for several reasons: WW II was won by the superior technology of the Americans, the Dutch infrastructure was ruined and the Netherlands lost Indonesia and therefore had to transform its economy.

The need for technology was considered to be so great that the DUT could not fulfil it alone. In 1956, a second Technical University was founded in Eindhoven, and in 1964 a third was founded in Twente. Meanwhile, the establishments of the DUT were enlarged and renewed. As the University of Twente was shaped in years of reform, its curricula were often rather experimental as compared to those at Delft. At the DUT, various people regarded their institution as being the only real engineering school, while they denounced Twente as a 'camping-site' and Eindhoven as the 'company school of Philips'. Curricula at DUT generally contained a negligible share of humanities and many people were proud of that. In the 1960s, the Department of Mechanical Engineering wanted to abolish its professorship in management because part of it was 'organizational psychology', which was brandmarked as 'pseudo-science'. The chair was only saved by the support of the KIvI and 4 large corporations (De Jong, 1992, p. 86).

All engineering studies in the Netherlands characterized themselves as 'tough'. At the welcoming address, freshmen were told to look at their neighbors; if the freshman was convinced that he would become an engineer, his neighbors would not, because half of the students failed. This attitude ('we are the best and therefore many students will fail) was part of the institutional pride of the Technical Universities. Within the faculties, there was hardly any attention paid to students who had fallen behind or had run into problems. The loss that resulted in human terms was taken for granted[8].

DUT remained by far the largest Technical University in the Netherlands. Nowadays it employs about 5000 people. There are about 13.000 undergraduate students.

Two Waves of Environmental Awareness

The uproars of the seventies affected the DUT considerably. By the introduction of new legislation in 1972, students and assistants could participate in the university decision-making processes. Many students spent much time on various left wing political purposes. Political debates in regard to technology and environment were focused on (nuclear) energy and energy consumption, industrial pollution, soil pollution by toxic wastes and the supply of energy and raw materials.

By the end of the seventies, environmental issues had affected some engineering curricula: in the Department of Architecture, a working group on town planning and environment was established. This group developed and introduced several activities within the curriculum of the Department of Architecture (this curriculum is based on multidisciplinary blocks of 2 months, one block in the second year of study was completely focused on the environmental aspects of buildings and their surroundings) and environmental issues were introduced within some

---

[8] For a general history of DUT, see Baudet, 1992.

specializations of Civil Engineering. In this Department, sewerage engineering and drinking water purification had been a specialization before. Control of the quality of surface water was fitted into this subject, while marine ecology was also added as a specialization course.

At the Department of Chemical Engineering, some basic environmental courses were introduced. All students had to participate in 'Chemistry and Society' courses in which environmental subjects, in their social contexts, were the main subject. Health and Safety effects of chemical processes also became integrated in the curriculum (Lemkowitz, 1992, 1996).

However, environmental issues only marginally affected most other engineering curricula at DUT.

A second wave of environmental awareness was triggered by the Brundtland report (World Commission on Environment and Development, 1987) and the first National Environmental Policy Plan of the Netherlands (NEPP, 1990). This renewed interest in environmental issues resulted in some new initiatives:

* The Faculty of Mechanical Engineering established a part-time chair in Environmental Technology. Dr.ir.J.L.A Jansen and Ir. H.P. van Heel[9] jointly fulfilled this new task. They introduced a successful course in 'Environmental Technology'.
* The Faculty of Industrial Design Engineering established a part-time chair in Environmental Product Design. This became the core of a research group.
* The Faculty of Mining established a chair in Recycling. Thereby, it more or less redefined its 'core business': from 'mining' to 'raw material supply'.
* In 1990, four Faculties established the joint research institute 'Interduct', the Delft University Clean Technology Institute. Later, three more Faculties participated in Interduct.

However, these initiatives were all additions; there were hardly any changes in the basic training programs of engineers, nor in research programs.

In the framework of the NEPP, important tasks were assigned to universities and in 1991 a university environmental policy plan was adopted. This plan included the introduction of an environmental management system and more scope for environmental issues in training and research. It also stated that guidelines for introducing sustainable development within engineering curricula and research programs had to be formulated within three years.

As the Faculties were rather independent in shaping their curricula, this was a hard task. A high level steering group was formed and in the summer of 1994 it published its report (Stuurgroep Duurzame Ontwikkeling TU Delft, 1994). The steering group aimed at introducing 'sustainable development' throughout the engineering training programs. The report was rather controversial within the university community. On the one hand, students and various staff members supported it. However, most Faculties did not want to support these plans. At that time, the technical

---

[9] Jansen and Van Heel are well known in the Netherlands. Both men are engineers. Jansen was an MP in the seventies (a green party) and held a leading position within the Ministry of the Environment. Van Heel was the director of Hoechst Holland, Vlissingen.

universities and the KIvI were struggling to convince the government that undergraduate training of engineers should be prolonged from 4 to 5 years. As the outcome of this debate was still unclear, one did not want to put an extra burden on the overcrowded curriculum. Moreover, the concept of sustainable development was for many people rather vague, and therefore contradictory to the self-image of an institute of hard core technologists. Priority was thus given to a plan to introduce ethics courses.

Although the steering group's report had not much direct impact, various activities followed and kept the drive for sustainable technological development very alive:
In 1994, the University Council adopted the strategic vision that was formulated by the University Board 'Towards a new commitment' (College van Bestuur, 1994). The mission statement was formulated as:

> *DUT will function as an internationally leading technical university, both in regard to education as well as research. DUT is committed to the main social and technologic-scientific problems and challenges. It contributes to the solutions of these issues and holds itself accountable for them.*

In addition, the University Council emphasized the importance of sustainable development for DUT. Various activities in relation to Sustainable Development took place. In 1994, a small group organized a successful congress on sustainable technology and religious acceptance (De Jong, 1994). In 1995, student groups organized a successful conference, 'TU Globaal'.

Clearly, new initiatives were needed. The government had consented to 5-year curricula for engineers and so there was scope for new courses. This scope was not to be filled by extra technology courses. Social skills of engineers were often regarded to be less than sufficient and therefore, developing social skills became important. Moreover, it became politically unacceptable that half of the students failed. Pressure on students had to be eased.

By the end of 1996, a new Committee was installed by the University Board to come up with new proposals for implementing "sustainable development" in the engineering curricula. This Committee consisted of fewer professors and more lecturers. The intention was that it had to philosophize less, and act more.

The main target of the Committee remained bridging the gap between (traditional) 'environmentalism' and 'engineering': sustainable development had to become a challenge for engineers and the engineering profession. In line with the strategic vision of DUT, engineers who graduated from DUT had to be prepared for the great technological challenges, especially solving questions related to sustainable development. This implied that DUT has to educate engineers who can operationalise 'sustainable development' in technical scientific designing and in the application of technology and technical systems.

In its approach, the Committee was inspired by the report 'Our Common Future' by the World Commission on Environment and Development (1987) and by the Copernicus Declaration (1993). Prof. dr.ir. J.L.A. Jansen chaired the Committee. His experiences as initiator of the research program Sustainable Technological Development, a program that started in 1993 and was sponsored by five government departments, gave inspiring examples of new paths to fulfil the needs of people in the next century. This requires a dramatic increase in so-called eco-efficiency, the efficiency by which the environment at large is used to provide for people's needs. The Committee therefore considered that sustainability should be an integral element of the designing process, as well as of the development and application of technology. In its approach, the committee regarded the responsibility for sustainable development as a line-responsibility in professional practice, i.e. it could not only be left to specialised engineers.

The Committee regarded the integration of sustainable development into DUT education and research as a challenge, which it had to meet in cooperation with the Faculties in a process of 'learning by doing'. For that reason, the committee consulted closely with various decision-makers within the faculties. This resulted in a plan consisting of three interconnected operations:

- The design of an elementary course 'Technology in Sustainable Development' for ALL students of the DUT.
- Intertwining of sustainable development in ALL regular disciplinary courses, in a way corresponding to the nature of each specific course.
- Development of the possibility of graduation in a sustainable development specialization within the framework of each faculty.

The elementary course 'Technology in Sustainable Development' (TIDO).

The objective of this course is:
- To develop consciousness among the students for the challenges that sustainable development poses to engineers,
- To develop understanding by the students of the role technology plays within society at large, and more specifically, in the process of sustainable development,
- To develop knowledge of the most relevant concepts, models and tools regarding sustainable development and basic skills for application during professional life.

The course will consist of two elements:
A general and theoretical part of 40 study hours covering the most relevant concepts, models and practical exercises and
A faculty-specific part of 40 study hours connecting sustainable development to their disciplines.

Intertwining of sustainable development in disciplinary courses.

Adequate intertwining of sustainable development in disciplinary courses will depend on the nature of the course. A design course demands a different approach from that of a fundamental natural science course. In order to 'learn by doing' how to set up models and methods to intertwine sustainable development in different categories of courses, one or two pilot- projects per faculty will be set up. Based on the experiences from these pilot courses, we hope to learn how the intertwining can be managed and how to develop a course for teachers of the university to enable them to meet the goal.

Graduation in sustainable development

As 'sustainability and environment' was considered to be a line-responsibility, the committee argued that it required, like other line-responsibilities (finance, quality management, personnel management etc), specialists to support it. On the other hand, some students may desire to specialize in the technology components of sustainable development (1 % would already entail some 10 to 15 graduating students per year). The committee wanted to offer those students the opportunity to specialize in sustainability during the last years of their course. The requirements will be a graduate paper which is clearly sustainability-oriented and follows the attendance of three to five sustainability-oriented courses. The courses selected will have to cover some 800 study hours.

This part of the plan triggered some resistance within DUT. Faculties feared losing students (although this was denied in the plan) and (probably) feared that the graduates in sustainable development would be too much social sciences oriented. Discussions with faculties were renewed and obscurities in the proposal were removed. Right now, decision-making on the proposal is in its final stage.

Sustainable Development for Aerospace engineers

The first TIDO course will take place between September and November 1999 in the Faculty of Aerospace Engineering. To give an impression of the course the following topics will be dealt with:

1. Sustainable development, what is it and what can engineers do about it?
   (Population growth, under-development, unjustified division of wealth)
2. Eco-efficiency, as the main challenge for the 21st century engineer. Technology as the cause of the problem or technology as problem-solver?
3. The environment as a system: cycles, equilibrium, carrying capacities, stability and exhaustion of raw materials.
4. Degrees of magnitude of effects in time and space. Examples of environmental problems from different degrees.
5. Atmospheric problems as an example: ignorance, uncertainty, conflicting interests and the precautionary principle. The greenhouse effect and the ozone hole as examples.
6. What do aircraft contribute to atmospheric problems? Emissions, trends, and possible ways of achieving reductions with different aircraft.
7. Space debris, an underestimated problem for future communications and space flight.
8. Man and Environment. Social and cultural backgrounds of man's use and misuse of the environment.
9. A local environmental problem: aircraft noise near airports.
10. Sustainable development in a global perspective: How do our decisions affect the world's poor? How could we help them to develop their societies?
11. Innovation and sustainable development in corporations: gaining from developing sustainable technologies.
12. Technology in interaction with society: social and cultural factors and the margins for a government technology policy. The course assumes that sustainable development is not just a

matter of acquiring some extra knowledge. Attitude is also important. Moreover, it is often necessary to change social structures. It is our conviction that it is not very effective to teach this by lectures. Social simulations will be used to give students insights into the difficulties involved in bringing about social change.

This TIDO course is scheduled for fourth year students. However, TIDO will not be the only element of sustainable development in this curriculum. Other components follow, such as:
- environmental management will be included in a second year course on aircraft production;
- LCA's are dealt with in a course on materials and design;
- the dynamics of public debates on technology are dealt with in a second year course on the History of Aerospace Engineering;
- sustainable development will be an important element in the third year Design & Synthesis exercise assignments;
- in the fourth year, there is a course on ethics of technological design.

All these courses are compulsory. Students might choose to do some more courses. However, scope for this is rather limited in the curriculum.

Concluding remarks

The University Board approved the plan in March 1998, and provided the necessary resources. An opening conference was organized on May 14th, 1998. Industry and government officials emphasized the need to train engineers in regard to sustainable development.

To train engineers who will be able to contribute to sustainable development will be a long process, for it will not only require new knowledge. It will also require the skill to integrate social and environmental issues into technological designs. This cannot be achieved by adding a course or (occasionally) paying attention to environmental effects of technologies. It can only be achieved by a change of paradigm in engineering; from technological design, as optimization within margins set by society, to technology as serving people's needs. New ways of training engineers are, therefore, to be developed. DUT has certainly not achieved that paradigm shift, but has taken a great step in the right direction.

References

Baudet, H. (1992) *De lange weg naar de Technische Universiteit Delft*. De Delftse ingenieursschool en haar voorgeschiedenis SDU. Den Haag.

College van Bestuur TU Delft (1994) *Naar een nieuw engagement, Een strategische visie voor de TU Delft*. TU Delft.

Commissie Lange Termijn Milieubeleid (1990) *Het Milieu: denkbeelden voor de 21ste eeuw Zeist: Kerckebosch*.[English edition: Dutch Committee for long-term environmental policy (ed.) (1994) The environment; towards a sustainable future. Dordrecht: Kluwer Academic].

Dickson, D. (1974) *Alternative Technology and the politics of technical change*. Glasgow: Fontana/Collins.

De Jong, E.J. (1994) *Maatschappelijke aanvaarding van invoering van duurzame technologie Techniek beheersen of erdoor beheerst worden*. Delft: Stichting Remonstrants Vizier.

De Jong, F. (1992) *Tussen tandwiel & Turbulentie De opleiding tot werktuigkundig ingenieur aan de TU Delft*. WBMT- TU Delft.

Habermas, J. (1968) *Technik und Wissenschaft als 'Ideologie'*. Edition Suhrkamp.

Hessen, B. (1931), The social and economic roots of Newton's Principia. Reprinted in: Dingle, H. (1972) *Science at the Crossroads*. London: Brian and O'Keeffe.

Hughes, T.P. (1986) The Seamless Web: Technology, Science, Etcetera, Etcetera. Social *Studies of Science* 16, pp. 281-292.

IEEE-Spectrum, Louis Harris Survey (1984) *Electrotechnology and the Engineer: A survey of attitudes of the IEEE membership*. Louis Harris & Associates, Inc.

Jansen, J.L.A., Vergragt, Ph. J. (1992) *Sustainable Development: A Challenge to Technology! Proposal for the Interdepartmental Research Program Sustainable Technological Development*. The Hague: Dutch Ministry of Housing, Spatial Planning and Environment.

Jansen, J.L.A. (1994) Towards a sustainable future, en route with technology! In: Dutch Committee for Long-Term Environmental Policy (ed). *The environment; towards a sustainable future*. Dordrecht: Kluwer Academic, pp. 497-523.

Lemkowitz, S.M. (1992) A Unique Program for Integrating Health, Safety, Environment and Social Aspects into Undergraduate Chemical Engineering Education. In *Plant/Operations Progress* 11, no. 3, pp. 140-150.

Lemkowitz, S.M., Lameris, G.H., Bonnet, J.A.B.A.F., Bibo, B.H. (1996) Integrating Sustainability into (Chemical) Engineering Education. In *Proceedings of "Entree'96"*, pp. 205-220.

Lintsen, H. (1985) *Ingenieur van beroep Ingenieurspers*. Den Haag.

Mulder, K.F. (1993) A useful tool turned into a monument: Controversies over Holland's Windmills in the first half of the 20th century. In *Journal of the Society for Industrial Archeology* 17-2,37-46.

National Environmental Policy Plan (1990) *To choose or to lose*. The Hague: Dutch Ministry of Housing Physical Planning and Environment.

Neef, W., Pelz, T. (1995) Ingenieurausbildung für eine nachhaltige Entwicklung. In *Wechselwirkung*, Dezember 1995, pp. 32-37.

Nelkin, D. (ed.) (1992) *Controversy, politics of technical decisions third edition*. Newbury Park: Sage Publications.

Rijksinstituut voor Volksgezondheid en Milieuhygiene, (1988) *Zorgen voor Morgen. Nationale milieuverkenning 1985-2010*. Samson H.D.Tjeenk Willink.

Schuuring, C., Tuininga, E., Turkenburg W. (eds.) (1983) *Splijtstof, Controverses rond kernenergie*. Amsterdam: SISWO.

SME Milieu Adviseurs, Lans, H, De Vos, J P (1998) *Duurzame ontwikkeling in het hoger onderwijs Milieuprijs Hoger Onderwijs 1998*. Elsevier bedrijfsinformatie bv.

Stuurgroep Duurzame Ontwikkeling TU Delft (1994) *De plaats van duurzame ontwikkeling in het onderwijs van de Technische Universiteit Delft*. TU Delft, June 1994.

Tenner, E. (1996) *Why things bite back. Technology and the Revenge of Unintended Consequences*. New York: Alfred A. Knopf.

Ulrich, O. (1984) *Wedstrijd zonder Winnaars In het slop van het industriele systeem*. Wageningen: De Uitbuyt.

World Commission on Environment and Development (1987) *Our Common Future*. Oxford: Oxford University Press.

Chapter 5

Sustainability Through Incremental Steps?
The Case of Campus Greening at Rensselaer

Steve Breyman

Abstract

This paper describes the Campus Greening experience at Rensselaer and some of the ways via which sustainability is integrated into its programmes.

Introduction

Although urgently needed, great leaps forward in environmental performance are not short-term prospects for most institutions. Those trying to build sustainable institutions are constrained by familiar impediments to organizational change: bureaucratic inertia, standard operating procedures, risk averseness, lack of vision and leadership, ignorance, narrow definitions of costs and benefits, and so on. Most architects and builders of sustainable institutions must thus press forward by small steps. They must, by necessity, propose and implement demonstration and pilot projects, incremental improvements in environmental performance, and expansion and transformation (broadening and deepening) of existing environmental programs. They must consciously link incremental steps into a "hop scotch" towards sustainability. "Greeners" have no other choice but to work within a paradoxical context to strive for sustainability within organizations for which sustainability is not a primary goal.

This paper argues that institutional sustainability *is* attainable through a concerted strategic campaign. Support for the argument is drawn from the ongoing campus greening initiative underway at Rensselaer Polytechnic Institute. The greening initiative centers on both the curriculum and the physical plant. Physical plant greening at Rensselaer is essentially a "sustainability within one institution" approach. This is the result of a conscious decision based on several observations: leverage for change is greatest close to home, synergy arises across projects within a single institution, and we are determined to become a model for those concerned with the internal sustainability of their own organizations. At the same time, curriculum greening is designed to help educate students who will become leaders of institutional and extra-organizational greening efforts after graduation. Our environmental education work is thus not an end in itself, but a means to "help society to be sustainable." The two greening streams intersect. Building a sustainable institution within an unsustainable society is, in the long view, no more than an "emergency measure." Individual sustainable institutions are valuable in their own right, but are most important as signals to society that alternatives to waste and excess, to myopia and disregard for the future are not only desirable and urgently necessary, but possible.[10]

The chapter paper begins with a history of past and current environmental programs at Rensselaer. The second section explains why our campus greening initiative can be considered applied sustainable development. The focus in section two is on assessment of our interim success in building sustainability within one institution. This narrow focus is reasonable given that no monitoring or assessment study has yet been done of our ability to help society become sustainable. We have a good sense of our "placement rate" (the success of our graduates at finding jobs or getting into graduate school). And it is relatively easy to quantify faculty sustainability research and community service. But the nature and quality of the work graduates are doing, and the actual usefulness of faculty publications is another matter we have yet to systematically investigate.

The chapter closes with a discussion of our long-term vision for the university, based on the four principles of ecosystem sustainability: (1) ecosystems dispose of wastes and replenish nutrients by recycling all elements; (2) ecosystems use sunlight as their source of energy; (3) populations are maintained such that overuse of resources does not occur; and (4) biodiversity is maintained.[11] These principles act as guideposts to help us navigate on the long journey that is the movement towards sustainability. They are not currently explicit goals for top university administrators at Rensselaer, nor is it likely they will be in the near future. Prior to our physical plant greening program, it was fair to say Institute operations were like the society of which they are part: completely out of line with each of the four principles. Our modest initial success has not been of sufficient scale to get anywhere near achievement of these goals, but those of us active in the greening initiative have internalized the principles. We realize they are the ecological bottom line. No greening program is on the right track unless it is moving the institution closer to these goals. And no society will be sustainable until it explicitly embraces the principles, and gears its national and international policies towards their collective realization.

The Greening of Rensselaer Initiative

Greening at Rensselaer has roots in the raised ecological consciousness of the early nineties (growing recognition of global environmental problems; Earth Summit in Rio de Janeiro), and in idiosyncratic factors unique to campus (peculiar mix of students and faculty; identity as a technical university). There had been, during the seventies, some administrative attention paid to campus energy consumption for reasons of cost containment and regulatory compliance. But

---

[10] Philip Sutton helped clarify the ideas in this paragraph.
[11] Bernard J. Nebel and Richard T. Wright, *Environmental Science: The Way the World Works* 6th ed. (Upper Saddle River, NJ: Prentice-Hall, 1998), p. 104.

neither the institutional commitment, infrastructure nor resources were in place by the 1980s to align Rensselaer with efforts ongoing elsewhere in the U.S. and around the world, symbolized by administrative allegiance to the principles of the Talloires Declaration.[12] Without the benefit of administrative adherence to these principles, we have forged ahead with incremental programs to green the curriculum and the physical plant at Rensselaer.

Greening the Curriculum

It is considerably easier to multiply environmental courses within disciplines, departments, and schools within a university than it is to devise new courses and curricula across them. And yet no single discipline has hegemonic purchase on analysis and resolution of environmental problems. What to do? Confront the unavoidable. Multi- and interdisciplinary curricula are indispensable if the "ecological literacy" (a working grasp of the extent and nature of environmental problems, and some clear ideas about alternatives to the political-economic status quo at the root of these problems) necessary for construction of sustainable societies is ever to be achieved.

Despite the difficulties inherent to curriculum reform, and despite the problems of organizing multidisciplinary course offerings (one of my colleagues describes organizing professors for a common purposes as akin to "herding cats"), we have made significant progress. The progress is mainly due to monetary support available to attract faculty time and interest through supplemental salary payments. Successful fundraising provided the material resources necessary to shift faculty attention from existing projects to curriculum greening. Without an infusion of fresh resources, curriculum reform leaders must rely on the good will and voluntarism of faculty participants. Professors may be eager to green course offerings, but they are very busy people, and the reward structure of the academy generally discourages unpaid labor.

Undergraduates at Rensselaer may now take multidisciplinary environmental studies courses as freshmen ("Introduction to Environmental Studies" or "Economy, Ecology, and Ethics" or "First Year Environmental Seminar"), sophomores ("Environment & Society"), juniors (a wide range of options including the innovative full-year course "One Mile of the Hudson River") and seniors (another broad range of courses including the capstone "Classic Writings on the Environment"). There is, as yet, neither a single *required* environmental course, nor any general green course requirement for graduation from Rensselaer.

Until recently, graduate students had fewer interdisciplinary offerings from which to choose. Beginning in Fall 1998, Rensselaer's Department of Science and Technology Studies (STS) and the Department of Economics began offering a Professional Masters of Science degree in

---

[12] As seen elsewhere in this book, the Talloires Declaration is a ten-point statement of university commitment to environmental literacy and ecological responsibility. The Declaration, originally signed by 22 college officers from 14 countries in 1990, was organized under the auspices of the Secretariat of University Presidents for a Sustainable Future. The Secretariat has since changed its name to Association of University Leaders for a Sustainable Future, and is based in Washington, DC. The Declaration now has over 265 signatories from over 43 countries on five continents. For a copy of the Declaration and news of the Association, see www.ulsf.org.

Ecological Economics, Values and Policy (EEVP). There is also an undergraduate EEVP degree, a dual Bachelors of Science between STS and Economics. EEVP proceeds from the premise that twenty-first century environmental education must be multidisciplinary, innovative and action-oriented. EEVP gives students a thorough understanding of the complex and often contradictory demands of today's highly technological culture, and concrete experience in applying this integrative understanding to real-world problem-solving through an explicit focus on environmental service-learning projects (about which more below). The EEVP program equips students with the knowledge and experience they will need in their professional lives to build a sustainable future. The EEVP faculty includes professors of ecological economics, environmental ethics and philosophy, environmental politics and policy, environmental law and culture, and many environmental science and engineering specialties.

EcoLogic and Physical Plant Greening

Greening the curriculum proceeds alongside, with growing points of intersection, efforts to green Rensselaer's physical plant, student life, and administrative policies. The former has been primarily a faculty-led effort, while the latter is mostly a student-led effort. Administrators play a necessary role in approval of proposals from both greening streams. The student environmental organization, EcoLogic, is officially a chapter of Student Pugwash.[13] EcoLogic has been at the center of the Greening of Rensselaer Initiative. I was recruited in Fall 1994 to serve as the group's faculty advisor. Through fundraising, negotiations with administrators, and much hard work we have made genuine progress toward building an environmentally responsible university. A partial list of our accomplishments includes:

- Growth of EcoLogic from a handful of well-meaning members to the premier student organization on campus;
- Establishment of an organic vegetable garden and greenhouse (imperfectly based on principles of participatory design and democratic control of technology) to raise vegetables and landscape plants, and planning for a small fruit tree orchard;
- Massive expansion of the solid waste recycling program for academic buildings and dormitories that has avoided tens of thousands;
- The hiring of a full-time student Greening Coordinator to manage the recycling program, oversee student interns working on greening projects, and generally advance greening efforts;
- Establishment of an Environmental Education Center (with books, periodicals, and computer) to serve as a clearinghouse for on- campus environmental information, operate the web-based "Eco-Hotline" to answer environmental queries, sponsor an Institute-wide greening newsletter (enviRenss), serve as the office for greening interns and as a gathering place for environmentally-minded students;
- Sponsorship of green events and conferences (like annual Earth Day events, and our "Greening the Campus" conference);

---

[13] Pugwash, which won the Nobel Peace Prize in 1997, is an international non-governmental organization of students and faculty dedicated to the socially responsible use of science and technology.

- Establishment of a greening internship program (through the Undergraduate Research Program and work-study program dozens of students have participated for pay, academic credit, or experience);
- Slow and halting effort to first enable and ultimately mandate green procurement policies on campus (which may speed up in the near future due to receipt of a grant that should permit the hiring of a full-time student Green Purchasing Coordinator);
- Establishment of the multiple award-winning EcoLogic homepage, and many other web sites, and an email list with hundreds of subscribers from all over the world for communication, coordination, and discussion;
- The hiring of a full-time student Water Conservation Coordinator to educate the campus about saving water and implement water conservation technologies and practices (we have to date saved Rensselaer over $100,000);
- Integration of greening projects with environmental curricula (e.g., my F98 "Environment & Society" students are conducting the second-ever comprehensive environmental audit of campus);
- Participation in local environmental controversies and causes (including opposition to a proposed garbage incinerator upwind of campus, and formation of a campus Green party chapter);
- Participation by several EcoLogic members in student government as the Student Voice party.
- Formation of an Environmental Action Committee within the Student Senate.

Campus Greening as Sustainable Development

Campus greening appeals to students provided they have a minimal level of ecological literacy from diverse ideological and political backgrounds. EcoLogicians include both radical deep ecologists, and free market conservatives. The ideological breadth of the participants is due to the nonthreatening nature of campus greening thus far. With further success and growth, it is distinctly possible that the program might take on a tone more critical of the political-economic status quo. The radicals believe, for example, that it is only a matter of time before the "is capitalism sustainable?" questions arises and requires a programmatic answer. In the meantime, the cross-worldview cooperation is a notable feature of the initiative.

The process of campus greening raises student consciousness it is both experiential environmental learning and often a student's first experience with social change. One of our mottoes here comes from Jesuit Henry Volken: "If you want to understand reality, try to change it." Working on projects, especially those with some real prospect of actual implementation, boosts a student's sense of political efficacy their assessment of their own ability to be heard, to have their voice count, to make a genuine difference. This new found confidence is an essential civic ingredient for construction of sustainable societies.

Some students have found that campus greening is an opportunity for technological entrepreneurship, a significant program underway at our business school. Sustainable societies will require a myriad of new technologies, many of which we have but the faintest ideas about. A computer science student is designing a software application that will permit instructors ready access to various tools for evaluating student papers on-line. The idea is to make assignment marking as easy on a computer monitor as it is on hard copy, thus ultimately eliminating the need to print out term papers.

The central insight for building a sustainable university is to view educational institutions as integral parts of ecosystems from local to global. We must think in terms of "campus ecology," and the four principles of sustainability. Our new Ecological Economics, Values and Policy program does just that. We have structured the undergraduate program around a series of environmental service learning projects to make steady progress towards sustainability.

Sustainability Service Learning Projects

EEVP majors will take the lead in Rensselaer's environmental service learning program. A student would begin as a freshman and see the project through to completion (likely to take several years). Students would leave legacies upon graduation making Rensselaer a model of institutional sustainability. The following list of five Ecological Economics, Values and Policy projects, upon which preliminary work has already begun, now serves as the focus of student work. Positive project outcomes will constitute genuine steps toward campus sustainability, and provide students with experience to build sustainable societies upon graduation.

(1) Forge a partnership between local farms and Rensselaer's dining halls. Rensselaer administrators have approved a pilot project for one dining hall. We are working with the Albany, NY-based Regional Farm and Food Project to identify the most reliable local suppliers and the appropriate local agricultural commodities. The goal of this project is to pioneer the role of the large institution in establishing a sustainable food system. Localization of the farmer-consumer relationship is a crucial first step towards this goal.

(2) Establish a yard and food waste compost program to reduce the solid waste stream and provide soil amendments to reduce cost and dependence of campus landscaping on external suppliers. Campus Planning and Facilities Design has granted us a site for the compost facility. Rensselaer administrators have approved a pilot project at one dining hall where processing "waste," normally dumped down food disposals, will be collected and deposited at the compost site (students must figure out how this will be done). Students will custom design a system to meet campus needs. Significant opportunities exist for students to do research on soil chemistry, cost-benefit analysis, vermiculture (worm composting), environmental decisionmaking (how and why do institutions decide to do the right thing), grant writing (to raise funds for site improvements), and other pertinent topics.

(3) Transform the campus landscape from one dependent on annuals, chemical fertilizers and pesticides, frequent watering and weeding, to one dominated by perennials, xeriscape, and chemical-free native plants. Students in environmental studies classes conducted initial investigations of sustainable landscaping. EEVP students will build on this foundation, and implement their initial findings to restore Proudfit Park, a once popular piece of campus greenspace destroyed during a recent building renovation, and made available to this project by Rensselaer administrators.

(4) Green Rensselaer procurement policy. Rensselaer purchasing officials have agreed to cooperate with students working on this project. Green purchasing aims to "close the loop." It is not enough to recycle; institutions must purchase products with high post-consumer recycled content. Institute purchasing must prefer products that conserve energy, minimize pollution and excess packaging, and encourage reduction and reuse. EEVP students will explore alternative products, investigate regulations governing campus procurement, design green purchasing guidelines, and hire a full-time student Green Purchasing Coordinator for one year. The Green Purchasing Coordinator would work in the purchasing department, and serve as a resource person for students working on this project. While other universities are working to green their purchasing, there is to our knowledge no college which has hired a dedicated student Green Purchasing Coordinator. After the first year, we will ask the administration to fund this position. Administrators have agreed to do so provided the position pays for itself through savings and cost-avoidance (a challenge we have already met for the Greening Coordinator and Water Conservation Coordinator positions).

(5) Build on the success of our Green Web project. Support for this effort could solidify Rensselaer's strength in this area (described by a national survey as the fourth "most wired campus" in the country), and place EEVP at its heart. The goal of this project is to demonstrate how the internet and the world wide web can be used to advance sustainability. Our Green Web project includes:

- the Environmental Gateway (master site for the complex);
- the Environmental Studies site (which focuses on academic programs);
- the EEVP site (designed to attract the attention of prospective students);
- a Virtual Second Hand Store for on-campus sale and exchange of goods;
- the electronic version of *enviRenss* (the newsletter of the Environmental Education Center);
- the Environment & Society Internet Resource Guide (which lists hundreds of sites all over the world, and records thousands of "hits").

Taken together, these and other EEVP projects yet to be imagined by the students themselves will constitute a solid sustainable development program. All solid organic wastes (yard and food) will be composted. Finished compost product will be applied to an organic landscape of native perennials. Dining hall food will come from local organic farms and Community Supported Agriculture (CSA) outfits. Ninety-five percent or more of campus solid "waste" will be recycled or composted (including electronics, and construction debris). Long-term opportunities for expansion of recycling markets will, with the help of regulations and mandates, be virtually limitless. Green purchasing efforts will ensure the vast majority of products and materials needed on campus meet strict standards for sustainable content and reusability, and that materials flows will be drastically slowed through a strong consumption reduction program. New revenues from sales of recyclables and disposal costs avoided will be reinvested in further greening. But even with this substantial program, several pieces of the sustainability puzzle will be missing.

Conclusion: The Future

To reiterate, the four principles of ecosystem sustainability are: (1) ecosystems dispose of wastes and replenish nutrients by recycling all elements; (2) ecosystems use sunlight as their source of energy; (3) populations are maintained such that overuse of resources does not occur; and (4) biodiversity is maintained. In the long-run, planetary survival depends on human societies learning and adapting their activities to these principles. At Rensselaer, we will not build a truly sustainable university until these four principles are integrated into all Institute operations.

I argued in this paper that environmental reformers within large, established institutions generally have no choice but to strive for incremental steps towards sustainability. This does not absolve us of the need to make the enormous changes necessary, only that the changes—barring some global catastrophe that speeds the process must come within the frustrating institutional context outlined in the Introduction. It is sometimes difficult to avoid the depressing thought that "things will have to get worse before they get better." And yet, "worse" in terms of climate change, biodiversity crisis, and other global environmental threats may mean the collapse of ecosystems upon which all life depends. Waiting is not an option for those of us working for a sustainable world.

Thus, the longer-term challenge for campus greeners at Rensselaer is to bring the university as close as possible to realizing the four principles. The waste disposal and nutrient replenishment principle requires us to construct a wetland for waste water treatment, probably for the City of Troy (which currently treats Rensselaer's waste). A wetland large enough to treat the waste of over fifty thousand people, and numerous firms, will provide the added benefit of preserving and enhancing biodiversity, and reducing air and water pollution (biosolids from Troy's plant are currently incinerated, and treated waste water is released into the Hudson).

The sunlight principle will require us to either develop complete energy independence through on-site renewable generation (solar, wind, biofuels, micro hydro) or the greening of Niagara Mohawk (our power utility). Given the recent "deregulation" deal struck between the New York State Public Service Commission and Niagara Mohawk that paid almost no attention to environmental issues, it may be easier to go it on our own. The Institute should also establish a program that leases electric vehicles which may be recharged from green power hook-ups in campus parking lots to faculty, staff, and students (this recognizes the centrality of the automobile in American life), and a home loan program that helps campus citizens convert their own homes into off-the-grid power generators. Incentives need to be granted to commuters (mostly faculty and staff) to ride bicycles, walk, car pool or take mass transit to work, and Rensselaer needs to work with other large employers to improve public transportation. All existing dormitories, academic and office buildings need to be retrofitted for maximum conservation, and for solar and wind power generation. All new buildings should strive to be pioneers in green building materials, passive solar architecture, and design to make recycling and other environmental activities as easy as possible.

Rensselaer's population of 8500 students, faculty, and staff has essentially held steady for the past five years, in line with the third principle of ecosystem sustainability. This is not the result of a conscious no-growth policy, but instead a consequence of student demographics and budget austerity. As the college-age student population in the United States is slated to increase significantly in the first decade of the twenty-first century, pressures to grow will surely ensue. We will have to decide on an optimum size (probably not much larger than we are now), and defend it against the inevitable desire to grow.

The maintenance of biodiversity may be the hardest principle of sustainability for a single institution to realize. Green procurement can help, ensuring that products purchased do not contribute to habitat destruction, deforestation, and other causes of species extinction. Rensselaer should require an introductory environmental studies class as a requirement for graduation, educating its students about the urgent and reversible threats to biodiversity around the globe. Administrators could make public statements in support of biodiversity protection, and seek research funds to support studies of sustainable development. Institute endowment investments could be made through a "green screen" to make sure that hundreds of millions of dollars become part of the solution, not part of the problem. The Career Development Center might inform students looking for jobs of the environmental records of businesses that recruit on campus.

Campus greening is much harder to do today than it would be through a new administrative agency: a "Greening Division" that oversees and works to green all campus operations. The Greening Division would have real authority, but would not operate through a top-down structure. While cliché, it is true that many good ideas and significant energy for moving towards sustainability come from people in offices, laboratories, and classrooms. The Greening Division would not only be a new layer of management, but a rich source of service-learning and experiential education projects, as well as a source for sustainability policies, and government, public and media relations.

Building sustainable societies will be the hardest and most satisfying work most of us will ever do. There are few if any more urgent tasks before us. Universities have the resources, vision, opportunity, and responsibility to lead themselves and their societies towards sustainability, one step at a time.

Chapter 6

Managing U.S. Campuses With An Ecological Vision

Alberto Arenas

Abstract

The following chapter focuses on several universities in the United States currently engaged in environmentally-sound practices in their day-to-day operations.[14] These campuses demonstrate that it is possible to adopt responsible fiscal decisions while minimizing environmental damage and protecting the local ecosystem. Whether it is sustainable transportation at the University of California at Davis, solid waste management at the University of Minnesota, Twin Cities, or organic dining at Bates University in Maine, they all demonstrate that creativity, commitment and patience can push forward the goal of reaching a high degree of sustainability in the operation of large institutions. We will look at different universities that, while exhibiting important differences (some are public, some are private, some have less than 2,000 students, some have more than 50,000) share the vision of transforming their campuses into ecological havens. Finally, all these practices serve as pedagogical tools to sensitize and inform students about the ecological impact of their own behavior and of the accumulated action of thousands of individuals placed together, and about the intricate connections between economic decisions and ecosystemic well-being.

Transportation

Over the years, the Parking and Transportation Divisions at major universities have shown increasing interest in encouraging their student and employee population to walk, bicycle, carpool or use mass transit as a means of diminishing air pollution, reducing traffic congestion, saving money (parking, gas, car maintenance), lessening commuter stress and eliminating parking headaches. Many US universities have also retrofitted their fleet of vehicles to be able to use alternative fuels. For instance, at the University of South Florida, four vehicles run with solar energy and after every 90 miles the cars recharge their batteries at a solar recharging station

---

[14] For the elaboration of this chapter, in addition to visits to several universities and information received from many department campuses, three other sources have been invaluable: Julian Keniry's *Ecodemia* (1995), the National Wildlife Foundation's Campus Ecology, and the World Wide Web.

located on campus (Keniry 1995). Clearly, finding alternatives to cars and establishing clean and healthy ways to transport the university community has become a priority for many campus officials. A successful search has invariably meant a close collaboration between different campus departments and non-university entities (City Hall, city bus company, local environmental agencies, etc.).

University of California at Davis

The University of California at Davis has one of the most inclusive alternative systems of transportation of any campus in the United States. Not only has the Transportation and Parking Services division been at the forefront of motivating campus members to use bicycles, mass transit, vanpools and carpools, but it has also been a leader in the use of cleaner and alternative fuels for its fleet, such as compressed natural gas (CNG), electricity and bi-fuel (TAPS 1997a). One of the advanced features in this regard is an on-campus CNG fueling facility inaugurated in 1996 (TAPS 1997b), which eliminates a problem experienced by many campuses that despite having CNG-powered vehicles, these have to fuel in distant locations.

Of all the transportation programs at Davis, none is as renown as its bicycle program. With a student population of 25,000, there are an estimated 15,000 bikes on campus in a regular school day (TAPS 1997a), earning the university and the city the title of "Bicycle Capital of the United States". Along with an extensive system of bikeways and cyclist-friendly facilities, the university has been involved in adding new services to encourage an even larger number of users:

- Storage lockers (located near campus shower facilities) are available for intercity bicycle commuters for free.
- Bike auctions are held twice a year where hundreds of abandoned and unclaimed bicycles are sold at low prices.
- Students can store their bikes during the summer.
- There is a bike repair shop on campus, and repair and maintenance classes are offered to students and campus employees.
- Lock cutting services are offered to students when they lose their lock key; locks are offered at discount prices at participating stores.
- Students cited for a traffic violation can have it written off by attending bicycle traffic school.

Inter-institutional cooperation has been indispensable for establishing many of the alternative transportation systems. In cooperation with mass transit agencies, the local bus service is offered for free to undergraduate students and at a subsidized price for graduate students, faculty and staff up to a 40 percent discount for the purchase of monthly passes or longer. Another example of inter-institutional collaboration is seen in the vanpool program. A vanpool consists of seven or more people who share one vehicle to commute to the university from outside the city area. Each vanpool has an assigned parking space in a lot of the riders' choice. All vanpool members are eligible to participate in the Emergency Ride Home, a program that guarantees transport home in an urgent situation. To encourage the formation of vanpools, Davis even pays for empty seats in the van during the duration of the pass.

A similar program to the vanpool one is the carpool system, which covers 11 percent of Davis employees (TAPS 1997a). A carpool consists of two or more people (be it students, faculty or staff) commuting to the university from outside the Davis area. Members are eligible to a reserved parking space, and even when pooling is not available, each carpool member is entitled to a few complimentary parking permits per month. Just as in the vanpool program, members are eligible to take advantage of emergency rides whenever a special situation arises and other transportation options are not available.

As part of its long term goals, Davis is actively involved in researching new alternatives to increase the number of users of alternative programs. For carpools, it started a part-time carpool pilot program that provides incentives to people who car pool at least twice a week. For vanpools, it is pursuing the strategy of reducing costs for all members by inviting companies to advertise on the van in exchange for subsidies. For mass transit, Davis is investigating the possibility of a universal transit pass for the entire region, which would cover all forms of public transportation. For anyone who does not purchase an individual parking permit, the university is studying the possibility of putting in place a discount card/coupon book to be honored at restaurants and convenience stores.

Energy and Utilities

Energy conservation plans that include a combination of less fossil fuel use and more renewable energy application are becoming widespread throughout campuses in the United States. In terms of economic savings, perhaps no other greening practice has been as successful. Since 1982, the State University of New York at Buffalo started an energy conservation program that has saved the university $3 million a year (Smith 1992). The program was launched when a study of energy consumption patterns revealed that the university produced every year 313,900 tons of carbon dioxide, equivalent to 10.5 tons for every person on campus! Strategies have included the installation of meters in different buildings to measure electricity, heat and water use; the implementation of long-term campaigns to encourage staff, faculty and students to use the least amount of energy and water possible; the installation of energy-efficient systems for cooling, heating, water and electricity needs; and the use of safe and renewable energy sources, given that it is now possible to harness solar and wind energy at efficiency levels comparable to those of fossil fuels and at a relatively low cost. Some of these projects were started by university officials on their own, while others were started by a collective effort between students, staff and faculty.

Brown University (Rhode Island)

With a student population of almost 8,000 students, Brown University adopted in 1990 the "Brown is Green" (BIG) scheme, one of the most extensive environmental education programs in the nation in terms of campus resource conservation, waste reduction, and increased ecological awareness. BIG, in association with the Department of Plant Operations, has been responsible for the identification of areas of high resource consumption and the implementation of economically-feasible environmental solutions. In terms of energy and utility use, two areas of concentration have been electricity and water conservation (BIG 1997).

All buildings on campus, old and new, are specified to have energy-efficient lighting. So far, about 20 percent of the buildings have received lighting upgrades. In one typical example, the Geo-Chemistry Building, the upgrade reduced annual consumption by 30 percent while the whole cost of the upgrade was estimated to be paid back in three years (Teichert 1996). All exit signs were also retrofitted by replacing the incandescent lamps by fluorescent ones; thanks to energy savings, total costs of the retrofit were paid back in less than six months. Utility rebates are often used to offset the costs of many of the environmental projects. When high-efficiency motors were introduced in 265 locations to replace the older, less efficient ones, utility rebates covered 50 percent of the costs; this meant that in less than 1.5 years the net cost of the project had been paid back. To ensure that energy consumption levels are kept low and to detect any abnormal increases, the Department of Plant Operations installed meters in all buildings and these are audited regularly to ensure proper functioning.

Students have been instrumental in some of the campus conservation programs. Every semester they participate in research that identifies areas of high resource consumption and recommends a feasible strategy for addressing the problem. These student projects are done in combination with faculty, staff and the environmental coordinator. While they have not done a comprehensive electrical audit system, students have participated in the research and analysis of more manageable energy-conserving issues (Teichert 1996). For instance, students from an introductory environmental class did a study on refrigerator electricity use in dorms, and they elaborated educational materials on how to conserve energy (particularly stressing the importance of using common refrigerators rather than small, personal ones) and recommended the replacement of old refrigerators with newer models. Another student project did a follow-up study and concluded that the main problem was not the behavior of the user but rather that the old models needed to be replaced. At the time of these studies, refrigerators with non-CFC cooling systems were not affordable, but the reduction of prices in recent years has allowed the university to replace most of its CFC-refrigerators. The new, more efficient refrigerators have allowed Brown to save 10-30 percent in electricity consumption.

In terms of water conservation, BIG has adopted a three-prong strategy (BIG 1997). First, between 1991 and 1992 it replaced the dorms' old showerheads and toilets with low-flow ones. Each head reduced the flow from 3.5 gallons per minute (gpm) to about 2 gpm, while the toilets flushed 1.5 gallons instead of the customary 3 gallons. As a result, yearly savings were estimated at 5.6 million gallons. In 1993, the headshowers of all gymnasiums were also changed but this time with a newer version of heads, ones that minimized problems associated with the earlier models i.e., clogging and cold aeration. Second, university personnel has been involved in renovating the laboratory building mechanical systems to minimize water use, specially in the area of cooling systems for laboratory equipment given their high water usage. And third, just as with the electric systems, BIG has been involved in doing a campus-wide water audit, which has included the regular maintenance of the campus' 292 water meters. A more recent student study found out that if more extensive retrofitting reforms are undertaken, a total of 120 million gallons of water every year could be saved. For Brown, it would mean annual savings of almost $300,000. Undoubtedly, the rebate programs of local utility companies have been instrumental in accelerating the rate of cost recovery, allowing the school to undertake more ambitious projects to minimize resource use and maximize savings.

State University of New York at Buffalo

With a student population of about 24,000 students and more than 8,000 computers, the State University of New York at Buffalo has devoted a great deal of attention to conserving energy in its computing systems (Simpson 1994). A typical PC computer can consume as much as 300 watts of electricity, and assuming that each computer is turned on during normal business hours, the annual cost of operating each computer is about $50, bringing UB's tab just to power the computers to about $380,000 every year. By implementing simple changes in behavior and technology, UB is reducing the energy bill associated with computer use by about 50 percent. The university's conservation campaign included the following: the publication of a booklet containing practical suggestions on how to conserve energy and paper; the designation of volunteers representing almost all offices and divisions on campus to make sure that, among other things, the green computing practices were implemented; the joining of efforts with private businesses to promote the 'green office' through public forums and conferences; and the purchasing of energy-efficient computers, monitors and printers.

The UB booklet, which has been ordered by dozens of universities, includes some of the following easy-to-follow tips: turn the computer and monitor off when leaving the office for more than an hour (contrary to popular belief, turning off a computer for a short amount of time will not damage or shorten its life span); if for some reason the computer needs to be left on when nobody is using it, turn off the monitor; and recycle used toner cartridges for laser printers. Regarding the purchasing of green computers, the U.S. Federal Agency in charge of environmental protection (EPA) has participated in the production of energy-efficient computers, sold under the "Energy Star" EPA logo. Energy star computers, monitors and printers have a built-in "sleep mode" which automatically lowers their wattage when not in use, reducing energy use by 60 to 70 percent. The booklet also suggests choosing monochrome monitors over color ones (black and white monitors use 50 percent less energy), smaller monitors over larger ones (14 inch monitor uses 40 percent less energy than a 17 inch monitor), and inkjet printers over laser ones (although slower, they use 80 to 90 percent less electricity).

In addition to all the financial savings, the Green Computing program at UB also hopes to reduce every year carbon dioxide emissions by 2.2. million pounds, nitrogen oxides by 7 tons and sulfur oxides by 4.4 tons.

To ensure that the Green Computing Project and all the other environmental projects at UB do not just remain on paper, UB has created the Building Conservation Contacts (BCC), a unique network of 150 volunteers from every office, division and building on campus. The BCC volunteers make sure that their area is in full compliance with the recommendations made by UB's Environmental Task Force. Volunteers have as specific tasks: the dissemination of information about UB's environmental policies; the informal monitoring and identification of problems; and the serving as liaisons between their division and the environmental units (Task Force, Recycling Program, and so on).

Solid Waste Management

In terms of environmental consciousness on campus, recycling was the first program to be implemented on a massive scale. Over the years, campus administrators have become more sophisticated and have established a hierarchy of actions to adopt what has become known as the Four Rs: refuse, reduce, reuse and recycle. One of the leading campuses in the nation to establish a program of this nature has been the University of Colorado at Boulder. With a main focus in reducing consumption and transforming all waste into a valuable commodity, CU-Boulder has generated more than $270,000 in revenues, saved about $150,000 in disposal costs and created more than 20 student jobs (CU Recycling 1996). Moreover, since 1980 it has saved more than 90,000 fir trees, 60,000 gallons of gasoline and 315,000 pounds of air pollutants. Its recycling program has been such a success that CU-Boulder established a national clearinghouse for college recycling information with the participation of approximately 450 colleges.

Miami University (Ohio)

A much more recent solid waste management program is the one found at Miami University, started in 1990 and serving a student population of 16,000. The impetus for recycling came with the convergence of three factors: the closing down of the city's landfill, a mandate from the Ohio State legislature to recycle, and a key interest by campus staff to engage in ecological practices. Year after year, the recycling program has increased the amount of solid materials recycled, so that the 25 percent of material recycled the first year was increased to 55 percent by 1997 (Physical Facilities Department 1998). Similarly, the types of products that are recycled have increased in variety. From starting with just office paper, newspaper and bottles, it now includes cardboard, aluminum cans, bi-metal containers, plastics and polystyrene. One of the most recent technologies added to the program was a glass pulverizer purchased in 1998 to recycle bottles on site. The machine first breaks all the bottles into large pieces; these then pass through a magnetic belt that removes any metal parts sometimes found in bottles; next, the machine pulverizes the large pieces into sand. The glass pulverizer not only reduces the costs of handling bottles but it also provides the university with an ice-melt material for the winter.

Notwithstanding its successes, the realities of the market have played some dirty tricks on the recycling business. In 1989 the university bought a polystyrene chipper to process plastic plates and cups. Five years later the program had to be stopped when market prices for plastic became too high for regional industries to buy Miami's product. In a similar vein, for several years Miami sold recycled shredded newspaper to local farmers as bedding for animals. In 1995 the price of straw went down so much that it outcompeted the price of shredded paper and the program had to be shut down. Despite these reverses, Miami has mostly seen gains in recycling. By 1998, the recycling program was saving the university every year $105,000 in disposal fees and generating up to $30,000 in revenues from the sales of recyclable materials.

University of Minnesota, Twin Cities

A much larger and more complex operation than the one at Miami is found at the Twin Cities campus of the University of Minnesota. As the second largest campus in physical size in the United States and a population of about 70,000 students, faculty and staff, U of M faces an enormous daily task in terms of reducing and recycling solid waste. In 1994 U of M generated 34 tons of solid waste every working day, of which one-third was recycled (Recycling Program

1996). To facilitate the recycling pick-up, the campus is divided into seven management zones, each with a few Operation Supervisors who are responsible for communicating directly with custodians about the Recycling programs on campus.

The program that collects most solid waste is called SMART (known locally as the QUAD system). SMART began as an outdoor strategy with 180 waste containers that could hold, in three separate sections, trash, newspaper and commingled bottles and cans. It was then adopted as an in-door system for the 200 buildings on campus, and the outdoor containers were converted to having four color-coded holes for trash, newspaper, commingled bottles and cans, and office paper. The idea was to make trash disposal and recycling equal in terms of effort and convenience. Thanks to these changes, an estimated 2,000 tons of waste every year are recycled through the SMART system.

Given that large-size waste such as cardboard, phonebooks, and scrap metal cannot fit in these containers, the U of M uses other strategies to dispose of these other materials. Cardboard, 600 tons of which are generated annually, is collected in dumpsites designated for cardboard disposal or placed by the custodians in the trash room or loading dock. Almost the totality of cardboard at U of M is recycled. The campus also recycles 100 tons of phonebooks every year through an exchange system called GAB-GAB: Give-A-Book to Get-A-Book. In other words, to receive a new directory, interested parties have to give the old one in return. For scrap metal, the recycling program recovers 200 tons every year from the debris waste. The rejects usually come from remodeling, construction or demolition on campus. Materials that cannot be reused are broken down into recyclable categories such as fixed ferrous (the largest category of metal scrap), aluminum, glass, copper and stainless steel. Eventually most of the scrap is sold to local and outside dealers.

In a similar fashion to UB's Building Conservation Contacts, U of M established in 1989 a series of Waste Abatement Committees. The committees, overseeing most of the campus, have as their main function the promotion of behavior related to the purchase of recycled materials, source reduction, and material reuse. In the area of purchase, their policy decisions have led to the following actions: 50 percent of the paper bought by U of M contains some percentage of recycled paper; a high percentage of non-toxic, non-hazardous, biodegradable products and chemicals are used at laboratories; and 30 percent of all toner cartridges are re-manufactured. In the area of reduction, the chemistry department at the university has cut down on hazardous waste generation by redesigning lab experiments and substituting old products, saving the department $35,000 in yearly disposal costs. And in the area of material reuse, the construction department reused the 15,000 tons of concrete and 600 tons of steel created in the demolition of parking ramps in 1993. The abatement committees were also instrumental in establishing a statewide chemical redistribution program, leading to more than 1,500 kg of chemicals being reused in 1993.

Food Services

Campus dining services are setting the trend in promoting cost-effective nutritious, organic meals and resource conservation plans. The intrinsic pedagogical role of providing organic foods and lowering expenditures without sacrificing quality, position campus dining operations at the forefront of fostering alternative food production, packaging and waste management. Although these changes are more recent and less widespread than those in the area of solid waste management, green dining operations are becoming increasingly common, specially at smaller campuses where a fewer number of organic farmers are needed to supply the campus' nutritional needs.

Rice University (Texas)

As in all the other environmental areas, students have been active in promoting food services both in upstream ecological practices (e.g., buying from environmentally-friendly companies) and downstream ones (e.g., composting food scraps). At Rice University, with a student population of about 4,000, courses are offered that allow students to understand the campus as an ecosystem. In 1995, a group of students examined the food service at Rice and provided the university administration with the necessary information to implement an economically-feasible and environmentally-sound dining service (BAKE 302 1995).

The students started by researching the dining practices at comparable-sized universities that were known to have adopted green practices. From this research students concluded that Rice was far behind other campuses, and that there was enormous potential for improvement. The students then designed survey instruments that were administered to other students to determine their level of interest in engaging in ecological practices. Some of the questions and answers were (BAKE 302 1995):

- "When you are returning your tray, would you be willing to separate your food into compostable and non-compostable categories? This would likely involve 3 categories: paper trash, meats/animal products, and all other compostable materials." Almost 80 percent responded that they were willing to separate their food as long as it did not take more time than their current routine.
- "To keep food quality a priority, would you be willing to be subjected to the seasonal influences and availability on some produce?" The majority of students (97%) said they would rather choose from seasonal produce than from a wider variety that is not fresh.
- "In order to keep cost and food waste down, would an 'a la carte' meal plan appeal to you? This would likely eliminate the pre-paid dinners so students would never lose money if they skipped dinner." 83 percent of the students responded in the affirmative, saying they often lost money with the pre-paid dinner plan.

With this information in hand, students contacted the kitchen staff at the different dining halls on campus, and together they prepared a plan to measure food waste. Students and staff divided the post-consumer waste (e.g., leftovers) into three categories: meat products (compostable depending on the technology used), all other food products (compostable) and paper/carton trash. During a period of time, the trash was separated, weighed and recorded, and yearly estimates were made. It was then concluded that 12 tons of meat products, 77 tons of compostable material and 22 tons of recyclable paper and carton were generated annually by students at Rice.

Students, dining services staff, and grounds services staff came up with a strategy to reduce compostable and recyclable waste. For the first type of waste, three composting options were analyzed, which would cover not just food but also landscape waste: centralized composting (requiring the purchase of just a single large system but waste has to be hauled from across campus); decentralized composting (requiring several smaller composting units spread throughout campus but transportation needs are reduced); and off-campus composting (requiring no purchase of system or space to be used on campus, but it entails disposal fees and buying back the compost for Rice's landscape needs). After studying the three alternatives in terms of cost, space required, level of staff expertise, maintenance, smell, and so on, it was concluded that a decentralized system would best meet the composting needs at Rice. As the university expands and compostable waste increases, it is easier to install a small composting unit than to modify a large, central unit.

For the second type of waste, three main recommendations for the dining services were proposed: first, large plastic cups should replace current paper cups, and reusable plastic mugs should be sold which can be taken in and out of the dining halls. Second, cloth napkins should replace paper napkins; a preliminary study showed that the long-term savings from reduced waste disposal costs would help pay for the purchase of cloth napkins, and it was estimated that the current laundry facilities were adequate to wash the increased loads coming from dirty napkins. And third, milk machines should replace milk cartons, and given that space limitations prevent the installation of milk machines in the current kitchens, all new kitchens should be designed with ample space to accommodate milk machines and other ecologically-friendly technologies.

Bates University (Maine)

A full-fledged green dining services program is already in place at Bates University, a college serving less than 2,000 students. Started in 1994, the program's intent is to reduce food wastes and costs, benefit the health of the university community, and support the local economy by buying organic foods produced in the region (Green Page 1998). Dining services created a loop that starts with the purchase of seasonally and organically grown food from regional farmers. The prepared food that is not served to students is delivered to organizations that provide meals to needy populations, and eventually all the food waste is composted outside of campus. The compost is then used as a soil improver for parcels that grow produce for Bates, closing this way the loop.

The Dining Services Department has focused its energies on three main strategies: responsible purchasing, composting and distribution/recycling. Whenever possible, the purchasing strategy seeks to support local, environmentally-friendly companies instead of national, wholesaler ones. As a member of the Maine Organic Farmers and Gardeners Association, Bates has helped to set up a loose co-op of farmers that once a week delivers food to the university. In addition to receiving fresh and pesticide-free food, one of the advantages of being associated with the co-op is the possibility of discussing with the farmers ways of reducing packaging. For instance, the cereal supplier agreed to place the product in large tupperware containers rather than the traditional cardboard packaging. The yogurt supplier also places its product in large plastic containers that are later returned to the company to be re-used. Despite the obstacles associated with using only organic products (i.e., higher costs, and in Maine's case, a short growing season), so far all the parties concerned have expressed great satisfaction.

Supplies for dining services are also taken into account at the moment of purchasing. The napkins available in the dining halls are made from 100 percent unbleached, recycled paper. With regard to dining tables, these are refurbished by a local company that reuses old table legs and replaces the tops. This same company supplies the university with chairs, all of which are made from ashwood grown sustainably in Bates' home state.

Composting, as the second strategy, focuses on preconsumer food waste (e.g., potato peelings), postconsumer waste and napkins. The university collects the napkins and the preconsumer waste and takes it to a local farm, which uses it to make compost, some of which is later bought by Bates for its landscaping needs. For the university it is also less expensive to take the food scraps to the compost farm than to pay the fees associated with disposal in a landfill.

Distribution/recycling constitutes the third strategy. The distribution component comes with the food that is not served. Every day, a local organization picks up the uneaten food from Bates kitchens and uses it to provide meals to poor and homeless people. Finally, all recyclable materials (e.g., tin cans, bottles, cardboard, plastic) are sorted in the cafeterias and later hauled away. Bates is involved in a continuous source reduction campaign to encourage all divisions to use only reusable plates and cups, and to influence students to put in their plate only the food they will eat and to employ the minimum amount of supplies as possible (e.g. napkins).

Purchases

We have already seen several examples of colleges that have used their purchasing power to support companies that provide environmentally-benign products, materials, equipment and food. Despite the importance of green purchasing, it is ironic that many universities pay scant attention to this topic. It is common to find colleges or single departments that, while having mature recycling programs in place, often buy virgin paper. Changing these practices becomes even more imperative when one considers the gargantuan purchasing power of U.S. institutions of higher education. According to the Campus Ecology program of the National Wildlife Federation, total expenditures by universities and colleges exceeded in 1990-91 $140 billion (Campus Ecology 1996). Tapping into this pool of money in ways that encourage a comprehensive program entails paying attention to source reduction (buying less of what eventually will become waste), waste stream diversion (once something is discarded, making sure that it is used longer, recycled or reused), recycling (far beyond paper, bottles and aluminum), closing the loop (buying recycled products), and local purchases to support the regional economy (Keniry 1995).

James Madison University (Virginia)

Given that colleges discard more paper than any other material (about 45 percent of a typical campus waste stream), James Madison University decided to start its green purchasing program here (JMU Recycling 1997). Three main groups - a student environmental group, the recycling department, and an environmental committee - joined efforts to draft a recycled paper purchasing policy for the 13,000 student campus. The policy came partly in response to legislative mandate which ordered state agencies to purchase recycled goods whenever economically feasible. The main rationale behind the JMU policy for buying recycled paper was to reduce the demand on scarce and biologically-rich virgin resources, and at the same time to decrease the price of recycled paper as demand augmented over time.

After the policy was put in place, instead of forcing individual departments to buy recycled paper, the tripartite coalition deployed an aggressive educational campaign to raise environmental consciousness among students, faculty and staff. To change the negative perceptions of many campus users that recycled paper was of poor quality for printing, the environmental student group gave free test reams of recycled paper to 22 campus departments. A follow-up performance survey was then conducted and it showed that the recycled paper worked as well or better than the virgin content paper. Moreover, the students were able to demonstrate that prices for both reams were comparable, and if the whole university were to buy recycled paper reams, prices could even be lower than for virgin ones. The campaign was so successful that the majority of departments at JMU have decided to switch to paper with at least a 10 percent recycled content.

Rutgers-State University of New Jersey
A procurement program involving many products and services in addition to paper is the one found at Rutgers-State University of New Jersey. With a campus population totaling about 65,000 people and an annual budget in the hundreds of millions of dollars, Rutgers has the economic leverage to purchase large volumes of ecologically-friendly products and even require its vendors to provide packaging and services that cause the least environmental impact possible. The procurement office first started to green its practices in 1988 - partly motivated by a mandate from the state of New Jersey to recycle - by revising the waste and recycling contract (AULS 1996). The new contract required the service provider to assist Rutgers in improving its recycling program and to participate in the university's Environmental Public Awareness Program through the placement of ads in the campus newspaper calling for greater participation and featuring successful case studies at other campuses. The central procurement office was in a particularly advantageous situation given that it oversees most university contracts for the 700 academic and administrative units at Rutgers. Similar contracts to that of waste and recycling have been forged with vendors servicing the departments of dining, construction and custodial services.

To switch all its paper products to unbleached, 100 percent recycled content paper, dining services first started with an educational campaign - including a promotional visit from the manufacturer - to coax students to accept the new products. Then it replaced all napkins with unbleached, recycled ones, and is gradually replacing all the other paper products as well. Moreover, the staff at dining services tries to cater to the most environmentally-sensitive companies it can find, and it communicates to all companies its interest in reducing excess packaging. Regarding construction services, contractors are required to report to Rutgers waste reduction strategies as well as the amount of materials they have recycled. For paving contractors the university goes even further by requiring them to reuse and recycle all excavated materials. To close the purchasing loop, many of the products bought by construction services are made from recycled material, such as ceiling tiles, insulation, roofing products, snow fences, and parking bumpers.

With regard to custodial services, the procurement office works in close coordination with it to purchase non-toxic, alternative products and train staff. Whenever possible, changes are adopted that do not add new responsibilities to the custodial staff, but if that is the case, the changes are weighed and discussed between both departments. One such example was the replacement of virgin plastic garbage bags with recycled plastic ones. The old bags were color-coded by size but all the new, recycled bags were clear. Given that the required sorting meant extra work for custodians, both departments agreed to asked the vendor to label the boxes with the corresponding size, something the manufacturer agreed to do.

Students have been instrumental in helping staff to do research on alternative products and identifying potential suppliers. Instructed by staff and faculty, students have been involved in conducting campus-wide waste audits and developing procurement surveys for department chairs. Students have also been involved in establishing a cooperative agreement with extramural institutions so that they can all maximize their purchasing power. By making a single, collective order for a given product (e.g., recycled paper), the volume discount would allow all institutions to obtain a high percentage of recycled content in their product at a very competitive price.

Building Design

One exciting aspect of eco-architecture is related to combining various fields into one, in this case joining the disciplines of environmental studies, architecture and design. Environmental building sites are also intended to be visible models of ecological design, serving the campus community as a pedagogical tool by which everyone can learn about the appropriate selection of materials, alternative technologies, resource conservation and public participation. When the buildings are renovated instead of being built from scratch, as in the two examples below, they have the added advantage of avoiding the clearing of new spaces and of retaining many of the original architectonic features.

Humboldt State University (California)

Humbolt State University, with a student population of 7500 students, houses one of the first and most energy-efficient campus buildings in the United States. The Campus Center for Appropriate Technology (CCAT), founded in 1978, is a student-initiated, student-funded and student-run home devoted to sustainable living (CCAT 1996). It started when a group of students shouldered the task of retrofitting an abandoned house on campus. The students, along with faculty and staff, design and implement alternative systems of waste, heat, water, food and electrical systems that have become models of minimal environmental impact. Many of their technologies are a combination of ancient practices with modern ideas. The main goals of the center are to contribute to a healthy environment, examine social and ethical consequences of different technologies and provide a space for experiential learning. Among some of the technologies used at CCAT are human-run appliances, solar refrigerators, greywater treatment marsh, thermal curtains, wind turbine systems and various ecological designs.

Since 1991, when the center cut ties with the local utility company, power has been generated on site through a mixture of four energy systems. The main energy generator comes from 22 photovoltaic panels, but since sunlight is not received year around in this region, CCAT also employs a wind turbine to generate electricity. In addition, during the days when there is no sunlight or wind, it uses a natural gas generator as a backup power system, and finally, it uses a Human Energy Converter (HEC) which provides electricity for many of the outdoor events in the area. Designed by one of CCAT's residents, HEC consists of 14 bicycles attached to a generator, and the constant pedaling generates up to one kilowatt of electricity.

For heating the house, CCAT uses a combination of ecological designs and appropriate technology. Annexed to the center is a greenhouse that is used to provide passive solar heating for the house, and garden space for warm weather crops. Separating the greenhouse and the center is a rocky wall that acts as a thermal collector: it stores solar heat during the day and releases it at night. The heat rises and enters the home through openings at the top of the wall. Moreover, to prevent heat from escaping at night through the home windows, residents installed thermal curtains. The curtains, which are inexpensive and durable, are composed of four simple layers: the first layer against the window is a light colored fabric that serves to attract heat; the second layer serves as an insulator for which an old blanket is used; a piece of plastic serves as the third layer to stop vapor; and the last layer, the one facing the room, is used for aesthetic purposes.

Another important feature at CCAT is the manufacturing of ultra energy-saver refrigerators for commercial purposes. The refrigerators, running on 12 volts, are 600 percent more efficient than conventional ones. In conventional units, the compressor, located at the bottom, creates a heat blanket that surrounds the refrigerator, forcing it to generate more electricity to compensate. Humbolt State's model does away with this problem by relocating the compressor to the top. In addition, it eliminates the fan found in conventional refrigerators and uses extra-thick insulation for the refrigerator and freezer walls.

In terms of water conservation, along with using low-flush toilets and showerheads, the center employs other technologies such as a waterless composting toilet (a small can of sawdust is used after every use), an outdoor solar-heated shower (for summer days), and a rainwater catchment system (used to water the gardens). All the water used in the house - from the sinks and showers - is treated in the greywater marsh and then reused in gardens and lawns. In all, there are so many appropriate technologies and ecologically-sensitive behaviors at CCAT that the center has become a model worldwide for sustainable living.

Denison University (Ohio)
A more recent example of ecological design than the one at Humbolt State is Barney Hall at Denison University, a campus with less than 2,000 students. The building, which opened its doors to classes in the Fall of 1998 and will house the Environmental Studies and English departments, was the result of renovating a building originally built more than a century ago (Denison University 1998). The renovation project included the participation of more than 100 students who did research on green materials and products to be used in the construction, and several of their ideas were incorporated by the designers and architects. As part of the renovation, many of the original features of the house were restored and kept, including hardwood floors, solid wood furniture, windows, doors, cabinets, and tiles. The total cost of the project was estimated at $3.6 million.

To ensure maximum natural lighting, the original large windows were kept, skylights were installed, and windows that had been blocked with low ceilings were uncovered. In terms of solar energy, the building has photovoltaic panels to store up to 5 kw, but it is expected that in the near future more panels will be added to cover all the lighting needs of Barney Hall. To conserve additional energy, occupancy sensors were installed in all the classrooms which turn the lights off when the room is empty. For heating the building, Barney Hall installed two stand-alone natural gas heaters, which are much more efficient and less pollutant than the coal-fueled campus central heating plant. Over time, it is expected that the Hall will discontinue using non-renewable resources and be completely self-sufficient.

One of the main goals of Barney Hall is to serve as a real-living laboratory to educate the campus community at large and test different environmentally-sensitive technologies. Thus, in a bathroom one finds three different models of toilets and two different types of faucets. The project also specified that, whenever possible, products bought should contain some recycled content. For instance, the carpets are made from recycled plastic and the wallboard from recycled plasterboard and paper. Barney Hall officials adopted a non-toxic policy, which covers all materials used in construction and maintenance. To avoid sources of toxic gases, special considerations were made when choosing the carpeting, plywood, furniture, paints and adhesives. For cleaning products, only biodegradable, phosphate-free, and non-chlorinated detergents are used.

Conclusion

The above examples, while including some of the most well-known cases of environmental practices at campuses in the United States, constitute a small percentage of the actual number of universities that have revamped their daily practices along ecological lines. Nonetheless, if one considers the full 3,700 institutions of higher education in the U.S., those involved in comprehensive environmental programs that look at the campus as a vibrant ecosystem are just a drop in the bucket.

To be sure, numerous obstacles come in the way of instituting solid programs that take into account topics as varied as transportation, energy and utilities, solid waste management, food services, purchases, and building design. Opposition from decision-makers, administrative inertia, apathy from the student body, economic disincentives to try out new products, and old physical structures and administrative flow charts that did not lend themselves to easy restructuring, are among the main hurdles encountered.

To surpass these problems, an initial impetus has been given by rulings from state legislatures that force institutions to engage in recycling and waste reduction initiatives. With the backing of these mandates, the more successful programs have included campus-wide audits with the participation of students, staff and faculty. They have also entailed meticulous planning and the search for economically-viable technological advances. They have involved ingenious and persistent educational campaigns to educate the whole educational community. And they have all benefited from the tenacity of a few talented individuals who considered the campus as their turf to be uplifted and safeguarded.

References

AULS (1996) Positive Purchasing Power Gaining in U.S. The Declaration. *Association of University Leaders for a Sustainable Future, 1(2), May-August.*

BAKE 302 (1995) *Understanding Environmental Systems: Food Groups.* Rice University, Texas. http://www.owlnet.rice.ed/~bake302/food. Last updated December 10, 1995.

Brown is Green (1997) *Brown is Green Summary Program.* Brown University, Rhode Island.

Campus Ecology (1996) *Campus Environmental Yearbook.* Washington, DC: National Wildlife Federation.

CCAT (1996) *The Campus Center for Appropriate Technology.* Humboldt State University, California.

CU RECYCLING (1996) *Year End Report FY 1995-96.* Solid Waste Advisory Board, University of Colorado, Boulder.

Denison University (1998) *The Barney Green Renovation Project.* Denison University, Ohio.

Green Page (1998) *Bates Dining Services.* Bates University, Maine. http://www.bates.edu/people/studpubs/green/green_page/commons.html. Last updated May 9, 1998.

JMU Recycling (1997) *Utilization of Recycled Paper.* James Madison University, Virginia. http://www.jmu.edu/recycling. Last update unavailable.

Keniry, J. (1995) *Ecodemia: Campus Environmental Stewardship at the Turn of the 21st Century.* Washington, D.C.: National Wildlife Federation.

Physical Facilities Department (1998) *Miami University Recycling News.* Miami University, Ohio.

Recycling Program (1996) *Recycling Program Fast Facts.* University of Minnesota, Minneapolis-St.Paul.

Simpson, W. (1994) *UB Guide to Green Computing: How Your Choices Can Make a Difference.* State University of New York at Buffalo.

Smith, A. (1992) *Campus Ecology: A Guide to Assessing Environmental Quality and Creating Strategies for Change.* Washington, D.C.: Living Planet Press.

TAPS (1997a) *Long Range Access Plan, Transportation and Parking Services, 1997-2005.* University of California at Davis.

TAPS (1997b) *TAPS Bulletin1(2)*. Transportation and Parking Services, University of California at Davis.

Teichert, K. (1996) Brown Is Green Program at Brown University: Electrical Efficiency. In *"Ball State Greening of the Campus Conference 1996"*. Muncie, Indiana.

Chapter 7

Institutional change and leadership in greening the campus[15]

Aaron Allen

Abstract

How do institutions change? How can change occur at an institution of higher education such as Tulane? What (or who) prevents well-meaning changes from occurring? This chapter uses environmental concerns at Tulane University as a case study to examine the institutional change process. Agents of change should be able to use the examples and conclusions in this study as a basis for making changes at Tulane or any institution. The thesis is that *the inability for Tulane to make the campus environmentally sustainable in terms of operations and education is due to the lack of an institutionalized internal lobbyist and leader dedicated to environmental issues.* The argument is supported with a model for institutional change (developed from an extensive literature review), a historical analysis of non-environmental and environmental change initiatives at Tulane, a review of campus greening programs in institutions of higher education in the United States, and a series of interviews with Tulane students and employees. In conclusion, an Office of Environmental Affairs (OEA) with an Environmental Coordinator is needed to provide continual and focused leadership. Policies, resources, means and ends, and education are also lacking and should be procured and developed. These elements, from the model for institutional change, are incorporated into a „Blueprint for a Green Tulane," which outlines the steps necessary for institutional environmental change to occur. The central component of that change is leadership from the Environmental Coordinator and from students, who will in turn carry their leadership in the environmental sustainability movement beyond the campus and help create a more sustainable world.

Background information on „greening the campus" and on Tulane University

„Greening the campus" means increasing environmental awareness and / or action on campus – in the operational facilities and processes of the campus as well as in the human communities of the campus and surrounding areas. Greening the campus involves working towards some or all of the

---

[15] This article is excerpted from a larger study entitled *Greening the Campus: Institutional Environmental Change at Tulane University*. It is available from the Tulane Environmental Studies Program (address above) and on the Internet at http://www.tulane.edu/~env_stud/greening.htm.

goals set forth in the *Blueprint for a Green Campus* (see Table 1). Although the fundamental theme of greening is education, this study focuses on campus operations, the greening of which is pedagogical, not just educational. The economics of campus environmental initiatives in higher education are well documented: *greening the campus saves money* (see Table 2). Investing in campus greening is therefore an economic, educational, and environmental investment with handsome returns – both financial and social.

Table 1: The *Blueprint for a Green Campus* (1995) outlines a „green" campus as one that:
- integrates environmental knowledge into all relevant disciplines;
- improves undergraduate environmental course offerings;
- provides opportunities for students to study campus and local environmental issues;
- conducts a campus environmental audit;
- institutes environmentally responsible purchasing practices;
- reduces campus waste;
- maximizes energy efficiency;
- makes environmental sustainability a top priority in campus land-use, transportation, and building planning;
- establishes a student environmental center; and
- supports students who seek environmentally responsible careers.

In addition to saving money, campus greening allows students to learn how to infuse environmental sustainability into the larger society. Students must be able to practice (and see the University practice) the lessons of environmental sustainability which they are taught in the classroom. Tulane has committed to environmental studies, along with three other areas of interdisciplinary interest: urban studies, international studies, and information technology. Together, the four are conducive to environmental responsibility and stewardship.

Tulane University is located in uptown New Orleans in the state of Louisiana; the distinction „uptown" comes from the area being up-river from the historic French Quarter, the original and southernmost French settlement on the 2,552-mile-long Mississippi River. The Mississippi River Basin drains 30 states, or 1.15 million square miles of land (41% of the landmass of the continental United States). The River is the dominant feature of New Orleans, and Tulane is beginning to design research agendas and teaching curricula around it. Doing so is particularly appropriate, since Paul Tulane, the benefactor of the University, was a River pilot.

Tulane was established in 1834, with 11 students and 7 faculty in a rented hall, as the Medical University of Louisiana to study and treat „the peculiar diseases which prevail in this part of the Union" (Tulane University 1997). Tulane is now diversified into 11 academic divisions[16] with approximately 6,500 undergraduates, 4,800 graduate students, and 8,000 employees, of which approximately 1,750 are full- or part-time faculty. A University-sponsored study determined that 24,000 Louisiana workers owe their jobs directly and indirectly to Tulane. Additionally, the

---

[16] The 11 academic divisions are as follows: three undergraduate and one graduate Liberal Arts and Sciences colleges with 30 degree-granting departments, and schools of Engineering, Architecture, Law, Medicine, Public Health and Tropical Medicine, Business, and Social Work.

University injects approximately $1.5 billion into the local economy each year (Strecker 1998). With its historical location on the Mississippi River, traditional focus on health and education, and significant impact on the local economy, Tulane has a formidable presence in the southern United States.

Table 2: Annual revenues and savings for 23 campus conservation projects from the National Wildlife Federation's *Green Investment, Green Return* report (Eagan and Keniry 1998).

Transportation

Reducing Car Use at Cornell	$3,123,000
Increasing Bus-Riding at UC-Boulder	$1,000,000

Energy Conservation

Saving Energy at SUNY-Buffalo	$9,068,000
Retrofits at Elizabethtown College	$247,000
Energy Reduction at Brevard Comm. College	$2,067,000
Laboratory Renovations at Brown University	$15,500
Better Lights in Dorms at Dartmouth	$75,000
Solar Panels at Georgetown	$45,000

Water Conservation

New Water Fixtures at Columbia	$235,000
Water-Saving Showerheads at Brown	$45,800

Dining Services

Washable Cups at Harvard	$186,500
Refillable Mugs at UW-Madison	$11,400

Re-Use

Surplus Property at UW-Madison	$241,800
Re-Refined Oil at UI-Urbana-Champaign	$3,500
Chemical Re-Use at the Univ. of Washington	$14,400

Management of Hazardous Chemicals

Reducing Weed-Killers at Seattle University	$1,300
Fewer Lab Chemicals at the Univ. of Minnesota	$37,000

Composting

Fertilizer from Food Waste at Dartmouth	$10,000
Landscape Waste & Scrap Wood at UC-Boulder	$1,300

Recycling

Award-Winning Program at UC-Boulder	$107,000
Dining Services Recycling at Harvard	$79,000
Paper Recycling at UW-Madison	$120,000
Analyzing Wastes at UW-Madison	$21,000
Total Savings & Cost Avoidance:	$16,755,500

Presently, Tulane is in a time of profound change: a presidential transition. Tulane's new President, Dr. Scott Cowen, sees the academic year 1998-99 as a „Renaissance of thought and action" to redesign Tulane for the future. The present state of strategic planning is an opportune time for institutionalizing the greening process. An initial assessment of the Tulane environment (an environmental audit, discussed below) shows that much needs to be done, even though Tulane is not at ground zero with respect to greening. Environmental change, however, will not happen spontaneously; a bold change agent must take an active approach to ensconce environmental values into the core of Tulane's mission: its educational, service, research and operational structures.

Institutional Change
A Model for Institutional Change

Figure 1 is a model of institutional change. It is derived from the literature on institutional change in higher education.[17] Additionally, case studies in non-environmental and environmental change at Tulane and in academia support the model. The key element is a leader who is an administrator or faculty member but not a student, because students lack power and connections and are temporary (students, however, do play absolutely integral roles in the change process, as discussed below). In addition to the leader, leadership from the administration is necessary to support the change agenda.

The model is a conceptual framework for understanding and implementing change. It is dynamic: the dark arrows represent normal „flow" whereas open arrows represent feedback. The model is dynamic not only in itself but also between applications; different circumstances result in different paths. For example, education (the „end") may result in further advocacy for new changes (thus the dotted line, effectively making the model cyclical); also, procuring policy may return the advocates to the advocacy stage before getting resources. The model is not rigid; for example, policy may be skipped entirely – but the results of the change may not be permanent as a result. Dividing the change process into the segments of the model is artificial but necessary. Institutional change is not spontaneous, and greater understanding of the process will increase the likelihood of success for change movements.

Advocacy is the impetus to begin change. It is the product of diffuse, irregular efforts of (primarily) students and faculty found in the „shadow" of the university – the area outside of the „mainstream" of campus life and separate from the traditional governing structures of the institution (David Ehrenfeld, personal communication, 1998; Mansfield 1998; Bowers 1997). Advocacy is usually a grassroots or bottom-up effort, but top-down advocacy is just as important: the two converge in the middle to create the integrated advocacy required for institutional change.

Advocacy results in policy. Development of specific and general policies should be consensual, with the input of all appropriate parties. Policies should be applicable, enforceable and non-rhetorical in order to support, justify and communicate the change goals. Additionally, policy

---

[17] The complete literature review is available in the *Greening the Campus* study.

development and having policies in place is a form of education (a mean and end) about the change agenda (Creighton 1998, MacTaggart 1996, Strauss 1996, Keniry 1995, Smith 1993, Hamburg and Ask 1992, Lane 1990, Cerych and Sabatier 1986, Fantini 1981, Gitell 1981, Altbach 1974).

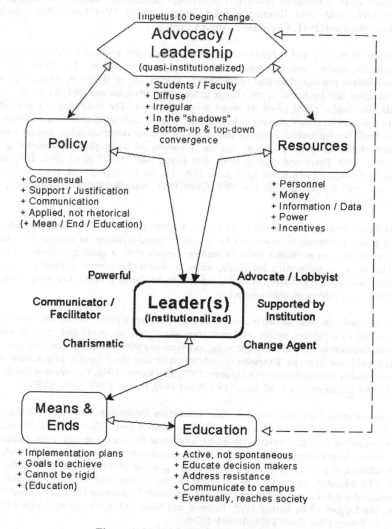

Figure 1: Model for institutional change

Advocacy and policy procure resources. Roughly prioritized, the primary resources are personnel (a leader, support staff, an office), financial resources, information and data, power (or direct access to power), and the ability to offer opportunities and incentives for improvement and positive change. Resource allocations should be in line with the missions of the institution, and a continual supply of necessary resources will maintain the desired changes. (MacTaggart 1996, Keniry 1995, Smith 1993, Hamburg and Ask 1992, Dominick 1990, Lane 1990, Cerych and Sabatier 1986, Gitell 1981, Fantini 1981, Altbach 1974).

Leadership is the key and defining element of the model for institutional change. Advocacy procures the leader, who is supported with policy and resources. The leader is in an institutionalized position dedicated to the change agenda. He or she is the change agent: the communicator and facilitator of the change process, the advocate and lobbyist for the change agenda. The leader needs power or direct access to power. The institution – especially the administration, who should also act as leaders for change – must support the leader. Finally, the leader should be charismatic: important character traits include communication, interpersonal and listening skills; visionary planning; and the capability to accomplish meaningful projects (Creighton 1998, Berry and Gordon 1993; also Riggs 1997, MacTaggart 1996, Dolence and Norris 1995, Keniry 1995, Smith 1993, Lane 1990, Farmer 1990, Dominick 1990, Wood 1990, Rainsford 1990, Cerych and Sabatier 1986, Gitell 1981, Altbach 1974; Orr 1990, 1992, 1994, 1995 and 1996).

While the leader is the key element to the model, it is also the place for the potential tragic flaw: how can one person do so much and be so great? Some solutions to address this potential weakness include an additional leader or leaders, support staff, a guiding committee (one that provides broad administrative leadership, ideas, a modus for communication and potential resources) and, most importantly, involving students in the change process. The integral roles of a committee and students are discussed below.

The leader develops well-defined means to achieve agreed-upon ends. Neither the means nor the ends can be rigid. Means are the implementation plans; they are many and specific, and they address education and process re-engineering (physical and administrative). Ends are goals; they are few and broad in scope. Examples of ends might be ecological literacy of graduates and an environmentally sustainable campus (Alinsky 1971; also Keniry 1995, Dolence and Norris 1995, Smith 1993, Eagan and Orr 1992, Lane 1990, Wood 1990, Farmer 1990, Altbach 1974).

Education is the primary mean and end. Campus decision-makers must be educated on the change agenda – on the mechanics of its means and its desired ends. The same issues should be communicated to the entire campus, since education about the change agenda is not spontaneous. For example, in environmental change, the campus community will not automatically understand the mechanics of a recycling program or the larger goals of environmental sustainability; they need to be educated. Eventually, the education reaches society, and such is the ultimate goal when attempting environmental change in higher education (Ackerman 1997, Brown and Duguid 1996, MacTaggart 1996, Keniry 1995, Dolence and Norris 1995, Orr 1994, Smith 1993, Orr 1992, De Young 1986, Gitell 1981, Altbach 1974).

Some theory ties together the model for institutional change in higher education: change does not happen spontaneously (Ackerman 1997, Bowers 1997, Williams 1991, DeYoung 1986). The changes pursued must be realistic. They will take time to achieve and will never be 100% complete (MacTaggart 1996, Steeples 1990, Cerych and Sabatier 1986). Operational changes affect some people significantly, while most are affected only minimally; transformation, not revolution, is needed. A two-dimensional framework of change is appropriate for Tulane[18]: depth is the degree to which a change requires a departure from existing values and practices, and breadth is the number of areas within the institution a change is expected to introduce modifications. Wide / deep changes result in opposition, whereas narrow / shallow changes do not take hold. Changes are most likely to succeed when they are moderate in depth and breadth of change (Cerych and Sabatier 1986). Institutional environmental change with regard to campus operations is moderate change (Hamburg and Ask 1992).

Institutional Change at Tulane (Non-Environmental)

Past change initiatives at Tulane show that, despite numerous barriers, both moderate and profound changes are possible – given an empowered leader (or leaders) with resources and policy who introduces means and ends to implement change. Six cases exhibit non-environmental change: Tulane's management of the Housing Authority of New Orleans (HANO); multicultural affairs; bisexual, gay and lesbian affairs; Tulane College's Programming Office; Tulane 2000; and the University Transformation Program. People did not immediately embrace these issues (they were not spontaneous); advocates and leaders convinced the campus that they were meaningful changes. For example, Tulane's management takeover of HANO was not a spontaneous move – the leader who initiated the project believed that Tulane's involvement was appropriate and in the best interests of HANO, Tulane, and the citizens of New Orleans.

Multicultural affairs; bisexual, gay and lesbian affairs; and programming issues in Tulane College show that it is necessary to establish offices responsible for oversight and implementation of changes. Advocacy began the establishment of all three, and all established policies and procured resources (an office, a budget, a director, etc.). Then institutionalized leaders implemented educational programs (means) to achieve broad goals (ends).

Two recent reforms were much more ambitious in their scope: Tulane 2000 sought to stabilize the University's budget (and subsequently focus the institution's academic priorities) with broad cutbacks, increased revenues and reallocations of resources; and the University Transformation Program sought to improve the quality of staff services and classrooms, along with starting an extracurricular program for first year students, instituting an information technology helpdesk, and establishing an international studies office. Both initiatives had a leader (the President and the Provost, respectively) and resources to develop and implement policy to make change.

---

[18] Cerych and Sabatier (1986) put forth a three-dimensional model, but the third dimension is for multi-institutional systems („level of change"), such as state schools with many campuses that are completely unconnected except for their central source of state funding. While Tulane has eleven different schools, they are all under the same administrative superstructure.

The necessary elements of achieving change characterize these preceding examples, and most fit into the strategic goals of the University (urban studies, international studies, environmental studies and information technology). Missing, however, is a concerted effort to make Tulane more environmentally responsible. While environmental research, and to some extent education, have improved (due to grant monies), the third and critical element of an environmentally focused institution of higher education – operations – has not been greened.

Institutional Environmental Change at Tulane

The above model shows that an institutionalized *leader* needs *policies* and *resources* in order to develop the *means and ends* and the *education* to move Tulane towards environmental stewardship. At Tulane, that leader should be an Environmental Coordinator in an institutionally supported Office of Environmental Affairs (OEA), which reports the Tulane Environmental Committee (TEC), the creation of which is the key advocacy needed to begin the institutionalization of the environmental change process at Tulane.

Tulane needs a general environmental policy and specific policies for certain greening projects such as recycling and procurement; the University cannot rely on the strategic goal of environmental studies to provide that policy. Resources (in the form of personnel, money, information, power and incentives) are needed for the greening initiative. The leader develops the means to achieve an environmentally sustainable campus that carries the message of environmental stewardship into society. Motivation (education) is critical: the OEA must communicate environmental concerns to the entire campus in order to accomplish greening goals. The leader should place special emphasis on key decision-makers to catalyze and maintain their support.

Institutional environmental change at Tulane is possible. Campus greening goals do not alter the basic mission of the University, in fact they complement them: environmental studies meshes well with information technology, international studies, and urban studies. Although much remains to be done, Tulane is not starting at ground zero. The environmental change needed at Tulane is moderate in the breadth and depth of change that would affect the University. With the advocacy to procure policy and resources, an institutionalized leader can provide the means, ends, and education necessary for institutional environmental change. An Environmental Coordinator is the key to coordinating environmental programs in the many divisions of Tulane.

The History of Greening at Tulane

The three divisions of the university are research, education and operations, and each has been greened to some extent. Case studies in each area support the model.

Environmental research has been the most successful division. It is a popular area because of the income associated with research grants and the opportunities for publishing. Also, quasi-policy (the environmental studies focus) and resources (multi-million dollar grants) led the development of extensive environmental research programs. The leadership of Dr. John McLachlan of the Center for Bioenvironmental Research (CBR) has developed, coordinated, and maintained environmental research program opportunities. The research division received a subjective grade[19] of „A-" in the spirit of the *Green Gradecard for the Green Wave* environmental audit (discussed below).

Tulane's Environmental Studies Program (ENST) has a history that epitomizes how institutional change occurs. In the early 1970s, students lobbied for the creation of the ENST. The coordinated major program (where students major in another field in addition to Environmental Studies) stagnated until the early 1990s, however, because the program was not allocated a budget and had only the devotion of one professor, who was not compensated for his involvement. As a result of the then new environmental studies focus of the University, the program progressed: new faculty became involved and established an environmental education committee, and grant monies provided the resources to offer course development grants, purchase equipment, hold training seminars,[20] and hire a part-time program coordinator. As a result, the program prospered, and enrollment increased dramatically.

However, the faculty leading the program could not dedicate enough of their professional time to the program; they treated it as if it were a University Senate committee. The student environmental organization, the Green Club, worked cooperatively with the ENST on numerous projects, including the campus environmental newsletter the *Environmental Forum*, the development of campus environmental e-mail listservers, and the design and publication of the *Enviro Counter Culture Catalog: A guide to environmental classes at Tulane*. The *Enviro Catalog* has received wide acclaim from within and outside of the University.[21] In 1998, the grants ended, and the University refused to provide a budget for the ENST and its more than 50 students. The CBR stepped in to fund the Program, but that funding also came from grants. Thus, the future of the environmental education program at Tulane is in question because of the lack of institutional support (*i.e.*, a budget). Additionally, the program is still directed by faculty members who are over-extended in their administrative commitments. While the ENST has potential to be a top program at Tulane and in the southern United States, the lack of administrative support and the absence of a full-time dedicated leader are hindering such success. The education division received the subjective grade of „B-".

The Green Club and the Tulane Environmental Project (TEP) have been significantly involved in the greening of one operational aspect of Tulane: recycling. Recycling at Tulane began in the 1970s as a volunteer effort. In the late 1980s the Green Club formed to address more institutionalized recycling. In the early 1990s, the Green Club leadership petitioned the University to establish a committee to green the campus. Tulane's President at the time, Dr. Eamon Kelly, established the TEP and appointed Professor of Environmental Law Oliver Houck as chair. The TEP was active for two years. In the first year the members of the TEP researched and implemented a recycling program, hiring a full-time coordinator and receiving a minimal

---

[19] The *Green Gradecard* did not use any standardized grading procedure; the students who conducted the audit relied on subjective judgement to grade each area of the institution. The same subjectivity was used in this study, although the research behind the subjective decisions was much more extensive.

[20] For more information on Tulane's innovative faculty enrichment seminars, visit http://www.tulane.edu/~efes.

[21] The *Catalog* is on the Internet at http://www.tulane.edu/~greenclb/catalog/.

University budget. In their second year they began a recycled procurement program to „close the loop," but that initiative was limited to a few paper products). Peaks and troughs in student leadership and activism (advocacy), the coming and going of numerous recycling coordinators over the years (leadership), and variable administrative support (resources) have led to peaks and troughs in the success of recycling operations. The Green Club has attempted other operational greening programs (*e.g.*, a „Green Dining" initiative in Tulane dining areas that has had minimal impact), and the administration took on an economics-based lighting retrofit (which did not include any education initiatives for saving energy and had no explicit environmental motives), but no other significant environmental operations initiatives have been institutionalized. The operations division received a subjective grade of „D-" / „D".

Table 3: Gradecard from the *Green Gradecard for the Green Wave: Environmental Sociology Audit Project, April 22, 1997*

AREA	GRADE	NOTES
Curriculum	A-	Strong, growing, funded
Buildings	C	New buildings OK, old poor; no renovation plans
Energy Use		
lights	A-	Upgrade program underway
heating/AC	D	Leaky buildings, overuse
Water	C	Overuse, poor conservation
Food Services		
Bruff Cafeteria	B-	Mostly reusable dinnerware, some vegetarian meals, low food waste, no donation, some recycling
University Center	C+	Mostly disposables, improving, as Bruff
Recycling		
academic buildings	B	Program needs more workers, infrastructure
dormitories	C	Need more institutional follow-up
campus grounds	F	Need bins on grounds
Composting	F	No composting of yard/food wastes
Procurement		
paper purchasing	B	2-sided / recycled paper policy exists, use varies
cleaning/pesticides	F	No environmental or safety considerations
hazardous waste		
policies	A-	Good policies exist
compliance	C-	Little or no awareness and action
Medical Waste	C	Good safety regulations; poor information gathering
Consciousness		
knowledge	B	Students aware of needs
action	D	Wasteful behaviors abound
Research	B	Much positive research, some poor funders
Investments		
business partners	B-	Pepsi, Marriott, BFI
endowment	F	No social/environmental screening
donors	D	Shell, Freeport-McMoran have poor envi. records
GREEN G.P.A.	C	1.97 Average Overall on 22 items

The history of greening at Tulane supports the model described above and reaffirms the need for a leader. Research has had a supported leader, and that division has been successful; numerous centers and laboratories at Tulane focus on environmental research. As for education, the Environmental Studies Program cannot rely completely on whimsical outside grants; it should be a University-supported program with a leader. Recycling and procurement programs are in need of improvement; each should develop coherent policy and comprehensive means to achieve those ends. Additionally, other campus greening programs for operations need to be established for Tulane to live up to its reputation as an environmental (research and education) university.

The Environmental Coordinator of the OEA could work closely with the ENST, CBR, Green Club, Recycling, and various schools and departments. The OEA could coordinate campus greening projects with students, staff, faculty, administrators, and the local community in the education, research, and operations divisions. All divisions need the support of the University administration and past greening leaders. An environmental audit of Tulane and lessons from academia offer support for the model for change and provide ideas for greening programs at Tulane.

The Greening Phenomenon in Higher Education

The *Green Gradecard for the Green Wave* environmental audit highlights many areas that are in need of improvement at Tulane, especially when it is compared with other institutions of higher education. Experiences in academia offer caveats, lessons-learned and examples on which Tulane can build – and even exceed. The greening initiatives in academia support the model for change, and they show the sound economic, social and environmental implications of such programs (Creighton 1998, Eagan and Keniry 1998, Keniry 1995, the *Blueprint* 1995, Smith 1993). Environmental audits are powerful tools for gathering information about the environmental quality of the campus. They are the starting point for environmental change, and they provide information to educate the campus, the community and especially those involved in the audit. Tulane's audit, the *Green Gradecard for the Green Wave*, which an Environmental Sociology class conducted in the Spring of 1997, evaluated various areas of the University and issued letter grades with respect to environmental performance. Environmental Studies, an energy saving lighting program, and hazardous waste policies received „A-" grades, while recycling, investment practices, and procurement of chemicals and pesticides received failing grades.

Overall, the audit graded twenty-two areas, and Tulane's „Green GPA" came out to a 1.9 / 4.0, or a „C" average (see Table 3). The audit concluded that the University should make an „institutional commitment to incorporate environmental decision making into all facets of [campus] operation . . . [and] establish a standing University Committee for Environmental Affairs." The *Gradecard* supports the model for change in that it advocates for institutional policy and resources that would allow for administrative (leadership) efforts to implement environmental change.[22]

---

[22] The *Green Gradecard for the Green Wave* is available on the Internet at http://www.tulane.edu/~greenclb/audit/audit.html. The term „wave" is used because Tulane's mascot is the „Green Wave."

Programs at other institutions concerned with environmental curricula and campus environmental consciousness illustrate the essential role of leadership to provide education; their success is reflected in campus environmental cognizance. Progressive environmental building, land-use and transportation (parking) policies have social, administrative and economic benefits. Energy and water conservation programs are financially sound and serve as education about the importance of conserving natural resources. The greening of food service operations has health, environmental, and economic benefits for the campus and local community. Waste issues (recycling, hazardous waste and medical waste) are visible to many in and out of the campus community; greening them is fiscally responsible, is educational, has positive impacts for the environment, and improves the image of the institution. Green procurement provides market stimulation to keep recycling and waste reduction initiatives available and economical. Finally, environmental research and socially responsible business and investment procedures have impacts that can be felt around the world. Case studies from progressive and innovative institutions in the above areas provide examples of what and how Tulane can green (see Creighton 1998, Keniry 1995, Smith 1993, Eagan and Orr 1992). Additionally, many of the case studies support the model for change. These greening initiatives contribute to achieving sustainability – on campus and beyond.

Hearing from the Tulane Community

A series of interviews with Tulane students, staff, faculty, and administrators further support the model. Five of the six questions support the thesis of this study, that a leader is needed to institutionalize and carry out greening efforts.

The four main institutional change barriers, as determined from the interviews, are:
- institutional / organizational (lack of communication, lack of advocacy and the lack of a leader)
- financial (lack of allocation of resources)
- cultural (lack of education)[23] and
- educational (lack of a modus for education).

Greening programs should relate to:
- operations (administrative and physical) and
- education (individual and community learning, both in and out of the classroom).

The results of the interviews clarify roles of each tier of the University community:
- students as learners, educators, and advocates;
- staff as learners and empowered „doers";

---

[23] The „cultural barrier" is complicated, and more research is needed on this subject. Many interviewees simply blamed the „culture of New Orleans" or the „Southern disrespect for nature" as reasons why environmental cognizance was minimal at Tulane. While such reasons may be true, the present author believes that other, more quantifiable, mechanisms are responsible, and a more detailed study could determine them.

- faculty as advocates and educators (who should practice environmental sustainability, especially if they teach it); and
- administrators as leaders in all aspects of the greening process.

The responses for the roles of administrators reiterated every element of the model and focused on the need for an Environmental Coordinator to lobby the administration on environmental issues. Finally, interviewees affirmed that it is possible and appropriate to green Tulane. With initial input from the Tulane community gathered, a proposal for greening Tulane can now become more formalized.

The „Blueprint for a Green Tulane."

The „Blueprint for a Green Tulane" is based on the model for change. The „Blueprint" is the outline of the steps needed to implement institutional environmental change at Tulane. Included in it is the proposal for the establishment of the Office of Environmental Affairs and the creation of an Environmental Coordinator position, both of which are explained below in more detail since they are the pivotal elements for the greening of Tulane. Residential approval and action are the final stages.

Advocacy

RE-ESTABLISH / REINVIGORATE THE TULANE ENVIRONMENTAL PROJECT (TEP) AS THE TULANE ENVIRONMENTAL COMMITTEE (TEC). It is necessary for President Cowen to initiate the new TEC. The TEC would be charged with approval of an annual agenda for campus greening and a review of the year's projects as coordinated by the Office of Environmental Affairs (OEA). A working group from the TEC and the OEA could develop the agenda and continually work with the OEA.

The Environmental Coordinator of the OEA would report to the TEC, and the Committee would, in turn, answer to the President (see Figure 2). It is necessary for the President to approve all appointments to the Committee, which would need a Chairperson of the President's choosing to act as the Presidential liaison. The TEC would meet once (perhaps twice) each academic year with representatives from the students (e.g. the Associated Student Body and the Green Club), the staff (e.g., the Staff Advisory Council), the faculty (e.g. the University Senate, the Center for Bioenvironmental Research and the Environmental Studies Program), and the administration (e.g., the Executive Working Group). The representation will also involve explicitly the three primary divisions of the University: research, education, and operations.

The representatives on the TEC should be the key players on campus with regards to environmental change. As such, the Committee will be the convergence of grassroots advocacy (which has been displayed for years) and top-down advocacy (which has yet to be shown) for environmental change. Simultaneously, the TEC will hold the power for making that change (i.e., the responsibility for planning in the OEA). The working group of the TEC could cooperate with the OEA throughout the year.

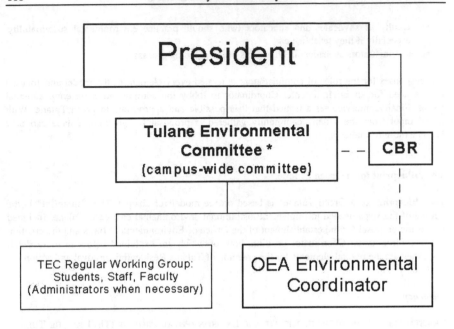

*Tulane Environmental Committee
*Appointed with Presidential Approval; Yearly Meeting for Agenda
Setting / Approval; Representatives from:*
Administration: Executive Working Group
+ *Operations:*VP Fin. & Ops., VP Admin. & Strategic Planning
+ *Education:* Provost, Deans, Environmental Studies
+ *Research:* CBR
Faculty: University Senate, CBR, Environmental Studies, faculty
Staff: Staff Advisory Council, staff
Students: ASB, Green Club, students

Figure 2: Proposed organizational chart

The TEC is the pivotal coordinating and advocacy body for environmental issues across the University, and the OEA is the leadership entity for carrying out environmental change. The TEC, the OEA and the Environmental Coordinator are interdisciplinary, interdepartmental, and interdivisional entities focusing on comprehensive institutional greening.

Policy

PUBLISH A STATEMENT THAT TULANE WILL BE A LEADER IN ENVIRONMENTAL RESEARCH, ENVIRONMENTAL EDUCATION AND ENVIRONMENTAL STEWARDSHIP. The statement should outline the core values of environmental responsibility that Tulane will espouse. With such a proclamation, the TEC working group would gather input from the University community via „town meetings" and would draft a University environmental policy statement for TEC approval. The President and the various legislative bodies of the University should then ratify the policy. Additionally, it would be necessary for the University to sign on to national and international environmental platforms, *e.g.* the *Talloires Declaration* and the *Valdez Principles*; such involvement brings national and international attention as well as assistance in implementing sustainability on campus. Finally, specific policies for projects such as recycling and procurement should be developed.

Resources

SEEK FUNDING FOR INSTITUTIONALIZING THE OFFICE OF ENVIRONMENTAL AFFAIRS. Funding sources should be internal and external. Internal funds could first come from a cooperative funding procedure, whereby each of the academic deans along with the Vice-Presidents who would be primary representatives on the TEC, would contribute $3,000 – $5,000 for the job search and first year's salary of the Environmental Coordinator. With a job search estimated at $3,500 to $4,000 and with salary and benefits estimated at $36,000 to $36,500 (for a senior program coordinator position), a total of approximately $40,000 is needed; with eight academic deans and three vice-presidents, the cooperative funding program could work. To date, no one approached about the cooperative funding measure has resisted it, however, they did mention that they would be more willing to participate once they know that the President is in support of the OEA proposal. This literal buy-in into the OEA is important for developing cooperation among the various entities.

External funds could come from alumni gifts and endowments for programs (such as scholarships and speaker series) and grants for projects and operating expenses. An endowment of $1 million would secure the OEA in perpetuity; the Office of Development could assist in such fundraising. Some grants pending in the ENST are already including such monies in anticipation of the OEA; the ENST has found, however, that granting agencies will not pay for employee salaries but will provide monies for students, programs and operating expenses. A study sponsored by the Nathan Cummings Foundation suggests that granting agencies and foundations fund specific campus projects that have the potential for success and could serve as a model for other institutions to use. Additionally, the report suggests that the monies be used as „seed money" for projects that will eventually sustain themselves (Strauss 1996).

Other potential funding mechanisms include a University budget, internal „loans" repayable with savings from cost avoidance programs, and a student environmental fee. The more innovative the design of the OEA, the more marketable it is; as such, the OEA could easily raise outside funding – especially from alumni.

Other important resources include personnel (especially a leader and student employees, discussed below), information and data, and an office. Initial sources of information and data on greening initiatives (or lack thereof) at Tulane are provided in the corpus and appendices of the study *Greening the Campus: Institutional environmental change at Tulane University* and in the *Green Grade Card for the Green Wave* environmental audit. In the future, an annual report of the OEA submitted to the TEC (*e.g.* the „State of the Tulane Environment") could chronicle important information and data. Finally, the OEA has been allocated office space in the new Environmental Science Building complex, where it will be in close proximity to most of Tulane's environmental research and education programs. The CBR, Green Club and Environmental Studies Program can provide necessary office supplies, including a computer, until funding is raised.

Leadership

EMPOWER THE OEA TO MAKE A POSITIVE IMPACT ON CAMPUS. The Environmental Coordinator of the OEA should work closely with various campus entities and constituents to develop and implement greening initiatives (discussed below.)

Means and Ends

EDUCATE THE CAMPUS ON ENVIRONMENTAL ISSUES. This education could be via large-and small-scale seminars and programs for students, staff, faculty, and administrators; continued research into and implementation of greening initiatives; a comprehensive measurement system; the development of an environmental management plan; classroom and curriculum initiatives; and other programs. The TEC should initially prioritize projects for the OEA to undertake, and after the first year the TEC will approve annual plans and review past performance. The „ends" should be outlined in general and specific policies. The Environmental Coordinator might also teach environmental classes, such as „Ecological Design" or „The Campus and the Biosphere."[24]

The Office of Environmental Affairs
Leadership

The OEA will house the leadership that will make environmental change at Tulane: the Environmental Coordinator. The Director of the OEA (the Environmental Coordinator) should report to the TEC. Dr. John McLachlan and the CBR would essentially provide a „home" and some day-to-day operational oversight for the OEA, while the TEC would provide the approval and guidance for long-range operations; Dr. McLachlan might also chair the TEC. Such an establishment is necessary because of the access to the varied power and resources of TEC members, in addition to the valuable experience with successful environmental change initiatives of the CBR and its director. The TEC would involve the people who guide the University in its daily and long-range operations and would insure that environmental concerns are heard. The TEC could appoint a working group (with ample student involvement) to cooperate with the OEA

---

[24] See http://www.tulane.edu/~enviro/pmba/enst481.htm for an example of such a class.

throughout the year on projects and programs. The organizational structure was already presented in Figure 2.

The OEA should be „bootstrapped" to each division and tier of the University: research, education and operations; and students, staff, faculty and administrators. Bootstrapping means creating official and unofficial connections which prevent atrophy or abolishment of the OEA and which foster collaboration and cooperation between all areas of the University. Such connections would be established via the TEC: research programs with the CBR; educational and service programs with the Green Club, the Environmental Studies Programs, and the deans of all the colleges and schools; and operational connections (the ones which will receive much of the focus) with the Vice-President for Finance and Operations and the Vice President for Administration and Strategic Planning. Many other connections would also exist, including those with Janitorial Services, Student Programs, Orientation, Admissions, Housing and Residence Life, Athletics, and campus institutes (such as the Center for Research on Women, the Payson Center for International Development and Technology Transfer, the National Center for the Urban Community, the Center for the Study of New Orleans and the Mississippi River, etc.). These connections will „bootstrap" the OEA to the core of the University and provide mechanisms for gathering and disseminating information and for effecting change.

Having an Environmental coordinator – the leader – is absolutely critical to the institutional environmental change movement. The leader should be a full-time employee with appropriate experience and degrees; the leader cannot be a student, although students are the second key to success in the movement.

Students

Students from the Green Club, ENST, student organizations and the general student population will be pivotal to the feasibility and success of the OEA. Not only would students carry out office duties in the OEA, they would also participate and benefit from the myriad programs of the Office. To maintain their involvement in the OEA, ENST and OEA fundraising endeavors could provide work-study funds for student workers, scholarships for leadership and academic excellence, and research assistanceships for student projects. Such funding could also be used to recruit incoming students.

As „customers," students are effective advocates for change; they could advocate and stand up for issues in student milieus by, for example, representing the OEA on various campus committees. Through the OEA, students would have an organized outlet for environmental activism, volunteerism and research opportunities as soon as they arrive on campus. They would provide a constant source of enthusiasm and ideas for the program, continually clarifying the *raison d'etre* of the OEA. Students in the OEA would be involved in an active learning and service community.

The students could gain valuable leadership and job skills in their time working with the OEA. They could take part in efforts to educate other students and employees through various programs, such as greening seminars, Internet sites, and publications.

Not only can students contribute to the success of the programs and projects of the OEA, but they will also be active participants in their own ecological education. Students in ENST courses could do service learning projects in the community as well as research on campus environmental issues, effectively using the campus as a laboratory for environmental problem solving – and for learning how to make positive environmental change.

Programs of the OEA can also help create connections for students, especially between students and place (i.e., Tulane and New Orleans). And the connections they make at Tulane through the OEA – with outside agencies, community members, with professors and, most importantly, with each other – would insure the lasting success of the OEA because of the broad and dedicated alumni support network that could develop. The innovative programs of the OEA and ENST would surely attract new students.

The OEA will depend integrally on students; it will also empower, support and educate them. The relationship will be one of symbiotic, collective leadership and learning. Campus sustainability programs are an extraordinary boon for the students, the entire university community and, subsequently, modern civilization: the students will carry their lessons and skills with them into society, disseminating environmental sustainability wherever they live.

Programs

Potential programs of the OEA range from large-scale projects (such as conferences with national or international organizations) to smaller-scale projects (such as office recycling education in a particular department), and they would encompass all the divisions and tiers of the institution, the areas of Tulane's strategic interest, and areas covered in the *Green Gradecard for the Green Wave*. All programs would strive for ecological literacy. Through the TEC, Presidential invitations could be sent to key faculty and administrators to strongly encourage them to attend the seminars and events, and in doing so, the OEA could be educating campus decision makers and crystallizing their involvement with campus stewardship programs.

The OEA would not necessarily run all the programs, but it would help coordinate efforts, provide information and experience, and advocate new programs. Students are an integral part of the programming function of the OEA, and they comprise the crucial links between the Office and the myriad departments, programs and organizations on campus and in the community. The successful projects of the OEA should be chronicled in campus newspapers and newsletters, as well as in local or national media. Projects of the OEA would likely begin focused on campus; once the Office builds momentum and accomplishes some major campus greening tasks, programming could move into the local community. The program possibilities of the OEA are seemingly endless (see Table 4 for some potential programs).

Table 4: Potential programs of the OEA

- Audits: Continue general and focused campus environmental audits independently and in classes.
- Recycling / Waste: Education about and coordination of activities for campus recycling and waste minimization.
- Procurement: Increase recycled and less hazardous product procurement, and develop a „Green Wave Seal" program, where local businesses and industries that conduct business in an environmentally responsible manner are awarded University contracts and receive local recognition for their accomplishments.
- Water: Retrofit water faucets and shower heads; organize watershed (Mississippi River) programs.
- Energy: Study and recommend the installation of energy efficient lighting (including solar), motion sensors, heating / air conditioning improvements, and other energy saving programs.
- Dining: Minimize use of disposables, increase locally grown food purchasing / consumption.
- Transportation / Planning: Address campus parking problems with a ride-share program or other appropriate transportation demand management program; cooperate with campus planning on new building designs.
- Grounds: Develop ways to maintain the campus landscape with indigenous flora and fewer chemicals.
- Laboratories / Research: Coordinate waste minimization programs and establish a chemicals exchange to save money and minimize disposal hazards.
- Publications: Assist with Green Club efforts and regularly publish the *Enviro Counter Culture Catalog* and the *Environmental Forum* newsletter; develop web sites focusing on Tulane's campus greening initiatives and student recruitment publications.
- Community: Coordinate projects with the Community Action Corps of Tulane University Students (CACTUS), the Campus Affiliates Program, and the National Center for the Urban Community, such as establishing greener playgrounds in local housing projects.
- Seminars: Developed seminars to train environmental and non-environmental administrators, faculty, staff, and students on campus stewardship projects or on incorporating environmental literacy into their classes, offices, and lives.
- Conferences: Green non-environmental conferences (less paper, fewer disposables, etc.). Sponsor conferences that are related to core themes of the University, such as the Mississippi River and New Orleans, or environmental, urban, international or Information technology studies.

Conclusions

An extensive literature of experience and research supports the development of the OEA, and if it is developed using the model for change from this study, then chances for success are greatly improved. While the proposed OEA and Environmental Coordinator position may not be the panacea for all institutions, it is relevant for Tulane. An alternative to the OEA could be to develop a new division at Tulane, for example, a „Dean of Environmental Programs" similar to the establishment Tufts University developed in the early 1990s. But such centralization would not engender the cooperation and *coordination* essential to the design of the OEA and Environmental *Coordinator* at Tulane, a university with many divisions, schools, and colleges.

Thus, the ideal situation for Tulane is a committee reporting scheme (the TEC) explicitly linking and coordinating efforts from the students, staff, faculty and administrators and in research, education, operations, and service.

It is estimated to take one year to establish the OEA: development and fundraising (fall 1998), fundraising and hiring (spring 1999), and implementation (and continuing fundraising) in the summer of 1999 in time for the fall semester, when programs would begin (and fundraising would continue). The three most important things needed immediately are:

- *Advocacy*: President Cowen's blessing, support and directive for establishing the TEC.
- *Policy*: a commitment from President Cowen that Tulane will be a leader in environmental education, research, and operations, upon which the TEC will expound to create an official University environmental policy.
- *Resources*: funding for the salary of the Environmental Coordinator (to come from a cooperative funding initiative supported by President Cowen).

With these three requests granted – with the convergence of grassroots and top-down advocacy – Tulane can begin a concerted effort towards institutional environmental change. That change will not happen spontaneously: only with dedicated policy and resources will institutionalized leadership develop the means and ends to educate the campus and move Tulane towards sustainability.

This year – which President Cowen has hailed as a „Renaissance of Thought and Action" – is the year to make environmental change at Tulane. Tulane has proven its commitment to „thought": environmental research and education programs are performing well. Now the administration must commit to the „action": taking active steps to being responsible environmental stewards on our planet, in New Orleans, and on our campus.

Acknowledgements

Many people contributed to the research and ideas that went into this study, and to thank all of them would be impossible. J. Timmons Roberts, Michael Zimmerman, and Charles Reith all contributed many dedicated hours of conversation, review, critique, and support. John McLachlan, Teresa Soufas, Yvette Jones, Christine Murphey, Dana Thomas, Melissa Vernon, and Kristin Traicoff all provided thoughtful comments and suggestions. Heartfelt thanks also go to the inspirational discussions with Julian Keniry and David Orr. And although any inaccuracies of logic or language are my own, Laura Robson supplied immeasurable support and countless editorial comments.

References

Ackerman, F. (1997) *Why Do We Recycle? Markets, Values, and Public Policy*. Washington, D.C.: Island Press.

Alinsky, S. D. (1971) „Of Means and Ends." In *Rules for Radicals*, pp. 24-47. New York: Vintage Books.

Altbach, P. G. (1974) *University Reform*. Cambridge, MA: Schenkman Publishing.

Berry, J. K. and Gordon, J. C. (eds) (1993) *Environmental Leadership: Developing Effective Skills and Styles*. Washington, D.C.: Island Press.

Bowers, C.A. (1997) *The Culture of Denial: Why the Environmental Movement Needs a Strategy for Reforming Universities and Public Schools.* Albany: State University of New York Press.

Brown, J. S and Duguid, P. (1996) „Universities in the Digital Age." *Change*, July / August 1996.

Cerych, L. and Sabatier, P. eds. (1986) *Great Expectations and Mixed Performance: The Implementation of Higher Education Reforms in Europe*. Trentham, Stoke-on-Trent, United Kingdom: Trentham Books Ltd..

Creighton, S. H. (1998) *Greening the Ivory Tower: Improving the Environmental Track Record of Universities, Colleges, and Other Institutions*. Cambridge, MA: MIT Press.

De Young, R. (1986) „Encouraging Environmentally Appropriate Behavior: The Role of Intrinsic Motivation." *Journal of Environmental Systems*, vol. 15, no. 4, pp. 281-292.

Dolence, M. G. and Norris, D. M. (1995) *Transforming Higher Education: A Vision for Learning in the 21st Century*. Ann Arbor, MI: Society for College and University Planning.

Dominick, C. A. (1990) „Revising the Institutional Mission". In   Douglas W. Steeples (ed) *Managing Change in Higher Education*. San Francisco: Jossey-Bass, Inc. New Directions for Higher Education, no. 71.

Eagan, D. J., and Orr, D. W. eds. (1992) *The Campus and Environmental Responsibility*. San Francisco: Jossey-Bass, Inc. New Directions for Higher Education, no. 77.

Eagan, D., and Keniry, J. (1998) *Green Investment, Green Return: How Practical Conservation Projects Save Millions on America's Campuses*. Washington, D.C: National Wildlife Federation.

Fantini, M. D. (1981) „On Effecting Change in Educational Bureaucracies." *Education and Urban Society*, Vol. 13, No. 4, pp. 389-416. Beverly Hills, CA: Sage Publications, Inc.

Farmer, D. W. (1990) „Strategies for Change." In Douglas W. Steeples (ed) *Managing Change in Higher Education*. San Francisco: Jossey-Bass, Inc. New Directions for Higher Education, no. 71.

Gittell, M. (1981) „Editor's Introduction." *Education and Urban Society*, Vol. 13, No. 4, pp. 389-398. Beverly Hills, CA: Sage Publications, Inc.
Hamburg, S. P., and. Ask, S. I. (1992) „The Environmental Ombudsman at the University of Kansas." In David J. Eagan and David W. Orr (eds.) *The Campus and Environmental Responsibility*. San Francisco: Jossey-Bass, Inc. New Directions for Higher Education, no. 77.

Keniry, J. (1995) *Ecodemia: Campus Environmental Stewardship at the Turn of the 21st Century*. Washington, D.C: National Wildlife Federation.

Lane, Jan-Erik (1990) *Institutional Reform: A Public Policy Perspective*. Brookfield, VT: Dartmouth Publishing Company Limited.

MacTaggart, T. J. and Associates with. Christ, C. L. (1996) *Restructuring Higher Education: What Works and What Doesn't in Reorganizing Governing Systems*. San Francisco: Jossey-Bass Publishers.

Mansfield, W. H. (1998) „Taking the University to Task." *World Watch*, May / June, 1998, pp. 24-30.

Orr, D. W. (1990) „The Liberal Arts, the Campus, and the Biosphere." *Harvard Educational Review*, vol. 60, no. 2, May 1990.

Orr, D. W. (1992) *Ecological Literacy: Education and the Transition to a Postmodern World*. Albany: State University of New York Press.

Orr, D. W. (1994) *Earth In Mind: On Education, Environment, and the Human Prospect*. Washington, D.C.: Island Press.

Orr, D. W. (1995) „Educating for the Environment: Higher Education's Challenge of the Next Century." *Change*, vol. 27, no. 3, May / June, 1995.

Orr, D. W. (1996) „Reinventing Higher Education." *Greening the College Curriculum: A Guide to Environmental Teaching in the Liberal Arts*. Washington, D.C.: Island Press.

Rainsford, G. N. (1990) „The Demographic Imperative: Changing to Serve America's Expanding Minority Population." Douglas W. Steeples, ed., *Managing Change in Higher Education*. San Francisco: Jossey-Bass, Inc. New Directions for Higher Education, no. 71.

Riggs, H. (1997) „Industrial Strength Academies." In *New Models for Higher Education*, Joel W. Meyerson and William F. Massy (eds.). Princeton, NJ: Peterson's.

Smith, A., and the Student Environmental Action Coalition (1993) *Campus Ecology: A Guide to Assessing Environmental Quality and Creating Strategies for Change.* Los Angeles: Living Planet Press.

Steeples, D. W. (1990) „Concluding Observations." Douglas W. Steeples, ed., *Managing Change in Higher Education.* San Francisco: Jossey Bass, Inc. New Directions for Higher Education, no. 71.

Strauss, B. H. (1996) *The Class of 2000 Report: Environmental Education, Practices and Activism on Campus.* New York: Nathan Cummings Foundation.

Strecker, M. (1998) „Tulane Makes a Billion Dollar Difference". *December 3, 1998, Press Release,.* New Orleans, LA: Tulane University Public Relations.

Tulane University (1997) *Undergraduate Catalog.* New Orleans, LA: Tulane University.

Williams, E. (1991) „College Students and Recycling: Their Attitudes and Behaviors." *Journal of College Student Development*, vol. 32, January 1991, pp. 86-88.

Wood, R. J. (1990) „Changing the Educational Program." Douglas W. Steeples, ed., *Managing Change in Higher Education.* San Francisco: Jossey-Bass, Inc. New Directions for Higher Education, no. 71.

Chapter 8

"ECOCAMPUS": a "Practice-What-You-Preach" European collaboration

J. Roturier[i], A. de Almeida[ii], E. Apostolidou[iii], D. Berbecaru[iv], J.F. Bonnet[v], R. Cazanescu[vi], P. Faucher[vii], S. Gabriel[viii], A. Gula[ix], M. Kwiatkowski[x], T. Laine[xi], Th. Lamouche[xii], J. Norgard[xiii], Ph. Outrequin[xiv]

Abstract

This paper describes the experience of a multi-university initiative on environmental conservation and sustainability and some of the results it has achieved.

Introduction

In the past five years, in a probable relationship with the UN Conference of Rio de Janeiro (1992), several initiatives have been taken within the scientific community aiming to increase the concern for sustainable development issues: (i) under the UNESCO's International Association of Universities sponsorship, a Declaration was published in 1993(Pietracci 1993) and (ii) another Chart has been submitted by the European COPERNICUS network (COP 97). Independently, participants in the Energy-University-Environment (EUE) Seminar, hosted by the University of Bordeaux 1 (France) in March 1995, have recognised that in most of their University Campuses or Research Laboratories, the management of natural resources, including energy and/or water use, is usually based on a "laissez-faire" policy. Such a situation was regarded by them as unwise, unfair and moreover unaffordable, so they decided to publish their common concern in the EUE-95 Declaration Statement , sharing it with the whole community of scientists and academic staff. In particular, three main reasons to implement and support a more conscious environmental management policy at universities were underlined:

- The financial costs associated with the daily operation of equipment to support both teaching or research activity continues to grow as more electronics are added to our laboratories and as more computers are added to our offices. The environmental degradation associated with the power production for the operation of heating, cooling (including cooling water for science equipment such as lasers, etc.) and lighting to support teaching and research activities has also grown as energy use has increased.

- The needs for the creation of new research and development programs are not being addressed in all countries around the world. This is due in part to artificially low energy prices and a lack of public awareness about the uncertainty of future energy supplies.
- Compounding this problem is the fact that research results are published in a multitude of obscure journals, often in a language foreign to the researcher. Hence, results from existing programs are not quickly distributed to others around the world. Furthermore, specific details about experimental set-ups and assumptions are often buried in unpublished reports and theses that it can take years to discover.
- Students are not receiving the best training because of limited, out-of-date texts, bad examples in campus buildings and isolation from others around the world who are interested in efficient building design and protection of the environment.

The EUE-95 Chart is regarded as the preliminary step of the ECOCAMPUS European collaboration, in which four main goals were assigned to participants: (i) Creation of a European Network of Environmentally Safe University Campus and Research laboratories (ii) Inventory of Energy-Efficient and Safe Technologies (iii) Definition of a Specific Methodology and (iv) Feasibility Studies. The present chapter, resulting from the EUE initiative, is devoted to presenting a brief survey of the main findings and conclusions obtained as part of the ECOCAMPUS European collaboration, a study partly funded by the EU DGXVII Thermie Programme[25]. Feasibility studies in seven countries are described, showing very different features: 5 are EU countries and 2 - from Central Europe- have obvious discrepancies in terms of economy and standard of living. However, another major difference is related to the weather conditions: very cold and long winters in Finland and Poland, mild winters in Denmark, France and Portugal and quite hot summers in Greece and Romania. Due to the high share of the thermal energy in the total demand, any forecast or comparison has to be done very carefully. The data presented here may only be regarded as a first step to be completed by a much deeper analysis.

Case Study from Denmark

Denmark is one of the EU countries where environmental concern is seen across the whole of society. At the Technical University of Denmark (DTU), environmental issues are prominent in research as well as in education activities, but until recently with little concern for the situation on the campus itself. In 1995, an initiative to carry out environmental management of DTU was taken by a group of teachers and students at the university. This «Environmental Management of DTU» project ran for two years, financed by the university. The purpose of the project was to engage students and staff in environmental problem-solving on their own campus, and to demonstrate, via some case studies, the situation on the campus and the options for improving

---

[25] under Contract STR 1006 – 96 FR (Project Manager : I. SAMOUILIDIS. A more complete analysis, and detailed data, may be found in the ECOCAMPUS final report (ROT 99) and/or from the co-authors who managed each case-study.

environmental management at DTU. About 25 teachers from different departments offered 16 subjects to about 80 students who undertook projects on water consumption, electricity consumption, heat savings options, hot water consumption, paper consumption, and many other subjects. A number of reports and seminars resulted. The understanding of the importance of the environmental problems seems to have increased among students as well as among DTU staff. Specially tailored for the ECOCAMPUS project, a more systematic and complete set of data was collected from both the Technical Division and the Central Administration of DTU. Time series of the consumption of electricity, heat, and water from 1980 till 1995 were established, as shown in Table 1. For shorter periods, data for the production of solid waste and chemical waste, as well as for the collection of paper for reuse were collected, too. In Table 1, the growth rate of electricity consumption, 4% per year, on average from 1980 to 1995, is shown. Heat consumption (Table 1), adjusted for climatic variation by the Heating Degree-Days parameter, shows no clear tendency up to 1992, but over the next three years, heat consumption increased by about 20%. Water consumption has shown a remarkable decline, amounting to around 30% over the 4 years from 1990 to 1994, followed by a 15% higher water consumption in 1995. Waste production has been growing and so has the production of chemical waste and the collection of paper for recycling, but the time series are shorter for these environmental indicators, and the data more uncertain.

	1980	1985	1990	1991	1992	1993	1994	1995
electricity(MWh)	16141	22880	24479	25464	26303	26249	27530	29447
heat (GJ)	195347	194199	198117	210417	199657	211110	233477	237841
water (m3)	206670	259825	226350	208097	182298	177776	156919	181011

Table 1: Resource consumption at DTU: History (1980-1995)

It makes little sense, however, to look at the resource consumption and other environmental indicators without taking into account the activities at the university, especially when comparing with other universities. The activities can be indicated by parameters shown in Table 2: number of students, number of employees, DTU's annual economic turnover and to some extent by the floor space area available. The most striking content of this survey is that the number of students declined by around 25% from 1990 to 1995. This obviously has a significant effect on the resource consumption per student, as shown in Table 3 for electricity, since these areas of consumption are more strongly associated with floor space and number of employees, and can only in the very long term be anticipated to decline with fewer students. These indicators, as well as electricity per turnover, are all shown in Table 3.

	1980	1985	1990	1991	1992	1993	1994	1995
area (m2)	363480	363640	369811	370265	370265	370349	373165	374867
students	4846	7024	8007	7904	7647	7109	6575	5916
employees	1797	2052	2414	2463	2476	2428	2401	2419
turnover mill. ECU	105	113	131	134	138	143	141	142

Table 2: DTU Key-parameters

Some of the increase in energy consumption in the form of electricity and heat, which is delivered from the combined heat and power plant at the campus, can be explained by a low general awareness, because the single departments are not billed for the consumption, which is paid by the university as a whole. More concrete reasons for the higher energy consumption are the increased use of computers and other electronic equipment, and environmental health and safety standards, requiring intensive 24 hour ventilation in many buildings, resulting in extra heat demand as well as electricity consumption.

	1980	1985	1990	1991	1992	1993	1994	1995
kWh/m2	44,4	62,9	66,2	68,8	71,0	70,9	73,8	78,6
kWh/student	3330,9	3257,3	3057,3	3221,7	3439,7	3692,3	4187,0	4977,6
kWh/employee	8982,4	11149,9	10140,6	10338,6	10623,2	10810,9	11465,9	12173,4
kWh/turnover	153,7	202,5	186,9	190,0	190,6	183,6	195,2	207,4

Table 3: Electricity consumption ratio (in kWh): by area, number of students, number of fulltime employees and annual turnover at DTU in thousands 1996-ECU.

Regarding trends in the near future, the DTU's Central Administration is now giving higher priority to reducing energy consumption and other environmental loads. One of the steps is to establish electricity metering and accounting for each single department. This is so far only as an experiment, since it requires some rewiring and other technical changes. One of the further measures suggested by the ECOCAMPUS study is that DTU should also engage in more systematic «Green Accounting» programs, keeping track of and publishing the development in environmental parameters, as commonly put into practice by many Danish companies and public institutions.

Finland

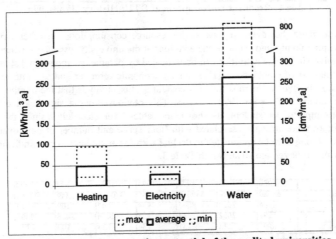

Figure 1: Average conservation potential of the audited universities

Olof Granlund Oy, a consulting company, analysed 7 universities or research centers in a co-operation with MOTIVA, the Finnish Information Center for Energy Efficiency. The standard Finnish energy audit procedure has successfully been used by consultants and other experts already for 5 - 6 years especially trained by MOTIVA, in a procedure that includes the gathering of basic information, field working, analysis of information and reporting. Based on the auditing reports, 5 universities or research centers were selected for a more detailed analysis (for a complete set of data regarding heating, electricity and water consumption and their conservation potential, see Chapter 3 in Roturier 1999). The present data shows that in some cases the conservation potential may be very high (up to 60 %) with very small investments resulting in payback periods as low as 1 month. Figure 1 shows the average conservation potential of the audited universities with the highest and smallest values. In one case (Helsinki University, Theoretical Institute of the Faculty of Medicine) all values are found to be much higher than in the other audited universities. The conservation actions are segmented into operational and investments demanding actions.

	Heating		Electricity		Water	
	kWh/m³	kWh/m²	kWh/m³	kWh/m²	dm³/m³	dm³/m²
Helsinki University, Theoretical Institutes Of the Faculty of Medicine	98,2	313,9	46,2	147,6	814,1	2601,0
Helsinki University of Economics	43,0		17,3		140,3	
Espoo-Vantaa Institute of Technology (functional unit of Espoo)	41,5	182,1	20,3	88,9	115,1	504,9
Espoo-Vantaa Institute of Technology (functional unit of Vantaa)	34,7	176,8	15,3	77,8	80,4	409,6
Helsinki Business Polytechnics Institute	49,4	186,7	34,0	128,3	220,7	833,6
KTV Residential Institute	23,0	100,4	20,6	89,7	96,2	419,3
Total average (all buildings)	48,7	200,2	26,0	111,1	265,4	1161,7
Typical average (without Faculty of Medicine)	35,8	149,2	20,7	94,7	122,1	516,2

Table 4: **Specific annual energy and water consumption levels in 5 Finnish Universities and Research Centres.**

Operational actions show short payback periods (mostly less than 0,5 yr). The average highest operational energy conservation action could be achieved by changing the operation time of air handling units. The average highest conservation actions that require investments are change of water ejectors to pumps (in one case) and change of control methods of air handling units. Figure 2 shows, subdivided into operational and investments actions, a list of possible conservation actions in universities and research centers. All conservation potential, translated into money savings, is analysed in terms of increasing the man-months relations. The average specific consumption for universities and research centers can be calculated from all data available. Alternatively, the data for the Faculty of Medicine can be left out so as to provide more typical figures. Based on energy audits, different energy and water saving technology is presented for universities and research centers. Conservation actions are classified by systems (HVAC, electrical). The total specific conservation potential is 0.58 ECU/m3, the average payback time being 1.6 years. Average money savings and payback time also evaluated for both HVAC systems (ventilation, heating and water) and electrical systems (lighting, cooling, other) are 0.48 ECU/m3 – 1.4 years and 0.10 ECU/m3 – 2.6 years respectively.

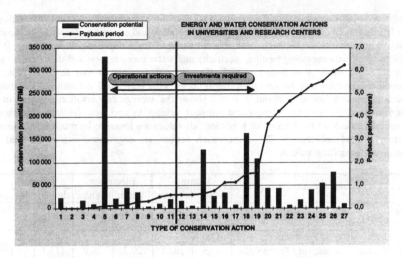

Operational actions
1. Removing humidifier from air handling unit
2. Decreasing domestic water temperature
3. Reducing luminous intensity
4. Changing operation time of lighting
5. Changing operation time of air handling units
6. Changing electricity tariff
7. Renovation of heat recovery unit/ changes of setpoitns
8. Reducing water flow rate of district heating
9. Changing use of PCs in classrooms (switch off)
10. Checking combustion efficiency
11. Limiting the peak power

Actions that demand investments
12. Changing control method of cooling pump
13. Changing use of boilers/ efficiency
14. Changing control methods of air handling units
15. Changing incandescent lamps to flourescent lamps
16. Changing indoor temperature setpoint
17. Sealing
18. Changing water ejectors to pumps
19. Limiting taps discharge rates
20. New cleaning method for laboratory instruments
21. Changing operation time of lighting
22. Renovation of doors to cold storages
23. Changing / renovating water taps
24. Installation of heat recovery unit
25. Occupancy sensor for controlling lighting in classrooms
26. Renovation of radiator valves and line control valves
27. Condensated heat recovery from chiller

Figure 2: Conservation actions in universities and research centers

France

The Chair of the ECOCAMPUS Work Group, CENBG-University of Bordeaux 1, in addition to managing the different steps of the feasibility study since the beginning of the academic year 1996-97, was committed to:

- establishing contacts with many Universities and Research Centers worldwide in order to permit a careful exchange of information;

- creating the network of European Universities, relying on present ECOCAMPUS partners and potential future members identified through new contacts;

- disseminating a basic knowledge on ECOCAMPUS issues to French Universities, and collecting results from initiatives independently performed.

As part of the present study, gauges and tools have been defined aiming to:

- analyse and follow electricity and/or water consumption by means of several indicators (consumption / price range / month / year / ten year period / m² / number of students / field of research activity / type of experimentation / contractual demand /etc...);

- find information on techniques and or energy-efficient equipment with examples of past projects and technical characteristics of possible solutions;

- support tools for new energy-efficient and environmentally-sound constructions which also encompass normalised procedures such as the Environmental Management Standard (ISO 14000) or those specific to French organisations (COE: Council on Energy Orientation and PEE : Plan Environment Enterprise).

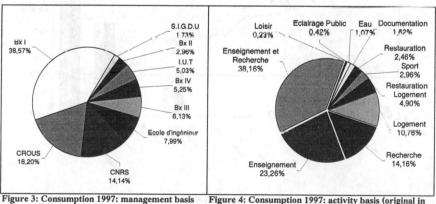

Figure 3: Consumption 1997: management basis   Figure 4: Consumption 1997: activity basis (original in French)

Almost all higher education activities in the Bordeaux region are located about 6 km south of downtown, in Bordeaux suburbs on the territories of 3 municipal authorities: Gradignan, Pessac and Talence (acronym GPT). With a total area of about 2.5 km², the whole campus is one of the largest in France. Each year about 50,000 students are enrolled in one of the higher education institutions available on the site, offering nearly all disciplinary fields, excepting medicine. Moreover, many services are also available, such as students restaurants and dormitories, a water supply facility, post office, culture and sports rooms and facilities,etc. As far as consumption is concerned, the annual electricity and water demand, for example, being about 25 GWh and 700.000 m3, makes the GPT area equivalent to a town of 10,000 inhabitants. In 1997, the total annual consumption of electricity was close to 24 GWh, the total subscribed power being 7,5 MW, the maximum power load reaching up to 8,5 MW.

The sum of all the electricity bills, from about 60 separate meters, that takes into account the cost of the subscribed power and electricity consumption, represents 1.5 MECUS (tax not included) not ignoring that overhead costs of such extra power are around 4.6 % on average. In Figures 3 and 4 the share of 1997 consumption for each administrative sector and for each activity, is shown. It may be seen that, altogether, the teaching and research activities, representing 80% of the total annual consumption, are the first end-use sectors. The students´ restaurants and dormitories sector, with about 18 %, ranks second. At first glance, the 1996-1997 growth is nearly zero. However, a more detailed analysis demonstrates that nearly all sectors, but the two most important, namely teaching and research, show a non-negligible increase (Figure 5). Also, in the long term, strong fluctuations appear that are probably associated with structural changes in some teaching and research activities i.e. a move to new buildings.

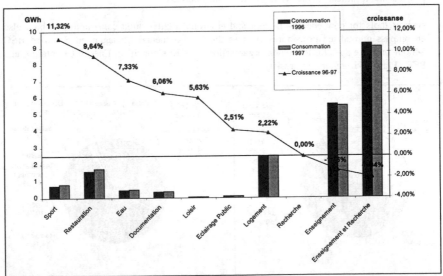

Figure 5: Consumption and Annual growth 1996-97

A very preliminary benchmark study is now being performed, these data bring compared to equivalent figures from the other feasibility studies relying on indicators such as F/kWh, kWh/m^2 etc. It makes easier a comparison of buildings with similar activities, i.e. students dormitories or restaurants. Also, as shown in Figure 3, an unambiguous and rather expected result is that R-D laboratories are # 1 in terms of consumption. Although such rough data, shown in Figures 3-6 are easily obtained, a few obstacles remain when a more comprehensive study has to be done (e.g. lack of a centralised source of information, large autonomy of management for almost all institutes, departments and laboratories, electricity and water use or waste collection available provided at no charge, complex electricity and water networks, technical managers working independently and so on). Such constraints need to be more deeply investigated and clearly identified as one of the main obstacles to future actions. For such reasons, the first step of the feasibility study has been started on the territory of the campus of University of Bordeaux 1, one of the higher education organisations located within the GPT area. It is important to underline here that the present work, part of a voluntary energy and environment policy defined by the President of the university, was successfully implemented in a close partnership with the staff.

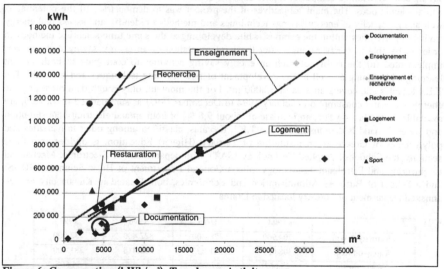

Figure 6: Consumption (kWh/m²)–Trends per Activity

In addition to the analysis of the electricity demand on a period covering the last past 10 years, other issues related to the University of Bordeaux case-study are introduced in the ECOCAMPUS final report (see Chapter 4 in Roturier 1999): (i) energy and water end-uses concerning in particular the scientific equipment, an electricity end-use usually ignored, while certainly responsible for most of the night and weekend consumption, so having a broad impact on the electricity bill and (ii) a survey of the waste management policies. A study concerning the water supply and demand issues is part of another, recently started (Fall 1998) project, partly funded by the Regional Water Authority.

The present first step, however, is now seen by many members of the university staff as a reliable and complete demonstration of the benefits resulting from the optimisation of electricity, water demand, and waste management, resulting in a significant decrease of the related costs, which presently increase each year.A policy aiming to implement, as a key part of the operation of a university campus, the Environmental Management and Audit System, now appears to be affordable and a quite obvious necessity, not only in terms of financial resources but also in order to offer an up-to-date environmental training of our students not neglecting new opportunities in research from the liberalisation of the energy and water markets to new waste management processes.

Greece

ECOCAMPUS´ goals were thoroughly examined in Greece, using the Technological Educational Institute (T.E.I) at Kavala, as a testing ground. Through the project, all aspects of an energy saving activity within a campus of higher education were considered: economical, environmental and academic ones. The main objectives of the project was to demonstrate (i) the potential as well as the capacity of energy savings techniques and methods to identify and assess real energy saving opportunities within the campus, while developing at the same time scientific methods in order to be able to verify savings, after the implementation of an energy saving measure was implemented (ii) the ability of such an energy saving activities to contribute to both student learning and training as well as the development of new teaching techniques and methods. The T.E.I Kavalas site covers an area of 32.000 m². For the moment, only rough data regarding the energy and water consumption (January 1994 to December 1997) as summarized in Table 5, are available. In the last 4 years, an increase of about 9,8 %, of both annual electricity consumption and water demand is demonstrated. The T.E.I. Kavalas, classified among other universities and polytechnics of Greece as an institution of Tertiary (Higher) Education, is divided into three sections: the School of Applied Technology (SAT) with departments of Electronic, Mechanical Engineering and Petroleum Technology, plus a General Department of Basic Sciences (GDBS) and a School of Business Administration and Economics, both located in Kavala city and an annexed Department of Forestry located in Drama.

	1994	1995	1996	1997
Electricity (kWh)	704.900	778.800	822.400	932.000
Heating oil (Kg)	308.039	341.832	252.418	381.400
Water (m³)	25.669	27.940	23.495	34.505

Table 5: Energy and Water consumption by T.E.I. of Kavala

The T.E.I. Kavalas campus is located on the western outskirts of the city in modern buildings covering an area of 32.000 m², set in a campus of total area of 136.000 m². The Campus serves approximately 1000 students and 210 scientific and administrative personnel. About 400 students reside in the dormitories during the school period, the number being reduced to 100 during the summer vacation. Energy and water consumption data, covering a period from 1/1/94 to 31/12/97 (summarised in Table 5), are strongly related to a few major determining factors (i) the floor area occupancy : 32,000 m² of floor area of campus buildings were fully occupied from academic year

1996/1997 and 25.300 m² before; (ii) the average number of days per month with classes in session and (iii) the maintenance works or end-uses: the 16% drop in water consumption, observed between the years 1995 and 1996 is mainly due to improving different parts of hydraulic network. In contrast, the 56% increase of the water consumption, observed in the year 1997, is attributed to a start-up of the new irrigation system of T.E.I´.s gardens which operate without any automatic control and the construction of a new building. Total 1997 expenses for TEI operations reached 4.78 million ECUs[26]. The electricity consumption and water demand segmented by end-uses (Tables 6 and 7 – Figures 7 and 8) and oil consumption for heating and hot water uses are analysed in the ECOCAMPUS final report.

Use category	kWh/year
Lighting	523940
Dormitory lights	224640
Outdoors lighting	21900
Educational facilities	277400
Pumps and central heating	27900
Recirculation pumps	21600
Burner electrical equipment	6300
Air-conditioning	43040
Heat pumps for cooling	20000
Fan-coil fans	23040
Direct heating	187500
Laboratory/Office equipment	150000
TOTAL ELECTRICITY	932.380

Table 6

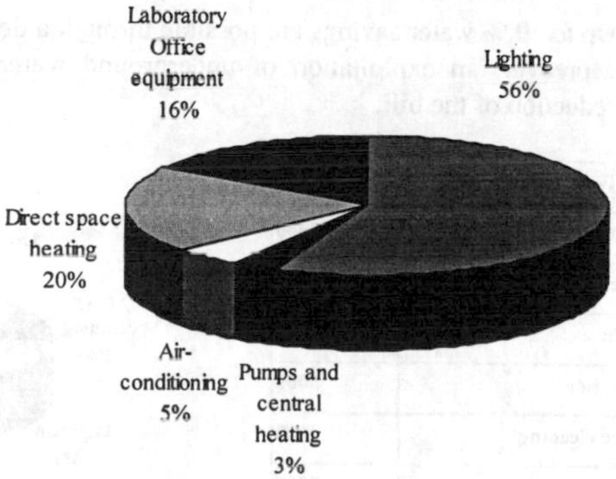

Figure 7: Electricity End-Uses

The breakdown of total expenses to major accounting centres shows that the utility costs (mostly energy) reached 5,5% of the total expenses for the fiscal year 1997, clearly demonstrating that such costs cannot be considered as insignificant even in relative terms. Therefore, energy management programs for the facilities higher education is now an urgent priority. Based on a more complete energy analysis and the main results presented in the ECOCAMPUS final report, several cost-effective measures are identified, some of which being:

A – Electricity demand - the total conservation potential is estimated to 8,8% shared as follows:
- Daylight savings of corridor lighting : Total electricity savings potential: 6,8%
- Lighting fixture revamping : Total electricity savings potential: 16,8%

---

[26] 1622 million drachmas (I ECU ≈ 340 drachmas).

- Minimise the use of electric space heaters: Total electricity savings potential: 10%
- Peak demand control : Total electricity cost savings: 8,7%
- Eliminating non-active (reactive) power in the main electricity board and minimising the growth rate of electricity, particularly the air-conditioning, the main reason for such growth.

B - Heating oil - non-negligible energy savings are also achievable through:
- improving operations of the central boiler room (savings 17%)
- installing appropriate room thermostats (savings 15%)
- a more appropriate boiler efficiency testing instrumentation (savings 7%)
- an upgrade and extension of the existing solar system for water heating (savings 5%)

C - Up to 10 % water savings are possible through a decrease of the losses in the supply network. Moreover, an exploitation of underground water resources should permit another 10 % reduction of the bill.

Water use category	m²/year
Dorm water use	19080
Office use	1015
Lab use	2000
Irrigation	5000
Space cleaning	2000
Losses	7500
TOTAL	36595

Table 7

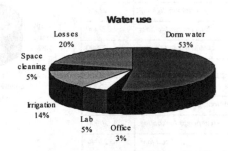

Figure 8: Water End-Uses

As listed above, the present results clearly indicate the need to establish and implement an energy savings program within a campus of higher education. Such a program can serve both economic and academic needs of participating institutions. From the economic side, this program has clearly demonstrated that there exists a significant energy saving potential within campus operations. From an academic point of view, this project has revealed the significant educational benefits that can result for both students and faculty. Through the co-operation of all campus members and outside experts, the project has convincingly demonstrated the need, and benefits, of extensive co-operation among various scientific and professional disciplines.

Poland

A preliminary energy audit has been completed and the energy savings potential roughly identified in a building of the Faculty of Physics and Nuclear Physics (University of Mining and Metallurgy -UMM). This work is being performed in partnership with staff and students of the

recently created (1995) Faculty of Fuels and Energy and with the FEWE, the Polish Foundation for Energy Efficiency. Part of the study includes:
* undertaking of energy audit in buildings of the Faculty of Physics and Nuclear Physics and Faculty of Fuels and Energy
* acquisition of new data related to heat, electricity and water consumption
* comparison of actual and calculated energy consumption
* identification of energy-efficient technologies demonstrated to be affordably used in such buildings

In the present study, energy audits of selected buildings of UMM were conducted in three buildings: Faculty of Physics and Nuclear Techniques - FPNT, Faculty of Fuels and Energy - FFE and Main Library - ML. So far, the research has focused on carrying out preliminary inventories of heating systems in the above buildings. General data on all three buildings are shown in Table 8. The second step, in the near future, should be devoted to assessing the entire possible energy efficiency measures for these buildings and to implementing the audits findings and disseminating the results to other Polish universities. Preliminary inventories of heating systems, that are equipped with two heated water pipes, were conducted. The heating installations being supplied from the Kraków district heating system, each building has its own district-heating substation. The heating systems do not have any automatic control at the moment, so the supply water temperature is not adjusted to the current needs. Heaters are not equipped with thermostatic valves, nor are there are any reflector shields on the walls behind the heaters. Furthermore, the insulation parameters of both walls and roofs do not comply with the currently valid Polish standards, the windows requiring sealing too. The maximum heating capacity demand for each building was calculated (calculations were conducted using computerised tools in compliance with applicable Polish standards). The theoretical end-use energy consumption for space heating purposes was also estimated. Readings of heating meters installed in the district heating substations in all buildings were taken during the last heating season, allowing the real energy consumption for heating to be evaluated (the heating meters show how much energy was supplied from the district heating system). The real energy consumption is higher than the theoretical end-

	FPNT	FFE	ML
Total heated area	5 180 m^2	2 302 m^2	5 067 m^2
Total heated volume	17 230 m^3	6 355 m^3	14 101 m^3
Max heating capacity demand	470 kW	158 kW	434 kW
Max heating capacity demand volume	27.28 W/m^3	26.37 W/m^3	30.78 W/m^3
Max heating capacity demand	90,73 W/m^2	72.80 W/m^2	85.65 W/m^2
Theoretical end-use energy	3 867 GJ	1 520 GJ	3 125 GJ
Annual Consumption	1 082 MWh	422 MWh	868 MWh
Theoretical end-use energy consumption	209.0 kWh/m^2	181.4 kWh/m^2	171.3 kWh/m^2
Real annual energy consumption (metered data)	4 256 GJ 1191 MWh	1 718 GJ 477 MWh	3 472 GJ 964 MWh
Real energy consumption	230,1 kWh/m^2	190.3 kWh/m^2	190.3 kWh/m^2]

Table 8: General Data on the FPNT, FFE and ML buildings

use energy consumption because the latter does not take into consideration the efficiency of the internal heating systems and heat exchangers. Built in 1989, the FPNT building is located in the neighbourhood of the UMM campus. It consists of 4 floors above ground level and a cellar that includes lecture rooms, laboratories and offices of the academic staff. The building has a relatively large number of windows, up to 60 % of the surface of external walls (depending on their exposure) consisting of double-glazed windows, certainly having a great influence on the heat demand.

Portugal

The main focus of the Portuguese case study, has been given to a campaign of measurements carried out in different buildings of the University of Coimbra: several departments, students' cafeteria, social assistance. Results from two of these buildings, namely the Departments of Computer Engineering (DCE) and of Electrical Engineering (DEE) are presented below, the following goals having been targeted: (i) achievement of consumption data collection, (ii) analysis of data resulting from energy audits, (iii) identification of energy savings opportunities. In this section, the consumption of some buildings is briefly analysed. Consumption data from two new buildings both devoted to teaching and research activities were collected and then divided into groups that are strictly connected to these activities. Items like water heating or space heating and cooling are included in the "others" sector. In order to evaluate the quality of the electrical grid, a small analysis of the power factor of each building is also presented. The DCE building is a three-storied building with 7 blocks: 5 blocks with classrooms and computer rooms, 1 block with a bar and a library, 1 block with the teachers' offices. During the metering period the electricity consumption was 3,500 kWh distributed as follows:

- Lighting was responsible for 54% of the total energy consumption, this high consumption being due to both the large number of lamps and the bad programming of the lighting controller, leaving the lights on unnecessarily in the common areas.

- Office equipment (94 PCs, 1 network server, 13 printers and 2 copiers) is responsible for 28% of the total energy consumption, with 50% of office equipment consumption due to computers. Another important issue, namely the power quality has also been specially investigated.

The load diagram and the power factor of the DCE building during the week under study have also been analysed. The increase of active power during weekday nights and during some periods on the weekend, is due to the presence of people working at these times. This DCE building presents a lower power factor that is permanently changing throughout the day. This low power factor is a consequence of the high concentration of office equipment and the type of lighting used. As previously shown, the compact fluorescent lamps, that have a very poor power factor (around 0,5) are always on in the common areas. The 5-storey DEE building , which houses both offices and teaching and R-D laboratories, contains about twice as much office equipment as the DCE building. However, the lighting share, although relatively high , for the same reasons, is a little bit lower at 42 % instead of 54 % for DCE. Unsurprisingly, both the load diagram and the power factor are quite similar in both buildings.

Romania

Like in Poland, the liberalisation of the energy market has induced a very important increase of the energy bills at least at the managers' level. Although decision-makers pay very great attention to the heat and electricity consumption, this is not necessarily taken into consideration at the user's level. Managed by IPCT - SA Bucharest, a Building Research Center, two case-studies: the "Tei" Campus – Technical University of Civil Engineering in Bucharest (UTCB) and the "Observator " Campus - Technical University in Cluj-Napoca (UTC) have been analysed. Only rough data are shown below:

- the annual electricity consumption of the Bucharest Civil Engineering University, from about 2,278 MWh in 1991 reached 3,657 MWh in 1996, an overall increase by a factor of 1.6, about 10 % per year!

- an analysis of the specific power consumption of the Bucharest Civil Engineering University also shows interesting trends in the same period with, for example, a 30 % increase of the consumption in a students' hostel

The groups of buildings from UTCB include 5 Faculties, 5 hostels, 5 labs, a canteen and one administrative area, all located in the "Tei" University Campus. These buildings have their own thermal power stations, while the other buildings are connected to the city central heating system. The University Campus "Observator" has 3 Faculties, 6 hostels, 5 labs, a canteen and some additional structures. The hostels were opened to users in 1970, the canteen in 1972 and the CFDP buildings in 1983. The campus has its own thermal power station, working on gas, supplying heating and hot water to the buildings. The heating consists of cast iron radiators. The electricity supply is provided through several transformer points where the power consumption is also registered, since there are no distinct metering device for each individual building. The total useful area and developed area are about 30,000 and 50,000 m² respectively. The number of students in the hostels increased between 1996 and 1998 from 2100 to 3360.

From the present study, a few cost-effective measures aiming to increase the power efficiency at the Technical University in Cluj are identified, for example:

- In the "Observator" University Campus, the Technical University in Cluj, it is suggested to replace the present thermal power station (wear and tear) by 8 fully automated microstations for every campus unit. For 8 microstations, the investment is about 230.000 Euro which could induce important annual savings: 322 Nm3 of natural gas, 108.000 m3 of water and 86.4 MWh of electricity. The resulting money savings would be 31.700 Euro annually: the energy savings would cover the salaries of 6 professors.

- In the short term, the Technical Civil Engineering University in Bucharest intends to implement two measures expected to save 79.279 m3 annually in order to decrease the water consumption in students hostels, the major water users, namely (i) a retrofit of indoor water installations and (ii) a water meter in every (collective) sanitary hostel room. The total investment cost is 60.000 Euro showing a payback time of about 5 years while the resulting annual savings would cover the salaries of 7 lecturers

The ECOCAMPUS ROMANIA network will grow larger in the near future including other universities (Timisoara, Iasi) and co-opting other universities in Bucharest. The research findings show some specific consumption values related to thermal energy, fuel, water and electric energy between 1988 and 1996. These figures are now included in a database open to experts in universities and research centers. A comparison between these values and the standard figures shows a very high resource consumption (energy and water) in certain cases and calls for certain strict measures intended to reduce and control the situation. Some of these are expected to be implemented soon on both the Bucharest and the Cluj Napoca campuses.

Summary of main results

As shown in the ECOCAMPUS final report, similar studies also aiming to encourage sustainable development approaches are performed in universities worldwide. Most of them, however, only analyse the impact of waste production and management or, when energy or water issues are quoted, the data usually refer to bills only. In contrast to this, the present ECOCAMPUS analysis:

1. makes a permanent and explicit reference to the energy (heat, electricity) and water supply and demand, in physical units;

2. includes the efficient-use policies;

3. does not ignore the waste production and management programs.

In its present status, the ECOCAMPUS study enables a few conclusions to be drawn, even taking into account the large differences in size, climatic conditions or status of the economy in the countries involved. In any case, it seems appropriate to consider at least a few indicators, which may be helpful in a macroeconomic analysis:

- The value of all heat demand and electricity consumption data is in a 250-350 kWh/m² range, divided into about 60 % (heat) and 40 % (electricity). A more accurate analysis may probably show some differences possibly correlated to the teaching activity: i.e. Science and Technology are probably more energy-intensive than Law or Humanities.

- Concerning electricity, the data vary from 30 to 170 kWh/m² for teaching and 60 to 110 kWh/m² for students dormitories. Indeed, the ratios of annual consumption/m2 or students or employees also increase significantly e.g. + 4,5 % on. In most cases, this phenomena may result from a significant increase in the last decade of the rate of equipment of Universities and also the absence of an energy efficiency policy. So, the electricity consumption has increased over the past 8 years on all the universities sites under study: the annual growth rate is in a 3 - 5 % range.

- A high standby power load, about 90 kW or 40 % of the maximum demand, is called for at nights and week-ends in buildings where several large R-D laboratories are hosted. Such findings call for a deeper analysis of the energy efficiency of specific pieces of equipment used in the scientific process of research.Two possibilities should be investigated more thoroughly: (i) a possible energy/environment labelling policy for the scientific equipment in a similar way to those used for domestic appliances or office equipment (ii) the creation of a data bank aiming to provide the users with updated electric, and cooling, specifications of each apparatus or appliance used in the experimental set-up.

- Water consumption, including students dormitories and restaurants, varies from 0.5 to 0.9 m3 per year. The rate growth seems to be under control.

- Solid waste quantities are growing (about 1 kg/student annually) such growth being possibly related to a more efficient collecting programme. The chemical waste represents about 10 % of the total weight.

- No accurate correlation can yet be established between the increase in consumption and the variations of surface areas, number of students or net number of employees

Regarding the costs:

- the utility (energy/water/waste) bills represent about 3-5.5 % of the annual turnover

- heat and water bills do not show any significant growth while the electricity bills are continuously increasing

- payback time may be as low as 2.5 years

Other initiatives

During the past two years, other excellent initiatives launched in university campuses worldwide were identified that present some similarity with the present ECOCAMPUS study, aiming to attain the same goals: lowering the utility bills, showing perfectly conscious campus management to students, academic staff and visitors. Some of them are described elsewhere in this book, so that repetitions may be avoided here.

General conclusion: Sustainable Buildings

The studies or programs described in this chapter, illustrate many benefits, not exclusively in terms of money. It is, however, important not to ignore the fact that many sources of expenses, such as oversized equipment, improper management, misoperations or misfunctioning are avoided if a more accurate assessment of the needs and real conditions of use is performed.

Nowadays, such procedures, aiming to support a Sustainable Buildings Policy in Europe, do exist. Carried out in different ways in many countries, a rough overview of the situation is now provided from the information available:

- In Denmark, in order to improve the efficiency of actions and to allow more systematised and standardised analysis, three development programs have been used by the National Building and Housing Agency to implement new methods of management and control of the design, construction and operation of buildings. An Environmental Management Program is being built up around four basic elements: companies' decision-makers and managers must define an environmental policy; an environmental review should map the environmental factors; the preparation of an environmental action plan containing an activity schedule and time schedule for the actual environmental work, with responsibility, authority and environmental tasks assigned in accordance with environmental policy; and finally, an environmental audit should be carried out, via which it is checked that the environmental management system is working satisfactorily and that the targets set have been achieved.

- In Finland, a research program entitled « Ecological Community Project-Towards a sustainable city » has been in existence since 1994. Two pilot areas have been chosen: a new one and another which needs renovation. The Viikki area in Helsinki (pole of science-industrial arts in Finland including the Helsinki Science Park) has been chosen to represent the new housing area (13.000 new inhabitants and 4.000 new jobs), optimising conservation of natural resources, architectural quality, investment and operational costs.

- In Germany, approaches towards sustainable development are pursued by local authorities, whereas the Bundestag has commited the country to reduce greenhouse gas emissions to 25% by 2010. Several cities (Frankfurt, Thuringen, Freiburg, Heidelberg, Saarbrücken, Bautzen, etc) have carried out local environment and energy planning projects, in order to efficiently fight greenhouse gases.

- In France, several examples of actions supported by the « Plan Construction Architecture », a public body financed by both Research and Housing Ministries are performed in the framework of a « Ecologie et Habitat » program. It aims to favour research and real scale experiences regarding the interactions between buildings and their environment. The environmental quality of a building is then defined as "its capacity to preserve the natural resources and to satisfy the comfort, health and living quality requirements of occupiers, and this, at each stage of its life: scheduling, design, execution, use, renovation and demolition". Based on this definition, several high school projects, (unfortunately none from universities or research laboratories), chosen after being asked to submit proposals, have since been funded.

Finally, many contacts established as part of the ECOCAMPUS collaboration clearly demonstrate that the present work is one among other important actions. Such wider concern now aims to explicitly include environmental issues as one of the key priorities in the management of university campuses and research laboratories. Such actions, often based on local initiatives, deserve to be supported and encouraged for many reasons, especially because more and more members of the academic community now explicitly recognise that students will face the energy and environment challenges during their whole professional life in the first decades of the next century. Is not one of the most significant reasons for supporting ECOCAMPUS or similar programs, that one can thus ensure that students are more thoroughly trained?

References

Benke, G. (1998) "Efficient Universities: where do we go?". Conference Graz (Austria) Sept. 1998 (HYPERLINK mailto:benke@eva.wsr.ac.at)

Delport, J., Calmeyer, J. (1998) Private communication.
(HYPERLINK mailto:jdelport@postino.up.ac.za)

Faucher, P. et al (1998) Implementing Energy-Efficient and Environment-Safe Programs in the Management of European University Campus and Research Laboratories : Case-Studies from the ECOCAMPUS collaboration ". In ACEEE Summer study, Asilomar (CA) Aug. 98.
(HYPERLINK mailto:faucher@cenbg.in2p3.fr faucher@cenbg.in2p3.fr)

Haberl, J. et al. (1996) Measuring Energy-Saving Retrofit: Experience From The Texas Loan Star Program. Report ORNL/Sub/93-SPO90/1 (Feb. 1996)
(HYPERLINK mailto:jhaberl@esl.tamu.edu)

Pietracci, F. (1993) Private communication
(HYPERLINK mailto:pietracci@uno.org)

Harris, J. (1998) Private communication
(JPHarris@lbl.gov)

Roturier, J. (1998) Energy-Efficient Office Technologies In Europe. Final report of the MACEBUR Workgroup. (EC-SAVE/PACE Programme). (roturier@cenbg.in2p3.fr)

Roturier, J. (1999) ECOCAMPUS : a Practice-What-You-Preach European collaboration. Final

Report of the ECOCAMPUS Workgroup. EC-Thermie Programme (roturier@cenbg.in2p3.fr)

Authors
[i]   CENBG - Univ. of Bordeaux - BP 120 - 33175 Gradignan-Cedex (France) (e-mail: roturier@cenbg.in2p3.fr)
[ii]   Dept. Electrotechnical Engineering Univ. of COIMBRA - 3000 COIMBRA (Portugal)
[iii] TEI of KAVALA Alternative Energy Forms and Heat Transfer Lab St. Loukas 654 04 KAVALA
[iv]   IPCT SA - Rue Tudor Arghezi 21, Secteur 2 - 70 132 Bucarest (Romania)
[v]   CENBG - Univ. of Bordeaux - BP 120 - 33175 Gradignan-Cedex (France) (e-mail: bernard@lept-ensam.u-bordeaux.fr)
[vi]   IPCT SA - Rue Tudor Arghezi 21, Secteur 2 - 70 132 Bucarest (Romania)
[vii] CENBG - Univ. of Bordeaux - BP 120 - 33175 Gradignan-Cedex (France) (e-mail: faucher@cenbg.in2p3.fr)
[viii] Technical Univ. of Denmark Dept. of Buildings and Energy, Bldg 118 - 2800 LYNGBY (Denmark)
[ix]   Polish Foundation for Energy Efficiency FEWE - Ul. FLORIANSKA 55 - 31 019 KRAKOW (Poland)
[x]   Polish Foundation for Energy Efficiency FEWE - Ul. FLORIANSKA 55 - 31 019 KRAKOW (Poland)
[xi]   Olof Granlund oy, Malminkaari 21 - 0071 HELSINKI (Finland)
[xii] EOL - 1 Cours Fragonard, B 106 - 06 560 VALBONNE (France)
[xiii] Technical Univ. of Denmark Dept. of Buildings and Energy, Bldg 118 - 2800 LYNGBY (Denmark)
[xiv] EOL - 1 Cours Fragonard, B 106 - 06 560 VALBONNE (France)

OBS: *The full project text is available from J. ROTURIER, under Contract STR 1006 – 96 FR (Project Manager : I. SAMOUILIDIS. A more complete analysis, and detailed data, may be found in the ECOCAMPUS final report (ROT 99) and/or from the co-authors who managed each case study.*

Chapter 9

Institutional Commitment to the Environment and Sustainability: A Peak of Excellence at Middlebury College

Nan Jenks-Jay

Abstract

This chapter describes Middlebury College's long term commitment to excellence in environmental education and sustainable operations. Over 30 years ago, the College charted a course in environmental education that has grown to include the entire campus and now reaches into the surrounding community and region. An original focus primarily on a narrow definition of environmental education has evolved into a broader concept of teaching and practicing sustainability. Success has been achieved largely through shared institutional values, clearly defined purpose, vision and leadership demonstrated at all levels of the College from the Board of Trustees, President and senior administrators to the faculty, staff, students and alumni. The College's commitment and progressive attitude makes it possible to transcend boundaries and overcome barriers that otherwise stand in the way of success. A system-wide approach and structure that includes high, medium and even voluntary positions reinforce environmental excellence and sustainable concepts throughout the institution. Middlebury College recognizes the vast benefits of using the entire campus and surrounding area as a learning community providing an exceptional educational experience for its students while at the same time contributing to the well-being of Vermont and New England.

Introduction

Middlebury College ranked number one in a recent study, conducted by students at Dartmouth College, of five New England colleges and universities that are considered to have outstanding environmental reputations. The study concluded that Middlebury College, with its long record of commitment to excellence in environmental education and current support of sustainability, emerged as a winner among its peers. One might ask how Middlebury College has become a leader in this area. The Middlebury story is one in which various events, actions and attitudes come together to shape the context for excellence and innovation at a traditional liberal arts institution.

In 1965, Middlebury College (the College) demonstrated leadership by establishing the first Environmental Studies program (the program) at an undergraduate, liberal arts college in the United States. Coinciding with the early years of the Environmental Studies program, the Energy Council was established to reduce energy use on campus through facilities operations. This simultaneous attention to the environment, originating independently from the academic and operation sides of the College, represents the beginning of a convergence in philosophy and commitment that exists today. Middlebury College's administration, faculty, staff and students collectively contribute to a continuing tradition of environmental   excellence that radiates throughout the institution and into the surrounding region. For nearly three and a half decades, various factors have come together to form a nexus where the cultural values in Vermont, the vision of the College administrators, and faculty members' scholarly work and dedication as educators, as well as the innovation of facilities management employees and the ever present energy of students to reshape and improve the world they are inheriting. These elements in combination with a systems approach that integrates environmental education and sustainable practices throughout the institution contribute to Middlebury College's unique story.

A Vermont Ethos

A value system prevalent throughout Middlebury College is consistent with a culture that has long existed in Vermont. Middlebury College, founded in central Vermont nearly 200 years ago, is situated between the Green Mountains and Lake Champlain. The small state of Vermont in northern New England has long embodied characteristics associated with a clean environment and exceptional quality of life. Vermont is one of the least densely populated states in the United States with only two or three small cities that could be considered urban.

The remaining population still live in small towns with quaint village centers surrounded by a working landscape, consisting of valley farms and forested mountainsides producing fast running trout streams. Stridently independent, Vermont prides itself on being progressive and entrepreneurial while at the same time respectful of its history and traditions. In addition to the traditional dairy farms, Vermont is home to the Northeastern Organic Food Association whose members produce a bounty of organic products, as do the numerous Community Supported Agriculture farms. Large tracts of forest land are being transferred from timber and paper company ownership to state and private conservation with the condition that the forests will continue to provide hunting and traditional recreation as well as timber harvesting under more sustainable management practices. For many individuals, a direct connection the outdoors through work like farming or forestry or recreation. Year-round outdoor recreational activities abound throughout the State including skiing, snow-shoeing, boating, fishing, hunting, hiking, mountain biking, and nature watching. A commitment to strong environmental legislation and land protection demonstrate the politicians' and the citizens' commitment to protecting the environment of this state. Vermont enacted landmark environmental legislation in the 1970's that continues to control growth and development. Private land conservation organizations along with state and federal agencies have protected over 16% of the total land in the State including working farms and forests (Klyza and Trombulak, '99). Many Vermont industries and entrepreneurial businesses such as Ben and Jerry's Ice Cream have gained a reputation for being socially and environmentally responsible. Today, businesses that take local and regional sustainability into consideration are creating a new marketing edge and improving the ecological and economic well-being of Vermont and New England.

In general, Vermonters, both natives and newcomers, share a philosophy that is rooted in the State's clean environment and picturesque landscape. These characteristics are so appealing that they attract individuals to relocate from afar and cause others to remain in Vermont when they could have greater professional and financial opportunities elsewhere. This Vermont appeal must certainly influence decisions made by some faculty, administrators and students who choose to come to Middlebury College. Since the environment is integral to a Vermont way of life, people tend to adopt a behavior that reflects a high regard for the environment as part of the culture. This environmental consciousness is prevalent throughout Middlebury College from the first year students and grounds employees to the President of the College, as a positive factor in effecting decisions and actions. This Vermont philosophy has established a foundation of values that guides individuals' thinking and has contributed in part to the success that Middlebury College has achieved towards becoming a more sustainable campus and contributing toward a more sustainable region.

The Administrative Leadership's Bold Vision

The Middlebury College administration charted a course of leadership in 1965 when it approved a new major in Environmental Studies well before other undergraduate institutions of higher education in the United States. As the Environmental Studies program grew in size and national recognition, the Dean of Faculty had the foresight to sanction an external review for the program in 1988 which lent additional credibility to the goals that the program had identified. For example, one of the external review committee's recommendations quickly became reality with the approval of a new political science faculty position partially dedicated to environmental studies. In addition to critical evaluation and new insights, the outside recognition that external review committees bring often help to establish or renew the administration's regard for nontraditional, interdisciplinary environmental programs. In 1992, the President of Middlebury College was one of the early signators of the Association of University Leaders for a Sustainable Future - Talloires Declaration, a ten point action plan for colleges and universities committed to providing leadership to promote education for sustainable development and environmental literacy.

Charting an even bolder course outlined in a speech to the Middlebury College community in the fall of 1994, a new President of the College took a courageous step forward when he identified the environment as an emerging area of strength and importance for the College. He reaffirmed the institution's commitment to both the Environmental Studies program which already maintained a national reputation, and to teaching through example by making the College a model of environmental responsibility. He designated the environment as a "peak of excellence". Two previously designated peaks in the presidential range were academic departments and an interdisciplinary program: foreign languages and international studies, and writing and literature. The designation as a peak is not merely a paper title, but is a place of prominence within the institution that entitles peak areas to special consideration, for example, with dedicated funds for library acquisition, for student internships and for planning retreats, among other benefits. The new environmental peak was unique, however, because it was not bound to the curriculum and classroom as were the first two, but was to permeate all areas of the College, transcending institutional boundaries. To achieve this challenging task, the President appointed an environmental peak committee to make recommendations for the future. An outcome of the peak report on the environment was action taken by the Executive Vice-President and Provost of the College who created the new high ranking administrative position, Director of Environmental Affairs and Planning. The Director of Environmental Affairs and Planning reports directly to the Provost who reports directly to the President of the College. The position also maintains a faculty appointment affiliated with the Environmental Studies academic program. As stated in the contract, this new position "reflects the College's commitment to make the study of the environment - broadly defined- one of Middlebury's peaks of excellence". This unusually crafted position has responsibility for college-wide academic and non-academic areas related to the environment.

Many colleges responded to the energy crisis in the 1970s by establishing an energy committee, as did Middlebury College. The Energy Committee, established by the President, was to create a plan of action to reduce energy consumption and advance energy efficiency. Having accomplished its goals, the committee became inactive until resurrected by the Executive Vice-President and Treasurer in 1985. The committee expanded its influence across the campus in the 1990s after the President recommended a Task Force on the Environment, at which time the Energy Committee evolved into the Environmental Council which in, 1995, was made a College Standing Committee reporting directly to the President. The Executive Vice-President and Treasurer who saw the institutional need to establish the Environmental Council, has been and continues to be the guiding force behind sustainable campus initiatives, championing new energy technology and sustainable design, leasing agricultural land to local farmers, using green certified wood on campus, placing College forest land in green certification and by chairing the project review committee. The Executive Vice President and Treasurer also embraces the idea of the College acting as an agent of change and leader in capacity building within the region.

After the peak reports were issued in 1995, the President issued the following Environmental Mission Statement recommended by the Environmental Council: "Middlebury College as a liberal arts institution is committed to environmental mindfulness and stewardship in all its activities. This commitment arises from a sense of concerned citizenship and a moral duty and from a desire to teach and lead by example. The College gives high priority to integrating environmental awareness and responsibility into daily life of the institution. Respect and care for the environment, sustainable living, and intergenerational responsibility are among the fundamental values the guide planning, decision making, and procedures. All individuals in the academic community have personal responsibility for the way their actions affect the local and global environment. Environmental Studies is recognized and supported as a major component of the College's academic curriculum. Through its many environmental awareness initiatives and its diverse course offerings in Environmental Studies, the College seeks to ensure that its graduates will have the knowledge, skills, and values to become leaders in the worldwide endeavor to restore and protect the environment." The administration's strong support was clearly articulated in this statement.

The Board of Trustees of the College represent the highest governing body of the institution. Herein lies the greatest power and influence within Middlebury College. In 1994, the Board of Trustees sanctioned the President's recommendation to make the environment a peak of excellence. A resolution approved by the Board of Trustees provides a sense of how the College's highest leaders perceive the institution and of their courageous vision for the College as it enters a period of growth and expansion. The following is an excerpt from a Board of Trustees Resolution passed in 1995. The resolution in part states: "...The Board embarks upon this path with enthusiasm and confidence... we believe our chosen course the more exciting for its audacity. Middlebury College means to become the college of choice, and we seek to do so by embracing a vision that marks us as the "college of the future." We have crafted a strategy to achieve that goal. The strategy assumes that managed growth, with appropriate infrastructureal accommodations made beforehand, will not simply convey a sense of momentum, excitement, and improvement, but will result in a stronger and more excellent institution. We take up our task with purpose and singleness of heart." They also endorsed the College Master Plan in 1996 which contains guidelines for growth and development that give environmental and regional consideration high priority. As the Master Plan was being prepared, the chairperson of the Environmental Council presented the Board of Trustees' Buildings and Grounds Committee with seven reasons why the College should employ environmentally sound planning in a report entitled "Sustainable Development and Design for the 21st Century at Middlebury College". The strength of successful boards is their mix of individuals who represent a wide range of interests and backgrounds, as does the Middlebury College Board of Trustees. Several consider themselves to be active conservationists while others realize the importance of environmental values and sustainable concepts as they relate to Middlebury College, to Vermont and to sound business practices. Today we are experiencing an evolution of the Board. One of the most recent members to join the Board of Trustees is a 1983 alumna of Middlebury College who obtained her Master's degree in the environment, then a law degree and now practices environmental and general law. It is an asset to have individuals with such commitment, foresight and environmental awareness leading Middlebury College as it enters the next millennium.

The Academic Program: A Peak and A Paradigm Shift

Since Environmental Studies program's first graduating class in 1969, the enrollment has fluctuated, peaking in the early 80s and then again in the mid and late 90s. However, the overall popularity of the Environmental Studies major has increased dramatically over its long history at the College, with the number of graduates reaching into the forties each year in the mid and late 1990's (Figure 1). Today, student interest has increased to the point where Environmental Studies is the third to fourth largest major at the College. Environmental Studies is also one of the three top areas of interest currently selected by prospective high school students who are applying for acceptance to the College.

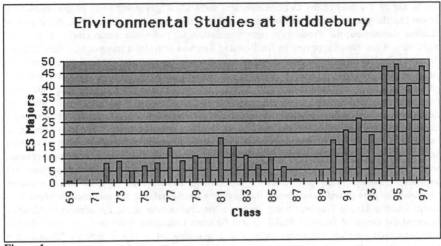

Figure 1

From 1965 to today, 419 students have earned their undergraduate degree in Environmental Studies from Middlebury College. Approximately 375 alumni of the College, representing graduates of the Environmental Studies Program and other departments, are currently working in a wide range of environmentally related occupations. An alumni network connects the program with graduates who are invited back to campus to give presentations and are listed as alumni who will sponsor internships and provide job opportunities for students and recent graduates. Communication between the program and alumni takes place through a newsletter and electronic e-mail exchange. Environmental alumni are considered to be a valuable resource who contribute strength to the environment as a peak.

A diverse faculty interest in the environment is essential to success. Faculty interest at the College is high. Forty-one full time professors are Environmental Studies affiliated faculty members. They represent 19 different departments and programs, which is just over half of the total number of 37 throughout the College. The faculty teach a wide range of environmental courses, advise student majors, and serve on the Environmental Studies Steering Committee. Three faculty members have joint appointments in both the Environmental Studies program and other departments. Within the past two years, four new faculty positions have been added in the Economics, Chemistry, Geology and Religion Departments which have appointments to teach courses that support the Environmental Studies Program.

The administrative directorship of the program rotates by design every three years among the senior members of the Environmental Studies affiliated faculty. Therefore, every three years a new director is appointed from the physical sciences, then the humanities or arts and then from the social sciences before returning to the physical sciences again. This strategy of rotating directors is designed to give the program greater objectivity and variety in the leadership representing the Environmental Studies program over time. It also prevents the program from becoming stale or allowing it to be run by a demigod. The Director of the Environmental Studies program and the Director of Environmental Affairs and Planning work closely together, consulting and communicating with each other to continue advancing the environment peak of excellence.

When the President of the College designated the environment as a peak of excellence, he also appointed peak committees to develop goals for all peaks areas and to suggest ways to achieve those objectives. Therefore, a group from the environmental studies academic program and alumni from the program formed the Environmental Peak Committee. The committee conducted an in-depth study which culminated in the preparation of a report for the President entitled "Report of the Committee on the Environment". The report presented 42 specific recommendations related to a broadly defined environmental education, some of which addressed: curriculum, establishing a summer graduate program, internships, creating a new off-campus program in another country, a colloquium series, the alumni network, environmental awareness, and safety and environmental impact. Many of the recommendations extended beyond the academic program to include campus-wide issues. A number of recommendations have already become reality including the colloquium series in which faculty, staff, alumni or speakers from outside the community give a lunch presentation each week. This forum creates opportunities for an informal exchange of ideas and information. It has also established a sense of community for the interdisciplinary program which it previously lacked. Another outcome of the report was the new position of Director of Environmental Affairs and Planning.

The Environmental Studies program curriculum integrates the natural sciences, social sciences and humanities/literature. Students studying Environmental Studies concentrate on one of eleven focus areas including: conservation biology, environmental chemistry, geography, US environmental policy, environmental economics, environmental chemistry, human ecology, international environmental studies, environmental history, environmental ethics, environmental literature and non-fiction writing. Many students study off-campus or in another country during their third year. They participate in any of 50 off-campus, environmental study programs approved by the College. Last year for example, 35 students studied in 28 different locations across the globe. Student internships during the January term or summers provide students with valuable life experiences and professional opportunities not available in the classroom.

In addition to internship experiences and honors theses that take student's education beyond the classroom, the senior seminar was developed to enable students to apply theory in practice by working on real environmental projects both on campus and in the surrounding region as a learning laboratory. The senior seminar is a capstone course that brings students together from the 11 environmental focus areas to address an environmental problem or issue. This integrated course draws on a wide range of individual knowledge and perspectives to develop a collaboratively achieved solution or outcome on campus or within the surrounding community.

The emphasis that the Environmental Studies program places on applied learning represents a shift in educational paradigm. Institutional paradigm in higher education includes the values and practices shared by the college community that defines its culture and the accepted mode of operation. In order to better prepare students for the challenges of the future, a shift in paradigm has taken place in Middlebury College's environmental studies program and is gradually also occurring within even the most traditional colleges and universities. The foremost shift in educational paradigm has been away from the pedantic emphasis exclusively on book learning, and towards an education that includes experiential learning. It has moved away from a focus on individual excellence and disciplines towards interdisciplinary team success, from single objects to relationships; from individual parts to the whole; and from structure or the final product to the process. (NAEP 1995)

An early example of this shift in educational paradigm at Middlebury College took place in 1985 when students in the Environmental Studies senior seminar studied waste on campus. The project resulted in specific recommendations to significantly upgrade the College's recycling program. After implementing the recommendations, the increased volume of recycled materials produced cost savings for the College and also reduced pressure on the region's aging landfills, a benefit to the College and the region. As a result, the College received the State of Vermont's "Recycler of the Year" award for recycling 50% of the College's waste. This senior seminar project was the first of many that study problems and issues using the campus and surrounding region as a laboratory. Today's projects have become increasingly more complex, for example looking at large scale watershed issues, and students use more sophisticated technologies such as geographic information systems and global position systems. The senior seminar uses the campus and the surrounding region as an extended classroom, often establishing partnerships with nonprofit conservation organizations, municipalities or other departments on campus that collaborate to solve environmental problems.

Student independent study projects and honors research theses also provide opportunities for students to combine their lecture and textbook learning with applied experiences in the field. A student working on climate change research in Alaska with his professor, designed a thesis around an educational CD ROM for local indigenous schools in the region. It described current theory on climate change and then provided the results of their study on the effects of climate change on boreal forest vegetation. This student project became a prototype for an on-campus project to create a web page and CD ROM for five Vermont schools in the region of a 16,000 acre (39,536 hector) swamp that the Environmental Studies program is studying in partnership with the Nature Conservancy. The schoolchildren will learn how this large wetland community in their own backyards contributes to a more sustainable ecosystem. Another student's senior project which studied the differences between air drying clothes hanging on a clothes line or tumbling them dry in a clothes dryer also had an eventual impact on regional sustainability. Following graduation, this student started a nonprofit organization in Vermont, coincidentally named "Clothes Line", which advocates reduced use of energy, explores viable alternative energy sources in the region and attempts to influence state policy on energy deregulation. These few examples from the senior seminar as well as student independent study projects and honors theses, demonstrate ways in which the Environmental Studies academic program is designed to create a nexus where the academic and operational parts of the College connect and where the College and the greater surrounding community link to achieve a more sustainable campus and region.

Campus Operations' History of Commitment

The College's facilities management and operations' long history of commitment to improving energy efficiency and environmental quality on campus have been critical to the environment becoming a College-wide peak of excellence at Middlebury College. A new energy consciousness on campus resulted from the 1970's oil embargo. At Middlebury College, the Vice-President for Administration and Treasurer established the Energy Council to recommend conservation strategies and to track energy use on campus. Some of the cost saving techniques included: window caulking, replacing old boilers with more efficient heating systems, and retrofitting lighting by installing energy saving lights and detectors for use only when needed. New Englanders take pride in their long standing reputation of being extremely "thrifty", a pattern of behavior which was a perfect match for energy conservation on campus and in the surrounding region. Personal behavior was changed through education and awareness campaigns that relied on the dissemination of information and positive incentives such as contests and competitions to conserve energy. Even though reduced fuel costs and the achievements of the College created a period of inactivity for the Energy Council in the 1980s, the mold had been cast. From that time forward, the College administration for operations and facilities management became committed to energy efficiency and environmental concerns as they related to the campus. However, due to growth of the campus and the age of computerization, energy demands have increased, but the College's conservation and energy efficiency efforts, including co-generation, have actually reduced the therms (therms - a quantity of heat equal to 100,000 BTUs or British Thermal Units) consumed per square foot for heating, cooling and electricity which today are comparable with those of the late 1970s (Figure 2). Although water is not a scarce resource in New England, a trend on campus has been to reduce consumption due to use of water-conserving technology and changes in personal behavior.

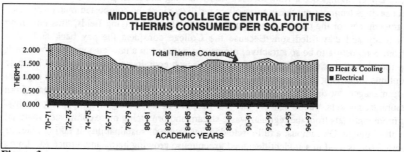

Figure 2

The College's recycling program was reorganized and expanded in 1989, and a Recycling Coordinator position was created as a direct result of the Environmental Studies senior seminar's report entitled "No Time To Waste". These new waste management measures significantly increased the volume of material being recycled to off- campus markets or local charities. Today, approximately 400 tons (440.92 tonnes) of waste materials are recycled, which accounts for between 35-40% of the total solid waste including: paper, cardboard, glass, tin/aluminum, plastic, Styrofoam, batteries, toner cartridges, automobile oil, scrap lumber & metal, furniture, books, student clothing, and other materials, as markets are identified (Figure 3). When the recycling program became institutionalized, the Recycling Coordinator's position shifted to include other environmental areas on campus. At the recommendation of the Environmental Council, the position was upgraded and expanded with a new title of Environmental Coordinator, who primarily reports to the Director of Environmental Affairs and Planning and works a quarter of the time for the Assistant Director of Facilities Management on education and outreach for the recycling program. The Environmental Coordinator has a wide range of responsibilities aimed at advancing the greening of the campus through facilities management initiatives; campus outreach and awareness education which include environmental orientations for new students, faculty and staff; and advising student environmental projects and research involving the campus. The Environmental Coordinator also oversees a web of student and staff volunteers which creates a network of effectiveness throughout the campus. These include the student Environmental Monitors in each residential building and staff Environmental Liaisons in each office.

One of the examples of leadership existing at all levels of the College is a case in which the Assistant Director of Facilities Management identified food residuals as a major portion of the College's waste being deposited in local landfills, after conducting a waste audit in 1993. He developed a pilot composting program to remove pre- and post-consumer food waste from the dining halls to be composted. After some trial and error and advances in composting technology, a passive aerated windrow system was found to be the most suitable for composting food residuals. Nearly 300 tons (330.69 tonnes) of the College's food residuals are being composted, accounting for 75% of all food waste and about 25% of the College's total waste (Figure 3). A combination of recycled materials and composted food waste amounts to approximately 61% of the total College waste being recycled. The composting program has saved the College $102,000 (US dollars) since the program began and has also produced large quantities of rich soil amendment. Direct savings occur from reduced waste hauling and landfill fees. In addition, there are indirect savings from not purchasing topsoil or fertilizer since the composted material is used as a soil amendment for the campus landscaping, greenhouse and playing fields, thus enriching Vermont's rocky and clay-filled soil. Because the College considers the pay back and other benefits from composting to be so attractive, it recently invested in a new custom-designed truck to pick up food waste on campus and purchased a high tech container with biofilter and leachate tank to continue improving the composting process. A partnership was initiated with the regional solid waste management district, a public service agency, to begin delivering food waste from local restaurants, markets, public schools and the hospital to the College's composting facility, removing more materials from the regional waste stream and producing more composted material for use by the College. On campus, a full-circle demonstration of sustainability is taking place as the composted soil is used in a student-designed greenhouse growing herbs and lettuce for dining services meal preparation. Here is an example where a student research project is integrated with the facilities management composting program and dining services food preparation in a sustainable demonstration of food to waste to compost to food again.

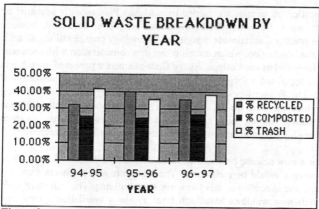

Figure 3

The College-owned lands include the 225 acre (91 hectare) main campus and playing fields, but Middlebury College also owns large tracts of forests and farmland totaling over 5700 acres (2306 hectares). The agricultural lands are leased to local dairy farmers and much of the forest area is managed for timber production. Guided by the Executive Vice-President and Treasurer, the overall goal of managing College land is to protect intrinsic values, historic and traditional landscape use patterns, aesthetics, biological diversity, wildlife habitat; and to provide educational and research opportunities. The College is in the process of having its forest land put into Green Certification in partnership with Vermont Family Forests Program to ensure that ecological and sustainable forest practices are employed, benefiting both the regional ecosystem and economy.

Sustainable practices such as maintaining traditional land use, recycling, composting, energy efficiency and water conservation, have simply become a way of life on the Middlebury College campus. Recent advances include the green certification of forest lands and the use of integrated pest management practices on the campus landscape and lawns. Progress is also being made in mapping and making an inventory of campus trees in a joint project involving students and landscaping staff, using geographic information systems (GIS). The GIS tree maps and accompanying database will have multiple applications for faculty and student research and education as well as for the daily maintenance and long term planning of the campus by the landscaping department. An electric vehicle is being leased by facilities management as an educational demonstration project. It will be used on campus as a work vehicle during the day, and can be test driven by interested staff and faculty during evenings and weekends. The use and operation will be monitored by a student project with results produced at the end of the lease. Here again, is a linking of operations and academics and faculty, staff and students. Challenges to create a sustainable campus still exist with regard to operations and facilities management, but it is encouraging to note that without mandates, many individuals are striving to make continued improvements on campus in the course of their routine work and daily lives, as well as through the specially-funded projects.

New construction and renovation on campus are guided by a Master Plan recently prepared by consulting architects with input from the College community. The document outlines environmentally responsible practices, sustainable design and technology considerations, historic values, aesthetes and view shed protection, which are all taken into consideration with each new project being designed and reviewed by the College. As the College enters a period of growth and expansion, the President has appointed a Project Review Committee at the recommendation of the Environmental Council. The Project Review Committee is assembling a set of overarching principles as well as the best practices to be used when reviewing and monitoring new construction projects, to assure that all new construction and renovation consider green technology and design and employ environmental protecting safeguards during construction.

During the design phase for a new science center, the Board of Trustees requested that, where possible, green building concepts should be considered. The architects and engineers took this charge seriously in the design and execution of this large, six story building. The structure itself is quite energy efficient, containing windows have high r values and a ventilation system that recovers heat from outgoing air. The insulation was produced from recycled materials. Construction waste was separated and recycled before it was removed from the site. The exterior of the building is made of locally quarried stone, and the interior trim, paneling and finish work is all made from green certified wood. The architects agreed on using a mix of tree species from New England rather then using all oak, which architects traditionally request. They realized that a variety of lesser used species and the irregularities in some of the green certified wood were both features that produced "more character", which everyone has agreed provides a more appealing effect. The Bicentennial Hall Science Center used a total of 125,000 board feet of green certified wood largely harvested in Vermont. The successful use of green certified wood in the science center has influenced the proposed library construction currently in the design phase and this is now slated to use green certified wood as well.

The Environmental Council's Long Range Plan and Action

Under the leadership of the Executive Vice-President and Treasurer, the Energy Council was reactivated in 1990. As the Energy Council's agenda increasingly began to include a greater number of campus environmental issues, the group's role expanded and was renamed the Environmental Council. The Environmental Council's membership includes equal numbers of students, faculty and staff representatives. It is co-chaired by a staff member and a faculty member, one of whom is the Director of Environmental Affairs and Planning. As a College Standing Committee, the Environmental Council reports and makes recommendations directly to the President of the College. The President also makes all appointments to the Council, but members are nominated through the Student Government Association, the Staff Council and the Faculty Council. In recent years, the Environmental Council has been engaged in a number of long-range planning studies concerned with the greening of Middlebury College. In 1994-95, the Environmental Council prepared and published a special report for the President that provided a comprehensive overview of the current state of the College's environment with recommendations for advancing the process of greening the institution. The report entitled "Pathways to a Green Campus: The Environmental Council Report and Recommendations" (Pathways) proposed a mission statement for the College and 22 other major recommendations that outlined a basic agenda for the Environmental Council in the years immediately ahead. Some of these included: the Environmental Coordinator's responsibilities, College publications, community awareness and education, energy efficiency and water conservation, dining services practices and food acquisition, land stewardship, toxins and pollution, waste minimization, and traffic and parking. The Pathways report and the "Report on the Environment", prepared by the academic program, deliberately overlapped and supported each other's recommendations. Together, the two reports made a powerfully persuasive case to the President of the College regarding environmental matters both academic and in the College's daily operations.

The Environmental Council currently works from the Pathways report, implementing its recommendations and identifying new areas where the College can be an innovator. To measure its progress, the Environmental Council conducted a comprehensive environmental audit this year, using the Pathways report as a benchmark, to see how far things had come and to provide direction for the College's future. The results demonstrated that much had improved, but it also brought attention to problem areas. The audit is now conducted regularly, with the results published and widely distributed, to acknowledge both improvements and areas where effort is needed.

With the College entering a period of growth and expansion over the next 5-10 years, the Environmental Council recommended establishing a new Project Review Committee to develop guidelines for design, construction and land use that consider green technology and design. The committee will use the guidelines to review proposed projects and to monitor projects during construction. The President of the College appointed the committee's members from the College community, and the Executive Vice-President and Treasurer and the Director of Environmental Affairs and Planning co-chair the committee.

Students as Agents of Change Towards Sustainability

Strong student interest has always provided a means to justify the Environmental Studies academic program as a major. However, students also contribute much more in the form of their energy, new ideas and a wide range of agendas which comprise a critical piece of the Middlebury College picture on the environment and sustainability. Their high level of commitment often establishes entirely new programs and initiatives. Their input and perspective are essential for the environmental academic program to remain current and continue to evolve. Students' unique insights are greatly valued by faculty and regarded by the administration of this College.

In addition to new student initiated endeavors, there is a plethora of existing environmentally related activities, in which students can become involved. Students participate in a variety of campus organizations and community groups. Because of the rural nature and natural amenities of the region, the College attracts a high number of student outdoor enthusiasts who join the Mountain Club. Those interested in advocacy and education are members of the Environmental Quality student group or join the Rain Forest Alliance chapter on campus. Others serve as student members of the Environmental Council, working on more comprehensive college-wide issues involving sustainability. Those who are more inclined to write, sketch or take photographs edit and illustrate "The Otter Creek Journal", a student publication described as "a local forum for discussion of ecology, sustainable living---eating-perceiving-being-relating-seeing-buying and energizing". Since 1985, students have played a key role in the College's recycling program, participating in the program's implementation and education. Even as recycling becomes more institutionalized, students remain involved and provide necessary input.

The Dean of Students office, which oversees the student residential advisors, has sanctioned a system of Environmental Monitors within student residences who assist the Environmental Coordinator to regulate recycling, report water leaks and energy waste, and to help educate fellow students about campus sustainability.

Student projects have reorganized recycling, established a hiking trail around campus, identified and mapped trees on campus with GIS, produced a bicycling guide for the community, developed a brochure for a local watershed center and recently recommended to the Board of Trustees that four parcels of College forest lands be permanently protected as "wild lands". Our students enlighten the College administration, influence the Board of Trustees, respect and collaborate with the staff and invigorate the faculty. Their interests often help shape the academic program by giving new direction to the curriculum. In addition, they have had immeasurable impact on improving the campus environment. As a rule, students never fail to surprise and inspire those of us working in academia.

Within the greater surrounding community, students volunteer in service projects with the local land trust, with "at risk" high school students working on environmental projects, and with regional conservation organizations. Student input and energy has been so valued by a chapter of the Audubon Society that they created a regular position on their board to be filled each year by a Middlebury College student.

Each semester, 18 students choose to reside in Weybridge House, one of several student residential academic interest houses. In association with the Environmental Studies program, Weybridge House has as its advisor an Environmental Studies affiliated faculty member. The residents design a community or campus project each term, and grow vegetables in their garden and purchase the rest from an organic, community supported agriculture farm to which they belong. They also sponsor educational programs on campus. A proposal to replace Weybridge House, the current student environment residence, with a Center for Sustainable Living and Learning (The Center) is under review. Students in an Environmental Studies senior seminar course conceived the original concept. They then developed the principles though a College community charette. Students have been involved with the proposal from the onset and will continue to have a hands-on role in the process from this point forward. The Center will provide students with a unique opportunity to practice sustainable living while learning about the most innovative tools and new technologies available. Students will monitor the systems and conduct research on this model, providing feedback to the College for future sustainable campus efforts. Educational outreach for the greater community will occur through year-round tours and programs about new materials and technologies for sustainable building construction and renovation in the New England region.

Campus and Regional Sustainability

While many colleges and universities often make reference in their publications to the regional amenities near their campuses, they frequently consider themselves to be beyond outside influences, acting as separate, insulated institutions detached from their immediate surroundings. Middlebury College, however, recognizes its role as a member of the greater community and is critically aware that the College can have major consequences on the region, particularly with regard to its waste products, water management, land use practices and traffic.

Increasingly, Middlebury College consciously acts in a manner that benefits the region. As a way of supporting local agriculture, regional economic sustainability and traditional land use, the College leases over 1000 acres (2471 hectares) of rich farm land to dairy farmers from the surrounding community. It purchases all of its milk from a neighboring farm and purchases 75% of the food used by dining services from a regional distributor that buys from local farms when in season. The Environmental Council sponsors a popular annual feast for students, faculty and staff that celebrates locally grown products with a meal including delicious organic vegetables, free range turkey, fresh milk and apple cider.

The College's recycling program has benefited the region's aging landfills by diverting a large percent of campus waste to reuse and recycling. The College's composting partnership with the County solid waste district is another way of cooperating with public agencies in the area to work towards more sustainable solutions in partnership with the community.

Land owned by the College has been into permanently protected through cooperation with the National Forest Service to provide lands for public use and to the Nature Conservancy to preserve valuable wetland and riparian habitat. The College also has agreements with local trails organizations to place and maintain portions of their hiking, cross-country skiing and snowmobile trails across College land.

In the recent construction of the College's new science center, Bicentennial Hall, the use of regionally produced green certified wood had an enormous impact on the Vermont Family Forests Program, the cooperative that supplied most of the timber for the project. The volume required for trim and finish is the largest amount known to be used in an academic building in the United States. The decision by the College to purchase the wood within the region launched the fledging green certification business within Vermont. The forest property owners and foresters who harvested trees received substantially more profit as a result of removing the middle people who typically handle the wood and inflate the price. From the neighboring forests to Bicentennial Hall, over 30 small individual businesses within the State of Vermont received payment for working on some aspect of this project. The College's purchase of local, green certified wood has multiple benefits to regional sustainability by supporting the regional economy and the forest industry and by insuring that forests are managed in an ecologically responsible and sustainable manner. The Vermont Family Forests Program and the College are also working together to put the College's forest land into green certification and to co-sponsor an educational conference on green certification, forest ecology and environmental entrepreneurial businesses involved in the timber and wood products industry. The College also plans to use local, green certified wood in the upcoming construction of its new library.

Campus sustainability cannot be achieved without considering how the College's actions and decisions will either positively or negatively impact the overall sustainability of the surrounding region of which the College is a part. There is much that can be accomplished by the College partnering with others in the area to achieve sustainable goals for the campus, for Vermont, and for New England. As the largest employer, developer, tax payer, and land owner in the county, Middlebury College is increasingly recognizing that it can play a positive role in capacity building and as an innovative leader in facilitating regional sustainability as it strives to become a more sustainable campus.

Conclusion: An Integrated Approach to Campus Wide Sustainability

Middlebury College is unique in that the institution embodies a shared vision which is derived from having a clearly defined purpose set forth by the Board of Trustees and the President of the College as well as a foundation of core values. These both lead to a greater sense of community and commitment. This is not to say that the College is without the traditional academic stratification, but it is less obstructive. As a result, leadership is demonstrated at all levels of the organization, not just the top, but by individuals who grasp the purpose, embrace the vision and work towards creating the future that the College has boldly identified as excellence in all areas of the environment and sustainability. The College does not just espouse these ideas, it acts on them, closing the gap between rhetoric and reality. Strategies that have aided in creating this unusual academic situation include the institution's ability to see interrelationships and processes as necessary synergy, and to tap individuals' capacity to contribute to the greater good. It celebrates change and recognizes personal and collective initiatives that enable change to occur. Moreover, there exists a systems approach throughout the institution which includes a structure of positions, people and programs that continually reinforce the value of achieving sustainable and environmental goals. This integrated system guides decisions and breaks down traditional barriers. Here is an example where students and faculty influence operations though course work, where staff become educators as part of a whole system learning process, where the forests and the campus are used by students and staff as a combination of research, education and as managing landscapes which become shared learning laboratories resulting in positive outcome rather then conflicts.

There are downsides to being a large, cumbersome and bureaucratic institution with multiple levels and different jurisdictions. There are times that the College cannot manage to get out of its own way in order to move ahead. Progress can sometimes be painfully slow and frustrating. However, Middlebury College is on the right track, having an overall purpose that is clear, and vision that is within sight not just for a limited few, but for all. Here is a rare example of an institution which has a mission statement that speaks to environmental excellence and sustainability, but has no policies to back it up. It depends not on compliance to achieve its goals, but instead relies on the commitment of the College as a community. Middlebury College has taken three and a half decades to reach the level it has achieved towards becoming a more sustainable campus and a member of a more sustainable region. Change has not occurred overnight, but that which has occurred has made a difference in the day-to-day lives of those individuals living, working and learning on its campus. Like all institutions of higher education, the College has a long way to go to become the foremost leader of sustainable practices. It has much to learn from others, but it is on the right path by creating unique learning experiences while creating a more sustainable campus and region, of which the College is part.

References

Bedford, D., Buck, M., Deblois, M., Hazen, J., McBeth, A., Watts, J. (1998) *State of the Environment at Middlebury College*; Report and Recommendations by the Middlebury College Environmental Council.

Bogard, S. J., Hanson, C., Hood, S., Jadd, K., Johnson, L., Rogers, C., Sandvik, C., Schecter, A., Sheriff, S., & Wray, C. (1997) *It's Not Easy Being Green: An Environmental Audit of Five New England Schools*. Environmental Studies Program, Dartmouth College.

Byerly, A., Cookis, H., Davis, E., Farquhar, N., Hanscom, G., Kiyza, C., Larrabee, J., Meyer, G., Miller, Raoul, Pack, B., Rockefeller, S., Peterson, B., Sheldon, S., Trombulak, S., Woodbury, J. (1995) *Report of the Committee on the Environment*. Middlebury College.

Callenbach, E., Capra, F., Goldman, L., Lutz, R., Marburg, S (1993) *EcoManagement; The Elmwood Guide to Ecological Auditing and Sustainable Business*. San Francisco: Berrett-Koehler Publishers.

Collett, J., Karakashian, S. (eds.) (1996) *Greening the College Curriculum*. Washington, D.C.: Island Press.

Creighton, S. H. (1998) *Greening the Ivory Tower: Improving the Environmental Track Record of Universities, Colleges, and Other Institutions*. Cambridge: The MIT Press.

Eagan, D. J., Orr, D. (eds.) (1992) The Campus and Environmental Responsibility. *New Directions for Higher Education*, no.77, Volume XX, (1). San Francisco: Jossey-Bass Publishers.

Environmental Council of Middlebury College (1995) *Pathways to a Green Campus*. Middlebury College.

Heinze-Fry, J. (1993) *Green Lives, Green Campuses*. Belmont, CA: Wadsworth, Inc.

Jenks-Jay, N. (1997) Why Campuses are Turning "Green". In *AAHE (American Association for Higher Education) Bulletin,* 49 (7), 7-9.

Jenks-Jay, N. (1995) Higher Education and the Environment, How Colleges and Universities are Responding to the Challenge of Educating Future Leaders. *NAEP (National Association of Environmental Professionals) News*, 20 (5), 20-23.

Keniry, J. (1995) *Ecodemia; Campus Environmental Stewardship at the Turn of the 21st Century*. National Wildlife Federation.

Klyza, C. M., Trombulak, S. C. (May 1999) *The Story of Vermont: A Natural and Cultural History*. Hanover, NH: University Press of New England.

Koester, R. J. (ed.) 1996 *Greening of the Campus Conference Proceedings*. Ball State University, Muncie, Indiana.

Mansfield III, W. H., (May/June 1998) Taking the University to Task. *World Watch*, 11 (3), 24-30.

Orr, D. W. (1994) *Earth in Mind; On Education, Environment, and the Human Prospect*. Washington: Island Press.

Orr, D. W. (1992) *Ecological Literacy; Education and the Transition to a Postmodern World*. Albany: State University of New York Press.

Soto, C. (ed.) (1995) *Campus Environmental Yearbook*. National Wildlife Federation.

Smith, A.A. & The Student Environmental Action Coalition (1993) *Campus Ecology; A Guide to Assessing Environmental Quality & Creating Strategies for Change*. Los Angeles: Living Planet Press.

Strauss, B. H. (1996) *The Class of 2000 Report: Environmental Education, Practices, and Activism on Campus*. The Nathan Cummings Foundation.

Wallace, Floyd, Associates, Inc (1996) *Master Plan for Middlebury College*. Boston.

Note: Middlebury College Environmental Web Page: http://www.middlebury.edu/~es

Chapter 10

University support to local and regional agenda initiatives for sustainable development

Dr. Andreas Megerle / Assistant Professor, Applied Geography, University of Tübingen

Heidi Megerle, Dipl.-Geogr. / Training representative, University of Tübingen, Agenda moderator and environmental consultant

Abstract

The following chapter addresses the needs and opportunities for University support to Agenda 21 initiatives for sustainable development, both "within" but primarily "outside" the universities. Different approaches are illustrated by some activities of the Chair of Applied Geography[27] at the University of Tübingen (Southern Germany) regarding local, regional and interregional agenda activities.

Introduction: Discovering the implementation arena

Social science practitioners concerned with questions of planning processes, e.g. applied and social geography, are conducting more and more research in the implementation arena. This is not only for the purpose of testing evaluation or monitoring methods[28]. The scientists are conducting projects directly by interactive research activities[29]. Therefore, they are no longer only observers, but are participants who take an active part in practical projects.

There are different reasons for this development, which are not exclusively based in the field of methodological theory. Nowadays, the personal motivations of scientists, combined with the

---

[27] Referred to "Chair" or "Chair of Applied Geography" throughout the chapter

[28] for instance Megerle 1992

[29] Thieme 1997. Schaffer 1997

rising necessity to engage themselves in marketing activities both for their chairs or universities - and for themselves- makes it more and more necessary to orientate their work towards the public. Often, "accompanied" practical projects are initiated by the research staff themselves.

Beyond this background, the question of whether the aim of research activities is to solve practical problems or not, is practical rather than academic. Thieme (1997) proposes to offer "concepts" and "guidance for solving problems" but not to participate in the actual solving process of the problem. In our opinion, that sounds a little like a bad repairman who does not have the time to repair your car but gives you some tools to do it yourself. The solving of specific problems is one of the most interesting steps during the process of the local Agenda, because this is where the scientists learn whether their ready-made solutions will work and, if not, the underlying reasons for success or failure. Of course this learning process is an open one. And is this, perhaps, something some scientists are afraid of?

Sustainable development and local Agenda 21: Special Responsibility of the universities

There are two reasons for the universities to deal with the issue of sustainable development.

- The Agenda 21: Article 35 of the Agenda deals with the special role of science in sustainable development. Article 36 notes the importance for the universities to integrate environmental management systems in their curricula (36.17), especially to meet the demands from the labor market (36.18)[30].

- Many scientific problems in the context of sustainable development and Agenda processes are still waiting for solutions. Examples range from methods of developing criteria of sustainable development to methods regarding means of improving the implementation and acceptance of Agenda Action Plans.

Consequently, there are two directions for university actions towards sustainable development:
1. "within the university": Creation and implementation of environmental management systems within the organization of the universities.
2. "outside the university": As one of the important regional participants, universities should be engaged in not only the supervision of regional development projects, but also be an active participant in them.

Universities seem to be aware of their responsability: In their Local Agenda 21 Survey, ICLEI found out that in 58% of the local governments "scientific institutions (universities)" are "formally included in the process to plan, implement and monitor the Action Plan for Local Agenda 21 or sustainable development"[31].

---

[30] Agenda 21 (Bundesministerium für Umwelt, Naturschutz und Reaktorsicherheit)
[31] ICLEI 1997

However, in the new publication of ICLEI concerning the Local Agenda 21 in Germany[32], universities are not mentioned at all.

This contradiction demonstrates the fact that systematic surveys of the activities of universities in Local Agenda 21 processes are still missing, at least in Germany.

Agenda support on the community level: some examples

Article 28 of Agenda 21 deals with the special responsibility of the communities for sustainable development. But only a few communities worldwide achieved the Rio goal to begin an Agenda process before 1996.

Information and Documentation

One of the first steps in a local Agenda process must be the collection of all relevant data, preferably in the form of a structure analysis. This provides an objective image of the strong and weak points of the community concerned. But often communities, especially smaller ones, do not have enough personal resources to keep their own information management systems or even to do their own data collecting.

Universities, however, have relatively easy access to all kinds of information needed in local Agenda processes. Therefore, the assistance of universities can be vital for the communities.

Structure analysis for the community of Filderstadt

Filderstadt is a city of about 40.000 inhabitants, situated on the outskirts of Stuttgart next to the airport. Originally, in the seventies, five primarily farming villages were unified to form a new city. Today, Filderstadt is characterized by a high percentage of commuters and it is still experiencing problems in finding its own identity as a city.

The structure analysis, including a study of the economical structure of the community of Filderstadt, was carried out by the Chair of Applied Geography, but was initiated by diverse players: the Chair of Applied Geography itself together with the commissioners for the environment and for the local economy of this community. Therefore, two of the three forces of the magic Agenda triangle (ecology, economy, social welfare) for a sustainable development were included at the beginning of the process! Securing this support was made easier because all three actors have a common formation background: geography. So the communication in this "geographer network" played an important part in gaining acceptance for the study.

The results of this structure analysis will be used to start a local Agenda 21 initiative.

---

[32] Internationaler Rat für Kommunale Umweltinitiativen/Kuhn/Suchy/Zimmermann 1998

Inquiry into local Agenda processes in two regions in Southern Germany

In 1997 the Chair of Applied Geography carried out an inquiry into Agenda activities of the communities in two regions Neckar-Alb and Ostalbkreis in Southern Germany. The inquiry was carried out by means of a questionnaire, especially developed for this purpose.

The principal aim was to find answers to the following questions:

•   What do community authorities understand by the concept of Agenda 21?

•   How many communities have begun with an Agenda process?

•   What do the community authorities expect from the Agenda process?

•   What kind of assistance would be helpful for the communities, especially the smaller ones?

The results were rather disillusioning: less than 6% of the communities had previously shown any interest in Local Agenda 21. And nearly all the communities felt that Local Agenda 21 meant "environmental projects of the administration" and not "integration of economic, ecological and social affairs" or "consulting processes with their citizens". But one third of the communities were interested in receiving more information.

The results of such inquiries are interesting and important because they can be used as argumentation material for other Agenda actions. But this special inquiry had yet another important function: to initiate contact with the communities, to make Agenda a community issue and to start a dialogue. The results will also be used by the official Agenda office of the Federal State of Baden-Württemberg for a general survey.

The case study of Pliezhausen
Pliezhausen is a smaller community with about 10.000 inhabitants, lying between the dominant cities of Stuttgart, Reutlingen and Tübingen. Therefore it is characterized by a high percentage of commuters and a rural structure altered by newly-built districts. The community is a product of the German administration reform movement in the 1970s and unifies four different villages, all of them ancient independent communities. One can imagine many resulting problems.

The Chair of Applied Geography was asked to carry out a representative inquiry (issue: quality of life in the community) of the citizens of Pliezhausen. The customized questionnaire was created in collaboration with the community authorities and a working group formed of important local players such as teachers, heads of social congregations and soon.

During the process, the Chair of Applied Geography discovered that not only the results but also the inquiry itself could be used to initiate an Agenda process. The community administration accepted this proposal and so, parallel to the evaluation of the questionnaires, a plan for the public presentation of the results and for the beginning of an Agenda Process was worked out by the authorities and the Chair. The public presentation took place in form of a citizen-information-day, including a sort of performance show of the community involving all the clubs, associations, local businesses, administration as well as cultural and musical programs. The results of the inquiry were presented and information about Local Agenda 21 was given, also in direct communication with the visitors. There were mailboxes where interested people could leave their addresses and any wishes for the Agenda round-table meeting which was to be held some weeks later. This was in spring 1998.

People are still waiting for this round-table meeting. It seems that some members of the community council are still not very enthusiastic about the Agenda movement: they might fear a loss of influence. It seems also, that there was a lack of communication between working group and community council. Although the working group consisted partly of members of the community council, the working group was unable to persuade the community authorities to begin the Agenda process.

So the promotion function of the Chair continues: after several meetings with members of the commuinty authorities and NGO-members the persuasion strategy was successful - in some weeks, the round-table meetings will take place and the Agenda process will be initiated.

This project had an interesting side-effect: whilst talking to people at the citizen-information day, we discoverered that there were a lot of visitors from other communities, even mayors, who had come to get information on Local Agenda 21. One consequence was that the Chair was asked by more communities in the region to help begin an Agenda process.This shows the importance of university activities in the spread of Agenda innovations within a region.

Case study of Tübingen

The city of Tübingen with a population of about 75.000 and an additional 20.000 students is world-famous for its university. Therefore, the situation differed considerably from that in Pliezhausen.

At first, the community administration and the council were very critical towards the Agenda movement. The commissioner for the environment was asked to prepare the Agenda process "outside" the council. Among some other institutions, the main task for the Chair of Applied Geography at the beginning of 1997 was to provide information on the Agenda issue in form of public presentations, announced by press releases. The initializing of a process was successful. After the initialization phase, the Chair retired officially from the round table work to maintain an objective and critical point of view of the process. This was regarded as necessary in order to be able to carry out independent monitoring and evaluation work. "Officially retired" means that members of the chair continued to work in the Agenda process as moderators or as citizens of Tübingen. In this way, the information and communication flow was kept intact.

Members of the Chair criticized the non-representative composition of the round tables where representatives from ecological NGOs easily outnumbered the representatives from economic and social organisations.

As a result of the cooperation work of the chair, the University itself is concerned with two of the Agenda projects:

An energy conservation project for the buildings of the geographical institute. The local Agenda working group is supported by the geographic students vocational union.

A project to obtain acceptance from the University administration (Chancelor) to sign the Copernicus-charter for sustainable development at the university.

Function as Critical voice: the Case study of Uhldingen-Mühlhofen

As an objective and external player it is the task of the applied scientist to function as a critical voice in certain processes. This was the case in the example of Tübingen as well as in Uhldingen-Mühlhofen.

Uhldingen-Mühlhofen is a smaller community (7.200 inhabitants) on Lake Constance (German southern border). One of the most important economic factors is tourism, but in the high season the large number of tourists causes quite a lot of ecological and social problems.

Uhldingen-Mühlhofen is one of the pilot communities within the German project "Eco Audit for Touristic Communities", one important way of entering a Local Agenda 21-process. In this case, the function of the chair is a critical oversight of the audit process which is led by a consulting company.

Asked by an environmental NGO and invited by the community administration, the Chair persuaded the different players to complete the audit checklists of the consulting company. In particular, the criteria necessary to evaluate the specific local and regional situation of the ecologically highly sensitive landscape were included. One result was that the issue of local building zoning was integrated in the audit project.

Beside the importance of NGOs as "early warning systems" and for the integration of "non-issues" as discussion-topics , this example shows that universities with their relative neutrality and with their knowledge of regional and local environmental situations, can also play an important role as mediators in conflict situations.

Results

There are several reasons for the importance of the role of the Chair of Applied Geography as a moving force.

There was a large information deficit at the beginning of the Agenda movement (which did not start in southern Germany until 1995) as far as the Agenda in general was concerned. Community authorities were often not even aware of the meaning of local Agenda 21 or of the difference between this and Agenda 2000 (a program of the European Union for agriculture). It was only the innovation transfer by the university information process which closed this information gap.

At the beginning of the Agenda movement, there were few practical helpers such as planning guides, especially for smaller communities. But planning guides cannot replace the search for an individual way of initiating an Agenda process in a certain community. Here, good understanding of the different forms of typical political fields and knowledge of regional environmental situations meant the geographers were experts on these specific implementation issues.

Even in well organized process structures like the audit process in Uldingen-Mühlhofen, the university's knowledge of specific regional and local problems combined with its neutrality can improve this process in an efficient way. Together with a NGO, the university assumed the role of an early warning system for quality assurance of the process.

University work is cheaper than the help of professional enterprises. For smaller communities this is an important factor. As a consequence there are some conflicts such as the problem of disturbing the free market.

Coordination of local agenda processes and more: the regional level

Many of the Local Agenda 21-problems can only be solved in a satisfying way if there is close "Agenda"-cooperation between several communities, especially smaller ones. To initiate such cooperation, the chair tried several methods, as is shown in the case studies.

The case study of the region of Neckar-Alb

Neckar-Alb is a region in Baden-Württemberg, south of the capital Stuttgart and including the two major cities Tübingen (university town) and Reutlingen (industrial town).

As mentioned above, the Chair of Applied Geography carried out an "activating" inquiry into local Agenda processes in the region of Neckar-Alb. One of the results of this inquiry was the setting up of a regional Agenda cooperation structure by the formation of a community network in one region. Therefore, the interested communities were invited by the Chair to come together and to discuss two of the most urgent problems. The time was well chosen, because parallel to the efforts of the Chair, there was a competition "Sustainable regions", organized by the German Ministry of Space Planning. Unfortunately, the efforts of the Chair failed, mainly for the following reason:

Most of the representatives of the nine interested communities came from the "middle" community administration level with little or no decision-making power. Only two of the participants were mayors. That showed that the "chiefs" themselves are not sufficiently concerned by the issue of "regional sustainability". Nevertheless, the Chair intends to make another attempt.

The case study of the region of the Ostalbkreis
The example of the Ostalbkreis[33] shows the important role of the "chiefs" and involved persons for the initiation of Agenda processes. In this case, the chair was supported by the head of the Landkreis, the Landrat, who made the Agenda his personal issue.

In the same manner as in the region of Neckar-Alb, the results of the community inquiry were presented to those who were interested. In this case, however, it was not the Chair but the Landrat himself who invited the communities. Therefore, interest was much greater: nearly all communities were represented, most of them by their "chiefs", the mayors. During the presentation the chair informed the communities about another project: the competition "Local Agenda 21 for smaller communities", organized by a regional academy, the academy of Bad Boll. Several mayors spontaneously decided to begin an Agenda process in their community and to enter the competition. One of them even won it.

After this meeting the Chair proposed evaluating some important plans of the Ostalbkreis in form of a "test of sustainability". The goal was to identify some deficits of sustainable planning and to make proposals for avoiding them (as far as possible). A further aim was to gather information for Agenda cooperation issues, to stimulate a discussion with the administration and to "prework" for the initialisation of an Agenda-Process. After an explorative phase, different plans and programs were selected and checked according to a specific list (see Figure 1). Because a strictly formal evaluation did not work sufficiently (the heterogeneity of the chosen plans and programs was too large), the evaluation was carried out by the verbal-argumentative method.

Figure 1: checklist for the assessment of sustainability in concepts, plans and programs (first step assessment)[34]

participant: ....
document: ....
type: ....

Evaluation criteria
1. Equilibrium of all parts of the „magic„ triangle (economy, ecology, social demands) including interactions
1. Limits for human action
1. Intergenerative justice
1. Participation of important social groups
1. Consideration of gobal demands
1. Implementation strategies
1. Consideration of regional and supra-regional demands
1. Consideration of social, cultural, environmental and economic compatibility
1. Regulations for the use of material and for the creation of values within the region
1. Actual and possible use of resources within the region
1. Development of new resources

---

[33] In Baden-Württemberg, a Landkreis consists of a group of different communities and has its own parliament, whose head, the Landrat, is elected. The Landkreise have a relatively large administration and a wide variety of planning responsibilities which range from road planning to garbage disposal.
[34] Eberle/Megerle/Dispan/Lattner/Weisbauer 1998

Evaluation scale

?	=	not valuable or valuation not meaningfull
-	=	negative, counter productive contribution to sustainability
0	=	contribution not recognizable
1	=	contribution small, but recognizable
2	=	large contribution

Annotations

D	=	data insufficient
I	=	planning goals probably contradictory to requirements of sustainabilty
K	=	specific demand for clarification (expert questioning)

As the formal checklist evaluation had proved to be insufficient, the final evaluation was accomplished in form of verbal arguments. This evaluation form might contain subjective elements. Therefore, it must be performed independently by two or more scientists.

The evaluation result is discussed with the author of the plan or program. If necessary, the result is adjusted.

The final step of the evaluation is comprised of proposals for improvement strategies that are applicable to practical implementation in the region.

Upon completion of the evaluation, the Chair proposed some alterations to the evaluated plans themselves and to the development processes. The Chair also proposed additional strategies for top-down and bottom-up initiatives in form of an Agenda structure.

The Chair's activities also influenced the decision of the Ostalbkreis parliament to begin an Agenda process as one of the first regions in Baden-Württemberg. There are hopes that the project (including a research program) will be financially supported as a „pilot project„ by the Ministry for the Environment of Baden-Württemberg.

Figure 2: Sustainable Ostalbkreis - Proposal for an Agenda structure[35]

Time	Agenda Activities	Scientific Activities
Short term: Structuring the process	Initiating and monitoring of an externally moderated agenda network with communities and different social groups	Scientific research activities accompanying the Agenda process: Monitoring Consulting Data collection and interpretation Methods and techniques (for instance development of scenario-proposals)

[35] Megerle 1998

	Initiation and operation of an Agenda office within the administration of the Landkreis as an Agenda service-center for the communities and as a promotor. Other functions include: documentation of the agenda process, public relations work, networking with Agenda initiatives and competitions outside the Landkreis, training activities	
Short term: Agenda work (Round table working groups)	Common searching for Agenda issues, for instance on the basis of existing initiatives and projects	
	Project working: Agenda projects with interlocal or regional reference. Interlocal coordination of Local Agenda projects	
	Searching for first drafts of different scenarios for the long term development of the Landkreis	
	Analysis of aspects of sustainability within the plans of the Landkreis and the communities and propositions for the improvement of the plans	
Medium term	Development of a series of ecological indicators for sustainability leadership: regional planning office of the Ostalb-region	
	Development of a series of economic indicators for sustainability leadership: regional office for the promotion of economy (WIRO)	
	Development of a series of social indicators for sustainability leadership: authority for social demands of the Landkreis Ostalbkreis	
	Development of a method for the coordination of sectoral plans and concepts	
Long term: Balancing analysis etc.	Analysis and balancing of energy and material flows	

Annotation: the sequence of the table is not necessarily the sequence of the implementation time.

Bottom-up: Interlocal Agenda-network of tourism communities

For the Schwäbische Alb, a low mountain range in the south of Germany, tourism is one of the most important factors for the economy, but there are some problems:

- most of the tourists come from the nearby region of Stuttgart

- they normally stay only for a couple of hours

- transportation is mainly by car

- the tourists are concentrated in a few places

- and within short time periods (week-ends),

Therefore, the Schwäbische Alb suffers from ecological and overcrowding problems. Another problem in the planning process is the division of the Schwäbische Alb into several administration units. In the past, this division has made it almost impossible to find solutions for the whole natural area.

As a result of the positive experiences gained to date in using the competition form to initiate

Agenda processes, the Chair (research) created a competition with a regional (Schwäbische Alb) and a thematic (tourism) focus in conjunction with the state institute for civic education of Baden-Württemberg (communication facilities, organization). The three communities who present the best ideas for sustainable tourism projects, will each win a prize. This prize will consist of free communication facilities and money for external moderation programs for the Agenda process.

The idea of the competition is to enable smaller communities to start Agenda processes, to ensure a high quality level and to promote efficient cooperation between the different participants. To avoid the danger of confusing "Agenda" with "Environmental Protection", the communities are being asked to respond with ideas for the development of new tourism products. After the end of the competition, the plan is to structure the Agenda-work in form of a regional tourist community network.

Competition flyers are sent directly to the communities but also to the Landkreise, who help inform the communities. This is important, because in this way the communities will receive information about this competition from different sources.

The jury which is to choose the winners consists of one representative of the communities (a mayor), the managing director of the regional tourism union and the director of the statewide Agenda office of Baden-Württemberg. This composition guarantees optimal coordination with other Agenda initiatives.

There has been some conceptual thought regarding linking this kind of bottom-up-project with a top-down-project. Maybe, the project to create a biosphere parc on the Schwäbische Alb might provide the necessary instruments.

Development of a tourism product through statewide Agenda-cooperation: the "Network Earth History Baden-Württemberg"

As an example of supraregional Agenda cooperation, this network also deals with the issue of tourism, but works at the level of the state of Baden-Württemberg.

The network was initiated by the Chair during a conference on sustainable tourism in 1997. Members of the Chair asked two mayors, one NGO-member and the leader of a tourist information office whether they would be interested in exchanging their ideas. They were soon joined by others and decided that the target of the network was to produce a high quality geotourism product.

Close cooperation of all participants was, and continues to be, necessary to cover all the features of the tourism product offered, a "one billion year journey" through the earth history of Baden-Württemberg. Other goals are to achieve widespread support and to cover all three corners of the magic Agenda triangle. Consequently, a great variety of participants with different backgrounds are working together: in addition to the tourism partners, there are members of environmental associations, industrial associations, museums, authorities, universities and interested individuals.

In order to facilitate local input for the network product, the Chair initiated the foundation of different local networks. There are different models: some networks show characteristics like Agenda-networks (high degree of participation of different social groups, volunteering activities), and other networks show a low level of participation but provide professional consulting. As some network partners come from the Schwäbische Alb, there is an opportunity for them to use their local tourist network to enter a Local Agenda 21-process and to win free communication facilities (see "Bottom-up: Interlocal Agenda-network of tourism communities").

For the Schwäbische Alb region with its innumerable geotouristic attractions and the resulting special situation for geotourism ("Jurassic Park"), the Chair has tried to initiate a regional network. One module is the joint production of a regional geotouristical prospectus.

The statewide network is coordinated and mediated by the Chair, whose interest is in obtaining research results concerning the issue of "networking and tourism for sustainable development". However, the Chair also acts as an information clearinghouse for the geotourism resources of the network partners and, one of the most important functions, as a moving force for marketing and other network activities.

So far, the experiment has demonstrated some advantages but also some inconveniences:

- The opportunity for moderated involvement of participants with divergent views is of great importance to the legitimacy and acceptance of unanimous decisions. Moderation also helps to render a creative atmosphere possible, to discover hidden resources and to ensure the sustainability of the product and the process.
- Network Organisation helps to acheive practicable standards: All members have to accept the guidelines for sustainable development.
- They contain regulations concerning the collecting of fossils and minerals, the use of landscape names in the framework of touristic offers, standards for landscape interpretation and other issues.
- Networks provide "dense personal interaction and learning processes" and are one of the primary accomplishments of the accompanying research program. For instance, the tourism partners become more and more conscious of the special features of "their" landscape. They will, therefore, support nature conservationist activities in the future. On the other hand, conservationists begin to understand and to accept the necessity for economic activities.
- The university might be viewed as competition for professional consultants. On the other hand, there would be no network "Earth history" without the university, because up to now there has not been enough money for professional consulting.
- But network actvities are beginning to create the first jobs ranging from Web-Site-publishing to landscape interpretation.
- One important disadvantage of networking is the high cooperation costs because so far the German state has not supported such activities.

The networking activities on different levels demonstrate that the universities can play an important role as active promoters of Agenda cooperation activities.

Universities as "regional agenda support centers": possibilities and problems

The examples show that universities can play an important role as a moving force in the initiation of Agenda cooperation processes. Those university sections which are oriented in the direction of "Applied Social Sciences" (for instance, Applied Geography) have a great responsibility for sustainable development not only in but also outside the university.

There are several reasons for the importance of the university role. Some of them (not all) are listed below.

know-how: technical knowledge as well as knowledge regarding the structuring and analysis of political and social processes, knowledge regarding regional potentials and regional problems (above all of "their" region), knowledge of information pools and easy access to them, etc.

infrastructure: the easy use of communication facilities (world wide web, e-mail, etc.) plays an important role for networking projects

economic reasons: when starting new projects and processes, the economic basis is often very weak so the smaller communities profit from the relatively cheap consulting offers of the university.

regional level and shortcuts: the regional level demonstrates increasing importance for Agenda cooperation projects: Local Agenda 21 processes must be coordinated; transportation and communication ways are shortcuts to local and regional participation. Increasingly, the university may have the opportunity to take on the role of a "regional service center", e.g. for the dissemination of information and the adaptation of innovations coming from outside.

interest in public relations and marketing: Beside their research interests, the universities have a growing interest in public relations work. The regional impact of university work plays an important role because work on this level becomes visible and clear to the public.

neutrality: As a consequence of the above mentioned characteristics of the university, the university can play an important role in moderating, mediating and managing regional communication processes. The three "c´s" (communication, coordination, cooperation) belong to the most important issues in Agenda work. They are necessary not only in order to prevent or solve conflicts, but also to stimulate network contacts between participants, who do not know each other, because they never meet in administration routines. And often the neutral and respected university can even be successful in bringing participants together who normally would never work together.

contacts: universities have a lot of contacts, not only within a region, but also outside. Therefore, existing networks can be integrated, the initiation of new ones is relatively easy and the necessary horizontal coordination of regional networks is possible.

interest in teaching issues: Agenda projects are a wonderful training field for teaching. In innumerable issues students can achieve their first practical experiences. They are able to improve their scientific qualifications by applying knowledge acquired from different subjects but also by learning and practising new skills,such as: methods, techniques for communication, moderation, negotiation, and persuasion. They are able to improve their social qualifications by making contacts, learning to sense the needs and wishes of other participants and acquiring the ability to make compromises. Hopefully, creativity, flexibility and implementation oriented working will be no longer problems of university education.

On the other hand, there are also some problems:

- It is difficult to remain independent and neutral all the time. Sometimes it is not possible at all and the university is forced to form a party within conflicts. Then it depends on the strength of the university to resist the pressure of the opponents and to overcome the situation as soon as possible.

- The "Applied" point of view within Agenda projects demands multidiscipline cooperation within a university. For several reasons, this is very difficult especially in large universities. If there are not enough specialists for communication and project management, external professional communication assistance could be a valuable though expensive help.

- Often, the investment input in Agenda projects (personal and financial) is not compatible with the scientific yield. For example, there might be problems with the formation of scientific theories because Agenda processes are often idiographic and unrepeatable events.

- The university has to be aware of the already mentioned competition problem with professional consulters or the reproach that university activities obstruct the foundation of a specific institution. An important criterion in evaluating this problem is to sketch an alternative scenario: how would it be without university efforts? In many cases the projects would not be carried out at all. So the ideal way would be for the university to initiate a project which is then pursued by professionals or by a specific new institution such as an institutional network.

Both the number and the intensity of Agenda cooperation activities between communities and universities seem to be good indicators for measuring the regional know-how-spillovers of university Agenda 21 activities. But may be there are also Agenda spill-over effects from the communities to the university? These would, however, be hard to measure.

University Agenda work could be viewed as a sort of social work which will not be possible without great personal commitment on the part of the university staff. But if this can be ensured, the Agenda forms a wonderful instrument for combining the scientific work of the university with practice.

References

Audretsch, D.B., Feldman, M.P. (1994) *R&D Spillovers and the Geography of Innovation and Production*. Berlin: Wissenschaftszentrum für Sozialforschung (=Discussion papers, FS IV 92-2).

Bundesministerium für Umwelt, Naturschutz und Reaktorsicherheit (1992) *Konferenz der Vereinten Nationen für Umwelt und Entwicklung im Juni 1992 in Rio de Janeiro* - Dokumente. Bonn.

Eberle, D. , Megerle, A. (1997) *Lokale Agenda 21 im Ostalbkreis und in der Region Neckar-Alb, Ergebnisse von Befragungen*. Paper. Tübingen.

Eberle, D. Megerle, A. Dispan, J., Weisbauer, S. (1998) *Wirtschaftsstrukturanalyse Filderstadt*. Paper. Tübingen.

Eberle, D. Megerle, A. Weisbauer, S. Lattner, R. Dispan, J. (1998) *Lebensqualität in Pliezhausen*. several papers. Tübingen.

Eberle, D. Megerle, A. Dispan, J. Lattner, R. Weisbauer, S. (1998) *Abschlußbericht der Untersuchung zu Nachhaltigkeits-Defiziten in ausgewählten Plänen und Programmen, die den Ostalbkreis betreffen*. Paper. Tübingen.

Fürst, D. (1994) Regionalkonferenzen zwischen offenen Netzwerken und fester Institutionalisierung. In *Raumforschung und Raumordnung* 3, pp. 184-192.

Gugisch, I., Maier, J. Obermaier, F. (1998): Regionales Management zur Gestaltung und Koordination kommunaler und regionaler Entwicklungsprozesse. In *Raumforschung und Raumordnung* 2/3, pp. 136-142.

Gustedt, E., Kanning, H. (1998) Jahre später - Facetten der Nachhaltigkeitsvision und deren Umsetzungsproblematik. In: *Raumforschung und Raumordnung* 2/3, pp. 167-176.

Hauff, R. Megerle, A. Megerle, H. Dieter, A., Behmel, H., Kraus, U., Klumpp, B. (1999) Abenteuer Geologie. *Touristik-Gemeinschaft Schwäbische Alb*. Bad Urach

ICLEI (1995) *European Local Agenda 21 Planning Guide*. Freiburg:ICLEI.

ICLEI (1997) *Local Agenda 21 Survey*. Paper.Freiburg: ICLEI.

Internationaler Rat für Kommunale Umweltinitiativen (1998) Kuhn, S., Suchy, G., Zimmermann, M. (eds) (1998) *Lokale Agenda 21 Deutschland*. Berlin: Springer.

Kettnacker, A. (1998): Bürgerbefragung und Bürger-Infotag in Pliezhausen. In: *Die Gemeinde* 22/1998.

Lechler, M., Megerle, A. (1997) *Einige Thesen zum Start der "Lokalen Agenda 21 Tübingen".* Paper.

Megerle, A. (1992) Probleme der Durchsetzung von Vorgaben der Landes- und Regionalplanung bei der kommunalen Bauleitplanung am Bodensee - Ein Beitrag zur Implementations- und Evaluierungsdiskussion in der Raumplanung, Tübingen: Selbstverlag (=*Tübinger Geographische Studien*, H. 110).

Megerle, A. (1998) Sustainable Ostalbkreis - *Proposal for an Agenda structure.* Paper. Tübingen.

Megerle, A. (1999): "Landschaftsmarketing" als Baustein für einen zukunftsfähigen Albtourismus. *Paper for the conference "Wirtschaftswunder Schwäbische Alb"* in Tübingen.

Netzwerk Erdgeschichte Baden-Württemberg (eds) (1998a) *Erlebnis-Urlaub Erdgeschichte in Baden-Württemberg.* Brochure.

Netzwerk Erdgeschichte Baden-Württemberg (1998) (eds) *Leitlinien zur Nachhaltigkeit.* Paper. Tübingen.

Rösler, M. (1998) *Arbeitsplätze durch Naturschutz – Biosphärenparke in Deutschland. Fallbeispiel Mittlere Schwäbische Alb.* Dissertation. University of Greifswald.

Schaffer, F. (1997) *Interaktive Sozialgeographie. Zur Konzeption einer praxisbegleitenden Implementations-Forschung.* In DELA 12. Department of Geography. Faculty of Arts. University of Ljubljana.

Sibum, D. Thimmel, S. (1998) Nichtregierungsorganisationen in Lokale Agenda 21-Prozessen. In: *Internationaler Rat für Kommunale Umweltinitiativen.* By Kuhn, S. Suchy, G., Zimmermann, M. (eds): Lokale Agenda 21 Deutschland. pp 249-256. Berlin: Springer.

Thieme, K. (1998) Sozialgeographische Implementationsforschung - zum Stellenwert der Praxisbegleitung im räumlichen Gestaltungsprozeß. In Goppel, K., Thieme, K., Troeger-Weiß, G. (eds) *Experimentelle Geographie und Planung: Theorie - Manegement - Praxis.* Augsburg: Selbstverlag Fachgebiet Raumordnung und Landesplanung der Universität.

Trepte, L. Bürk, R. (1998): Uhldingen-Mühlhofen on the Way to the European Union´s Eco-Management and Audit Scheme EMAS. *Paper for the International Conference "Developments in Sustainable Tourism".* Rimini/Italy.

Chapter 11

Sustainability and Higher Education in Asia-Pacific

Jacob Park and Ted Tschang
1616 16th St. NW Apt: 306
Washington DC 20009 USA

Abstract

This chapter describes some trends and tendencies on sustaibaility in the Asia-Pacific region with ao overview of some areas where attention is needed.

Defining the Sustainable Educational Agenda

Building the necessary institutional and human resource capacity for sustainable development represents one of the most important global issues. Although there are a number of differences in pedagogical approaches (e.g. between environmental specialists trained in the social sciences versus natural sciences) and methodological issues (e.g. what is the best way to teach the concept of sustainability ?), there is almost unanimous agreement that additional time and effort will be needed to ensure that sustainable development is better integrated in the activities and curriculum of universities and advanced educational institutions.

The concluding declaration of the 1997 International Conference on Environment and Society: Education and Public Awareness for Sustainability noted that "appropriate education and public awareness should be recognized as one of the pillars of sustainability together with legislation, economy, and technology." One may also recall that Agenda 21, the 1992 Action Plan of the United Nations Conference on Environment and Development (UNCED) made a special reference to the issues of education, training, and capacity building:

> "Education, public awareness, and training should be recognized as a process by which human beings and societies reach their fullest potential. A major priority is reorienting education towards sustainable development by improving the capacity of a country to address environmental development in its educational programmes, particularly in its basic learning" (UN 1993).

Building the necessary capacity for sustainable development is not only an important global objective; it is rapidly becoming a policy priority on the regional level. Universities and tertiary academic institutions in the Asia-Pacific region have played an important role in many regional social, political, and economic issues, but mobilizing the intellectual and educational community to support the goals of environmentally sustainable development has acquired special significance in recent years.

The traditional focus of environmental education and training in the Asia-Pacific region centered on the ecological and environmental policy implications of rapid economic growth. However, as a result of the severe economic crisis that has engulfed this region for the past couple of years, there is less emphasis on identifying the environmental problems and more on coming to terms with what we mean by sustainable development. This shift in emphasis reflects the general confusion and mood change that surrounds the sudden change from the so-called Asian Economic Miracle in the 1960s - 1980s to the Great Financial Bailout of the 1990s.

This chapter will examine how universities and institutions of higher education in the Asia-Pacific region are promoting capacity building, facilitating environmental curriculum development, and designing a new sustainable development educational agenda. Three goals of this chapter are: first, highlight the major sustainable development challenges on the regional level; second, provide an overview of the environmental education and training trends; and third, discuss why the concepts of knowledge and sustainability are so important to Asian universities and academic institutions.

Making Development Sustainable: The Challenges

1997 marked the first time in nearly thirty years that the advanced industrialized countries grew faster than the Asian tiger economies (South Korea, Hong Kong, Taiwan, Malaysia, Indonesia, Thailand, and Singapore). Although much of the recent international attention has focused on the rapid decline of the Asian regional economy, it should be noted that Asian-Pacific countries maintained an average growth rate of 7 percent (compared to the world rate of 1.1 percent) for most of the 1990s and received more than two-thirds of all foreign direct investments flowing into emerging economies. Even taking into account the recent economic turmoil, it would be difficult to identify a corner of the globe in which the imperatives of economic growth and environmental protection are more inconsistent than the Asia-Pacific region.

The Asian Environment and the matter of development

Asia is home to more than half of the world population, 60 percent of the planet's tropic rain forests, and supplies approximately 40 percent of the world's inland and marine fish catch. While poverty is a growing socio-economic problem due to the severe economic downturn in many Asian-Pacific economies, the environmental consequences of the region's economic growth period are still visible and appear to be getting worse. Nearly all of Southeast Asia was covered with forests a century ago, but it is now estimated that only about one-third is still under forest cover and this percentage is dropping very rapidly. Ten thousand square kilometers of forest are lost every year in Indonesia, while 90 percent of Philippines' lowland forests have disappeared in the past thirty years, causing massive losses in biodiversity (Park and Lo 1997).

What separates the Asia-Pacific region from Western Europe and North America is that it encompasses several vastly different stages of the urbanization and industrialization process. Asian countries at relatively early stages of development (e.g. Vietnam, Indonesia, People's Republic of China (PRC), and others) face the challenge of environmental degradation from the slash and burn practices of subsistence farmers; land degradation from cattle grazing; air pollution from fuel or coal burning stoves; and water pollution from agricultural runoff and domestic waste.

The more industrialized nations (e.g. Malaysia, South Korea, Taiwan, and the coastal areas of the PRC) have a completely different set of environmental problems, including untreated industrial waste, air pollution from power plants and factories; and dangerous levels of airborne lead pollution from increased reliance on motor vehicles. Among the advanced industrialized countries (e.g. Japan, Australia, New Zealand, and perhaps Singapore), the focus is on improving the general quality of environmental policy and management standards; investing in green technology R&D; promoting an ecological consciousness of citizens; and strengthening the legal infrastructure and government capacity for implementing environmental protection efforts (Economy 1994).

Urbanization and Industrialization

Urbanization and industrialization represent the key drivers that underlie the ecological and environmental transformation of the Asian-Pacific region. The urban development pressures in Asia, including increasing economic opportunities in urban centers, and the shift of jobs from agriculture to industry, occurred before in many European and American cities in the early 20th century. What is unprecedented, however, is the absolute scale of change in terms of the number of countries and people involved.

In Asia, the urban population is expected to double (to around 2.5 billion by 2025) in the next thirty years, although more than two-thirds of the inhabitants will continue to live in rural areas. By 2010, more than half of the 26 largest urban agglomerations (defined as 10 million or more residents) will be located in the Asia-Pacific region. Of the seven cities with the worst air pollution problems in the world, five of them (Beijing, Calcutta, Jakarta, Shenyang, and New Delhi) are located in Asia. There is a strong likelihood that there will be more Asian cities added to the list of the worst polluted cities, since half of the world's urban population will be living somewhere in Asia-Pacific by 2025 (WRI et al 1996).

Rapid industrialization, fueled by high real domestic growth and private investment flows in the 1980s and parts of the 1990s, had two important environmental consequences. The first important environmental consequence of rapid industrialization has been a huge surge in the demand for energy. Although the increase has been somewhat tempered by the recent economic problems, the overall increase in the regional energy demand is still striking. The total primary energy demand in Asia currently doubles every 12 years, as compared to the world average of every 28 years. Between 1995 and 2010, East Asian economies will experience a larger increase in petroleum demand than all of the OECD countries combined.
Indonesia, Malaysia, Vietnam, and China have been until recently energy exporters, but are soon

likely to become importers of energy due to internal demand. Even with the economic stagnation, the total demand for electricity in the next 15 years is expected to more than double. As the result of this rapid increase in regional energy demand, East Asia is expected to account for a greater increase in carbon dioxide and sulfur dioxide emissions in the 1990s than all the other regions in the world combined (Calder 1997 and Fesheraki 1995).

The second important consequence of industrialization has been the increase in industrial pollution and related health problems. Many industrial and water-based pollutants have been growing three to five times faster than the overall economy. Paradoxically, even when the economy experiences a severe downturn like in the past couple of years, the overall level of industrial pollutants appears to be increasing in a number of Asia-Pacific countries. As the result of the decline in environmental monitoring and enforcement associated with severe cutbacks in government expenditures, countries like Indonesia are experiencing a sharp rise in the level of industrial effluents even as the overall economic output is going down (Afsah 1998).

Effective water quality management is likely to remain an important regional problem as only a small percentage of the growing urban population (e.g. the figure for Indonesia is 5%) is served by a centralized sewer system. The less developed Asian countries like Cambodia and Burma have also developed a reputation as an easy location in which to dump toxic industrial waste and as a consequence, there has been a sharp increase in waste dumping cases in recent years (Sophal 1998).

Environmental Education and Training in Asia-Pacific: An Overview

The underlying causes of environmental problems in the Asia-Pacific region - explosive growth in population coupled with rapid industrialization and ecological deterioration - involves political and economic issues that far exceed the scope and mandate of universities and academic institutions. Yet, these are the intellectual centers and training grounds for future specialists, managers, and leaders. The involvement of the academic and scholarly community in environmental education and training may therefore be one of the most important litmus tests of a society's commitment to the goals of sustainable development.

Although universities and research institutes will not be able to fulfill the goals of environmental research and training without the active cooperation of national governments, the private sector, and inter-governmental organizations, it is critical that the academic community in the Asia-Pacific region exhibits the necessary leadership to articulate the vision of environmentally-sound development into the 21st century (Park and Lo 1997).

The importance of having such an environmentally-sound vision does not mean that it is possible or even desirable that there has to be a single operating definition of sustainable development. There is, at times, an unfortunate tendency to examine the concept of sustainable development as a collection of environmental or socio-economic dilemmas that need to be resolved by society at large. Unfortunately, such an approach presumes that the important sustainable development challenge is simply to know what the answer is to a particular environmental or socio-economic dilemma.

What is perhaps more important, and what better articulates the sustainable development challenge, is to develop a mechanism to know how a particular problem might be resolved. The heart of that challenge is not to develop the best or the most cost-effective solution to the climate change or the deforestation problem, but to develop the proper means to sort out and address the problems as they develop. As there will always be new environmental and socio-economic problems, it makes more sense for universities and academic institutions to assist in developing the proper societal mechanism to respond to new and emerging sustainable development issues.

Financial Resources versus Educational Need

Can a limited number of universities and research institutions enable 2.5 billion people in the Asia-Pacific region to think beyond the parameters of the neo-classical economic growth ("always get the price right") paradigm and to seek a proper balance between human development and ecological protection ? This may be a difficult if not an impossible task in many less developed Asian countries because of the sharp disparity between the resources that are available for higher education and the educational standards they are supposed to maintain.

For example, India has nearly a billion people - largely impoverished masses who increasingly view a College Diploma as the admission ticket to the middle class. While only 3 percent of Indians between ages 17 and 23 attend college, this still amounts to 3 million students who are rapidly overwhelming the resource capacity of the country's 10,000 universities and colleges. Since India only devotes 3.8 percent of its gross domestic product to education (primary to tertiary), which is small even by the standard of a developing country, many Indian universities and colleges often have a difficult time paying for educational materials and can only offer US$280 a month starting salary for a university instructor.

Predictably, when a regional business magazine surveyed the best universities and colleges in the Asian-Pacific region, only those academic institutions from the wealthier countries like Japan, Hong Kong, Singapore, Taiwan, and Australia made the top 10 ranking. University of Tokyo spends on average US$43,000 per student, while a comparable student enrolled at Sri Lanka's University of Colombo receives only US$4,500 (Bacani 1998).

Sustainability Education and Training: Three Approaches

Despite this gap between educational resources and need, particularly in lesser developed economies of Asia-Pacific, environmental education and training does play an important role in the overall educational system. There are three primary types of environmental education and training approaches in the Asia-Pacific region: educational programs aimed at young scholars; environmental education and training initiatives based at a single university; and information technology-driven, regionally-linked green educational and training networks.

Ecology-oriented Scholarships and Fellowship Programs

One popular form of environmental education and training in the Asia-Pacific region is to use fellowships and scholarships to identify and nurture young Asian scholars specializing in ecological sciences and environmental policy. The International START (System for Analysis, Research, and Training) Secretariat has a long-standing program to provide research grants to finance the research of young Asian scientists who specialize in global environmental change research, while the six year-old Economy and Environment Program for Southeast Asia (EEPSEA) supports training and research in environmental and resource economics.

Through its official development assistance program, the Japanese government established the Eco-Frontier Fellowship (EFF) program in 1995 to provide young researchers and scholars with the opportunity to conduct research related to global environmental change at any of its national research institutes. Funded by a grant from the U.S.-based Ford Foundation and administered by the Council for International Exchange of Scholars, the ASIA (Asian Studies in Asia) was founded to develop regional expertise on Asia and to establish a multilateral network of specialists to strengthen Asian scholarship on Asia within the region. Although this is not exclusively an environmental educational and training program, the ASIA program does allow students and scholars, particularly those from lesser developed economies of Asia, to continue their research and education in North America, Western Europe, Australia, and Japan.

University-based Green Policy and Management Initiatives

Another approach to environmental education and training in the Asia-Pacific region is one or a series of initiatives based at an university or educational institution. There are several university-based environmental educational and training programs in Japan, South Korea, and other more developed Asian countries, but one of the most ambitious sustainable development research and training efforts on the regional level is being initiated by the Bangkok, Thailand based Asian Institute of Technology (AIT). Through its five schools (advanced technologies, civil engineering, management, and environment & resources, and development), seven research centers, and eighteen integrated programs, AIT has made a number of notable contributions to sustainable development research and education.

With the tightening of funds from foreign development assistance programs and international donor groups, coupled with the regional economic problems, one of AIT's key strategic focuses has been to facilitate academic and private-public sector cooperation in environmental and sustainable development planning. As a relatively new university that does not have a large endowment, AIT has to be resourceful in identifying new funding and institutional partners. It is currently working to strengthen business education programs in Vietnamese universities, in cooperation with the Swiss Agency for Development and Cooperation and the Government of Vietnam, and is developing new research and training programs on urban environmental problems in cooperation with the private nonprofit group, U.S. Environment Institute. With nearly 9,000 alumni based in all corners of the Asia-Pacific region, including Bhutan, Mongolia, and Kazakhstan, AIT is striving to become a global as well as a regional institution of higher learning.

Sustainability Research and Training Networks

An important environmental education and training trend in the Asia-Pacific region is the development of regional sustainability networks. Many of these networks rely on the latest internet technology to create an interactive electronic medium through which environment-related data and information are shared and discussed. A good example of such a regional sustainability network is the Southeast Asian Policy Advisory Network in Global Change (SEA-SPAN) [http://www.icsea.or.id/sea-span], which is managed and administered by the Global Change Impacts Centre for Southeast Asia research institute. The Bogor, Indonesia-based Global Change Impacts Centre has created an interactive community of environmental policy specialists and ecologists using electronic discussion lists, news updates, and electronic conferences. SEA-SPAN has provided the most comprehensive source of data and information on the outbreaks of forest fires in Indonesia, which have received a lot of attention from both policy makers and the international media in the last couple of years.

Working in cooperation with many tertiary and research institutions in the Asia-Pacific region, the San Francisco, California based Nautilus Institute for Security and Sustainable Development [http://www.nautilus.org] has in the past five years launched several policy networks (e.g. the Energy, Security, and Environment in Northeast Network and Asia-Pacific Environmental Network) that focus on the environmental conditions of the Asia-Pacific region. Using Internet-based information exchange & dissemination programs and traditional policy forums (e.g. working paper series), the Nautilus Institute is spreading much-needed awareness of important regional environmental dilemmas like the energy and ecological conditions of North Korea.

One of the most important Asian sustainability networks is the U.N. Environment Programme-sponsored Network for Environmental Training at Tertiary-Level in Asia and the Pacific (NETTLAP), based in Bangkok, Thailand. The NETTLAP network [www.unep.org/regoffs/roap/nettlap] consists of institutions and individuals active in environmental education and training at the tertiary (e.g. university, technical institute, etc.) level in the Asia-Pacific region, with the organizational goals of enhancing the environmental expertise of decision-makers, policy formulators, and university educators, and increasing the environmental skills and awareness of university-level students. NETTLAP sponsors electronic workshops, publishes training materials, issues reports on regional environmental trends, as well as active research programs devoted to environmental economics, hazardous waste management, and coastal zone management.

Beyond Greening of Schools: Building a Knowledge-based Framework for Sustainable Development

What these three different environmental education and training approaches reflect, is the complex interplay of information technology, knowledge creation/management, and environmental sustainability that occurs at the level of a university or an academic institution. As internet-based communication technologies cause revolutionary changes in the way in which many individuals and institutions access and generate knowledge, there has also been a dramatic surge of interest among academicians and policy makers in using knowledge as the basis of a general framework to understand management (Nonaka and Takeuchi 1995), international development (World Bank 1998), and economics (Foray and Lundvall 1996). Increasingly, attempts to create, manage, and disseminate knowledge are being used to further the goals of sustainable development (Mansell and Wehn 1998).

Although the discussion of knowledge (like sustainability) often gets side-tracked in a debate of terminology and definitions, there are a number of reasons why sustainability and knowledge are conceptually linked. One reason is that both sustainability and knowledge are trans-disciplinary, that is, they both require a broad systems-approach and an understanding of multiple fields of study. Just as knowledge transcends multiple levels of social and economic activity, there has been a growing recognition that the study of environmental sustainability requires a broader, non field-specific system of integration.

Another reason why it is important to explore the interconnections between sustainability and knowledge is that they both represent essential components of development and are conceptually linked. The ability of a country or a society to accumulate and disseminate "knowledge" - measuring air quality, evaluating health risks, and designing cost-effective environmental regulations - is a key factor in how effectively a particular society or country addresses the environmental policy challenge (World Bank 1998).

While it is becoming a widely-held assumption that the ability of a country to increase the quality of its human and other reproductive capital (i.e. knowledge) is essential to its economic success, it is less clear how the effects of knowledge-intensification in the industrial sectors affect the environment. One theory is that as products become more knowledge-intensive, they may have more adverse effects on the natural environment. Thus, it is critical that there is a necessary balance between the inputs of new knowledge with the "knowledge" of environmental impacts and possible solutions.

Universities and academic institutions may be able to accelerate the development of the second "green revolution" in the Asia-Pacific region by providing the necessary intellectual and institutional leadership for instilling changes in the pattern of economic growth, production systems, and consumption patterns. This would be similar to the way the first green revolution (the worldwide movement dedicated to the creation and dissemination of agricultural knowledge) enhanced food security in Indonesia and a number of Asian countries in the 1960s and 1970s.

In order to effectively address the Asian environmental challenge, a number of things obviously need to happen: national governments need to make environment more of a policy priority; the private sector needs to integrate environment as a strategic factor in industrial policy; and environmental groups need to do more than organize citizen protests. What a knowledge-based framework for sustainable development may provide for Asian universities and academic institutions is an intellectual prism through which many of the problems and issues can be discussed.

References

Afsah, S. (1998) "Impact of Financial Crisis on Industrial Growth and Environmental Performance in Indonesia" *Paper Prepared for the US-Environmental Partnership.* Washington D.C.: US-AEP.

Bacani, C. (1998) "Secrets of Success". *Asiaweek* May 15 p. 11.

Calder, K. (1997) "Fueling the Rising Sun: Asia's Energy Needs and Global Security". *Harvard International Review* 19:3 p. 24.

Economy, E. (1994) "The Environment for Development in the Asia-Pacific Region". *Paper Prepared for Meeting of the Politics Group of the Council on Foreign Relations Asia Project.* New York: Council on Foreign Relations.

Fesharaki, F. (1995) Energy Outlook to 2010: Asia-Pacific Demand, Supply, and Climate Change Implications. *East-West Center Asia-Pacific* Issue No. 19 Honolulu: EWC.

Foray, D., Lundvall B. (1996) "The Knowledge-based Economy: From the Economics of Knowledge to the Learning Economy". In Foray D. and B. Lundvall (eds) *Employment and Growth in the Knowledge-based Economy.* Paris: OECD.

Mansell, R., W. U. (1998) *Knowledge Societies: Information Technology for Sustainable Development.* New York: Oxford University Press.

Nonaka, I., Takeuchi H. (1995) *The Knowledge-Creating Company: How Japanese Companies Create the Dynamics of Innovation.* New York: Oxford University Press.

ark, J., Lo F. (1997) "Building a Sustainable Development Educational and Research Agenda". *Asian Perspective* 29:2 pp. 57-75.

Sophal, C. (1998) "Dangerous Waste Left in Cambodia".*Reuters News Service,* December 26.

United Nations (1993) *The Global Partnership for Environment and Development: A Guide to Agenda 21.* Post Rio Edition New York: UN.

World Bank (1998) *World Development Report: Knowledge for Development.* Washington D.C.: World Bank.

World Resources Institute. UN Environment and Development Programmes, and the World Bank (1996) *The Urban Environment.* New York: Oxford University.

Chapter 12

Promoting Environmental Citizenship and Sustainability in Regional Campuses: Experiences from a Consortium of 15 Colleges and Universities

Robert S. Whyte
Director of Environmental Programs
Associated Colleges of the South

"Meeting needs now and in the future requires a major shift in the relationship of the humans to the natural environment. Responsible citizenship in the twenty-first century requires a change in mindset. As Einstein observed, 'the significant problems we face cannot be solved at the same level of thinking we were at when we created them.' Such a shift in thinking, values, and actions of all individuals and institutions worldwide calls for a long term societal effort to make environment and sustainability concerns a central theme in all education."

- Dr. Anthony Cortese, President, Second Nature

Abstract

This chapter describes the experience of a consortium of Colleges in which common approaches to sustainability are pursued.

Introduction

"Environmental Citizenship for the 21st Century" is a recent environmental initiative of the Associated Colleges of the South (ACS), a 15 member consortium of leading liberal arts colleges and universities located in 12 states across the southeastern United States.[36] The ACS environmental initiative is designed to increase "environmental citizenship" among the ACS

---

[36] Birmingham-Southern College (Birmingham, AL), Centenary College of Louisiana (Shreveport, LA), Centre College (Danville, KY), Davidson College (Davidson, NC), Furman University (Greenville, SC), Hendrix College (Conway, AR), Millsaps College (Jackson, MS), Morehouse College (Atlanta, GA), Rhodes College (Memphis, TN), Rollins College (Winter Park, FL), Southwestern University (Georgetown, TX), Trinity University (San Antonio, TX), University of Richmond (Richmond, VA), University of the South (Sewanee, TN), Washington and Lee University (Lexington, VA)

campus communities to include the students, faculty, and staff. Environmental Citizenship may be defined in many ways. At the very least, it consists of having attitudes that are respectful of the earth, of being mindful of the need for a sustainable environment, and of being intelligent in one's understanding of interactions between humans and natural systems. Environmental citizenship is building the capacity for responsible and well-informed decision making in this area.

Formed in 1991, ACS's mission is to make the case for liberal arts education and strengthen academic programs of its member institutions. It accomplishes these aims through the collective use of the financial, intellectual, and physical resources of its members. Since its inception, ACS has coordinated programs, workshops, information exchanges, and services for faculty, staff and students. An emphasis in collaborative effort and the development and sharing of replicable models are trademarks of its activities, whether in academic or administrative areas.

Academic Institution	Program Type	Academic Institution	Program Type
Rollins College (Winter Park, FL)	Environmental Studies Department	University of Richmond (Richmond, VA)	Environmental Curriculum Committee, established
Trinity University Global (San Antonio, TX)	Environmental Studies minor	Hendrix College (Conway, AR)	S.A.G.E. (Sustainability and Education), faculty committee to examine environmental and cross-cultural issues that might be integrated into curriculum
Morehouse College (Atlanta, GA)	Proposed environmental studies minor	Furman University (Greenville, SC)	Environmental Curriculum Committee, established
Centenary College (Shreveport, LA)	Environmental Studies Minor	Southwestern University (Georgetown, TX)	Informal major through independent study (Environmental Curriculum Committee established)
University of the South (Sewanee, TN)	Proposed environmental studies concentration	Davidson College (Davidson, NC)	Center for Interdisciplinary Studies
Millsaps College (Jackson, MS)	Environmental Geology Major (proposed environmental concentration)	Rhodes College (Memphis, TN)	Earth Systems Science minor
Centre College (Danville, KY)	Environmental Curriculum Committee established		
Washington & Lee University (Lexington, VA)	Interdepartmental Environmental Studies Program (interdisciplinary concentration)	Birmingham-Southern College (Birmingham, AL)	Environmental Curriculum Committee, established

Table 1: Summary of academic environmental programs of member institutions of the Associated Colleges of the South

ACS member institutions have been active for many years in promoting environmental awareness through course development, sponsoring programs, and promoting activities that not only teach principles of environmental stewardship, but also put them into practice. All of the ACS members offer environmentally related courses. Rollins College has developed a formal environmental program, with as many as 41 related courses. The majority of ACS schools are in the early stages of developing environmental programs (Table 1), but all seek to address environmental concerns by offering relevant courses in the physical and natural sciences as well as in the social sciences and humanities.

While classroom instruction is instrumental to promote environmental citizenship, the colleges and universities realized that appreciation of the environment and the problems facing them benefit from direct involvement of students and faculty in active learning programs. Examples of this are the ACS environmentally related study abroad programs, creating on-site overseas learning laboratories in environmental concerns. Experiential learning closer to home is also encouraged through internships and career planning and placement guidance.

ACS institutions have been strong proponents of environmental research, supporting numerous projects on environmental issues. Furman University faculty are studying the impact of global warming on fauna of the southeast[37]; Richmond faculty and students are researching the effects of pesticides on soil microbial communities; and Rollins College faculty and students are analyzing greenway corridors and how green space can be protected and preserved (Rollins College, Environmental Studies Department 1998). Through research efforts such as these ACS seeks to work within the consortium and enhance collaborative environmental research opportunities across disciplines and institutional boundaries.

The consortium also recognizes the importance of complementing traditional academic programs with service based learning. Service to the broader society has been a touchstone for the consortium. Examples include the volunteer efforts of students at Southwestern University in their local River Watch program, the recent efforts by Rollins faculty and students to provide clean drinking-water to the residents of the Dominica Republic, and the development of unique "ecoscapes" - outdoor educational gardens and natural areas - in the communities of the city of Birmingham through efforts of Birmingham-Southern College. Efforts are currently being sought to enhance environmental activities of the ACS program in Honduras, run by Rhodes College and in cooperation with the Heifer Project International (Little Rock, Arkansas), which combines on-site student service with independent study projects.

Finally, the consortium realizes that individually and collectively, its institutions must demonstrate their environmental commitment in their daily practices. Positive examples include active recycling programs at a majority of the ACS institutions.[38] Recycling efforts at Birmingham-Southern College and the development of the Southern Environmental Center and ecoscape (outdoor herb and natural garden) on an area previously used as a dumping ground were awarded one of President Bush's "One Thousand Points of Light" awards. Collectively, the

---

[37] Presentation by: Walsh, S.J. and D.C. Haney. 1993. Assessing possible effects of global climate change on the southern Appalachian Ichthyofauna. American Society of Ichthyologists and Herpetologists, Austin, Texas.

Walsh, S.J., D.C. Haney and C.M. Timmerman. 1993. Thermal physiology of southern Appalachian fishes: Implications of potential environmental change. American Society of Zoologists, Los Angeles California.

[38] A summary of ACS recycling programs is provided at the URL
http://www.colleges.org/~enviro/survey/index.html

consortium benefited from a pilot energy conservation project at Rollins College, which identified $250,000 in annual energy savings for the college.

History of the Environmental Initiative

The examples and concepts presented above provide the framework for future consortium activities. Efforts in the areas of academic programming, research, service and institutional operations provide the basis for collective action and efficacy of meeting the challenge of today's pressing environmental problems and are the basis for the ACS program in environmental citizenship. It was these initial environmental efforts at the individual schools that fostered the present environmental initiative. Historically, ACS has encouraged and provided a forum for the various faculty to report to one another on campus programs related to the environment although no formal environmental program existed. One of the first ACS programs to focus on the environment was an ACS sponsored service learning project in Honduras in 1993. The Sustainable Development Program in Costa Rica was initiated in 1994, and provided a greater focus on the environment.[39] This interdisciplinary program remains an active component of the ACS environmental initiative and offers academic credit in political science, economics, anthropology, and forestry. A pilot program in energy conservation at Rollins College - referred to previously - was an early model for the cooperative efforts envisioned in the present ACS environmental initiative. An extensive energy audit of all buildings on the Rollins campus provided numerous recommendations for improvements in energy conservation. Direct benefits provided to Rollins College were extended to all ACS institutions through an ACS sponsored site visit and review of the energy analysis, providing numerous lessons and applications on the individual campuses.

The various individual campus programs and the initial ACS sponsored cooperative efforts led to a series of discussions in 1996 to formally create an ACS environmental program. The large number of schools involved - thirteen at the time - and their broad range of interests, required considerable coordination and a comprehensive process to identify appropriate environmental opportunities, establish priorities, and decide on a series of activities to pursue. Funding was secured from external sources, and program and technical assistance were provided by Second Nature, a Boston based non-profit organization. In 1997 the ACS environmental initiative Environmental Citizenship in the 21st Century was formally established.

Project Organization - A Mechanism for Institutional Change

To ensure effective program leadership, education and communication, policy guidance, and resources among the 15 ACS institutions, ACS began its environmental initiative by developing a comprehensive program network (Figure 1). Leadership groups were organized on all of the campuses and initiated the effort to review the ACS materials describing the project and develop potential consortium projects. A faculty program committee, representing all the member

---

[39]   Real World Issues: Learning sustainable development in Costa Rica's living laboratory. From the Rollins College Alumni Record, June 1998.

institutions, was appointed and a program director selected. The director and program committee work in conjunction with the ACS presidents, academic deans, and the ACS president. The program committee is instrumental in providing program guidance and policy development, and the development of long-range plans, encompassing a long-term environmental strategy for ACS. Because of this long-term perspective, each member of the program committee serves a non-rotating four-year assignment. It is the ACS environmental program director who is the catalyst and direct link, bringing together the various ACS groups, faculty, staff, students and others, and ultimately must provide the leadership necessary for the development of a comprehensive, coherent, and cooperative program of benefit to each institution.

Critical to this process has been the buy-in from the chief academic officers[40] and overall administrative support. The chief academic officers have played a critical role in reinforcing the importance of this initiative and the opportunities for faculty, staff, and students to make an impact on the environment and the cause for sustainable development. Throughout the development process and into year two of the program, the chief academic officers devoted considerable time and energy to the organizational development, subsequent implementation of the many projects and activities, and to setting the overall initiative direction in cooperation with the program committee and director. It is this critical administrative program support, which is often lacking, that has provided the ACS environmental initiative with the impetus to focus the institutions on sustainability and encourage broad campus community support (Strauss 1996).

The ACS environmental initiative is unique in that it seeks to serve the needs of multiple institutions geographically spread over 12 states, and is not campus based or focused on a single institution. There are many examples of single institution programs and activities (Keniry 1995; Eagan and Keniry 1998; Creighton 1998), but there are few examples of formally established consortia efforts in the area of the environment. To stimulate environmental and sustainable development activity on the campus, moving the campus toward the goals of the overall endeavor, a mechanism was required to provide the director with critical campus-based program support. To meet this need, ACS appointed campus faculty fellows - a rotating position from year to year - to serve as the key spokesperson for the environmental initiative on each of the 15 campuses. The faculty fellows provide essential program support to the program director. The fellows coordinate the gathering of information and the dissemination of information to other ACS institutions, collaborate with the project director to meet specific program needs, bring together the key environmental players on the campus to explore cooperative environmental initiatives, and assist with specific aspects of the project such as visiting lecturers and workshops held on the campus. Time committed to these endeavors is minimal as the faculty carry a full teaching load, in addition to other academic responsibilities.[41] Centre College has successfully experimented with release-time, freeing this person from a single course, and allowing the faculty fellow to devote a greater amount of time to the initiative. Currently, the fellows are compensated with a minimal stipend. In the future additional funds will be sought to provide faculty fellows

---

[40] May include: Vice President for Academic Affairs, Dean of the College, Dean of Academic Affairs, Provost, Dean of the Faculty, Dean of the College of Arts and Sciences among others.

[41] ACS college and universities are largely undergraduate teaching institutions.

release-time so that they may devote greater time to campus and consortium environmental efforts and enhance institutionalization of the program.

Leadership and advocacy efforts also extend to the students. ACS-appointed student interns directly assist the faculty fellows in bringing the environmental project to the attention of individuals and groups on the campus. The interns play a lead role in organizing student participation in the project, building on whatever is currently taking place on the campus, and stimulating further efforts among the students and others on the campuses to develop projects supportive of the mission of the initiative. They also provide an inter-institutional student network linking their individual efforts to those throughout the consortium.

Promoting Change through Collaboration

Collaboration may be defined as working together as in a joint intellectual effort, but more often in higher education it can take on a secondary definition of cooperating with an enemy invader. This latter view, while a bit of a stretch, underscores the traditional lack of cooperation across academic disciplines and between institutions. ACS member institutions all share a commitment to excellence in their programs, to the continuation of liberal arts education and to the growth and development of each of their students. These common goals are the foundation for ACS. ACS provides the mechanism through which member colleges and universities create and build programs cooperatively that would not be possible individually. Since its inception, ACS has coordinated programs, workshops, information exchanges, and services for faculty, staff, and students. Specific to the environment cooperative measures include:

- The creation of faculty information clearinghouses across ACS institutions. This allows faculty members to learn of professional interests, courses, and research activities of other faculty and share and explore areas of mutual interest.
- The expansion and coordination of international study programs. ACS offers 16 overseas study programs, all of which are open to students enrolled in an ACS college or university, and several of which are specific to the environment, including its summer program in Costa Rica, Dominica, and the Yucatan Peninsula.
- The convening of key administrative, faculty, and staff groups from ACS institutions. This is essential for purposes of sharing information, examining issues, and/or problem-solving.
- The creation of special projects to enhance the educational and collaborative opportunities on each of the ACS campuses. This includes special pilot programs and workshops to support faculty in terms of their ability to develop new collaborative projects and activities related to the environmental initiative. Workshops were a principal focus the first year of the ACS environmental initiative providing a forum by which faculty, staff and students could first and foremost develop a sense of community establishing key relationships with their peers.
- The initiation of cost containment measures, taking advantage of the efficiencies achieved when 15 institutions work cooperatively. Examples here of collaboration would include joint purchasing agreements, comparing or benchmarking administrative functions, use of joint consultants, joint memberships in educational organizations, and joint library database purchases.

Through these and other collaborative efforts, ACS hopes that in the future it can demonstrate the synergies that consortia can achieve when sharing information and models of cooperative action with other academic institutions and organizations.

Current Environmental Activities

Consistent with the consortium's emphasis on cooperation across institutional boundaries, the ACS environmental initiative focuses on collaborative efforts to enable the ACS institutions to make a broader and constructive impact on the environment, and ultimately help it produce enlightened and effective citizens for the 21st Century.

Project Title	Principal Institutions	Priority Area
Environmental Studies Curricula	University of Richmond	Curricula Development: workshop focusing on alternative ways of educating undergraduates in liberal arts colleges about the natural and physical environment in which they live. Representatives from higher education, business, government, and NGOs discussed the need for enhanced environmental education of undergraduates and the different curricula that address those needs.
Sustainability in the Liberal Arts	Hendrix College	Curricula Development: workshop - examined the role of liberal arts colleges in helping prepare students for a sustainable future; emphasis placed on disciplines in all academic divisions: the humanities, social sciences, and natural sciences; and examination of the various dimensions of education at a liberal arts college: curriculum, campus design and operations, career planning, social outreach, and research.
Greening of the Campus - Broadening the Classroom	Birmingham-Southern College	Campus Operations, Curricula Development: demonstrations and discussions showing effective environmental actions being taken on campuses within ACS and nationwide in an effort to stimulate other campuses to emulate such exemplary practices. Participants engaged in interdisciplinary environmental projects (framed within the context of ongoing environmental problems in the city of Birmingham), learning to effectively integrate these experiences into classroom learning for the students.
Sustainable Development in Local Communities	University of the South, Birmingham-Southern College, Rollins College	Course Development, Research, Service: sustainable development in a local and regional context
Living in the Yucatan: Building Environmental Citizenship through a Field-Based Research Course in the Northern Maya Lowlands	Millsaps College	Course Development, Research, Service: ACS stff fld. course in the Yucatan, utilizes critical thinking, problem-solving pedagogy while exposing students to three major areas of field based investigations: Impact of development on coastal ecosystems and coral reefs; Archaeo-ecology of the Classic Maya Civilization and Ecological audit and baseline classification of very rare remnants of old growth forest in the central Yucatan.

Project Title	Principal Institutions	Priority Area
The Effects of Economic Growth in the Rural South	University of the South	Research: investigation of the effects of economic growth in the rural South and how growth affects biodiversity.
Sustainable Campus Development Clinic	Davidson College, National Wildlife Federation	Campus Operations: (student initiative) workshop address sustainability in three specific areas of campus development: architecture, landscaping, and transportation.
Heritage Resources Management in the College and University Environment: Environmental Planning and Decision-making	University of the South	Campus Operations, Service: workshop to provide a Its Importance in usable level of archaeological knowledge to a large segment of the ACS academic and public sector by actively involving ACS university members (faculty, students, and staff) in archaeological classroom training and field trips; essential product of the workshop is a draft heritage resources management policy suitable for adoption by all of the ACS schools.
Systematic Analysis and Reduction of Costs Associated with Campus Paper Usage business	Millsaps College, Birmingham-Southern College	Campus Operations, Research: principal goal is to reduce the costs associated with a college's usage of office paper through the systematic application of information technology and analysis of campus

Table 2: Summary of projects initiated through the Associated Colleges of the South environmental initiative "Environmental Citizenship in the 21st century".

To foster collaborative interdisciplinary relationships, and help prepare the Campus Community, with a focus on the student, for environmental citizenship in the 21st century, ACS provides funding to its member institutions through a formal grant process inviting faculty, staff, and students to submit proposals. Since 1998 ACS has made available over $200,000, funding a total of 12 projects (Table 2).[42] The focus of these projects is on the study of environmental issues that integrate perspectives and tools of the humanities and arts, social sciences and natural sciences, and is concerned with issues on local, regional, national and global scales. Funded projects are those that demonstrate an ability to increase environmental citizenship through the systematic study of the interactions between humans and the biosphere, and use innovative and proactive solutions to environmental problems. Topics of interest include but are not limited to: conservation of biological diversity and ecological integrity; cultural diversity and environmental justice; effects and mitigation of human action on pattern and process in biotic and abiotic systems; pollution prevention and remediation; human population and consumption; environmental and natural resource economics; environmental history, literature, and arts; environmental policy and law; ethics, values, belief systems and considerations of the global community and sustainable livelihoods.

An essential consideration in funding projects is the nature and extent of collaboration. Collaboration must be inter-institutional and interdisciplinary. Projects are required to focus on a

---

[42] In 1997, ACS received a generous grant extending over four years from a private foundation, enabling ACS to make these funds available to its member institutions for collaborative endeavors.

topic or process of wide interest to the consortium as a whole as opposed to matters of concern on a single campus, and with the potential to transform institutions, individuals and the environment.

Specific to the grant process and the overall environmental initiative are four priority areas: (1) environmental education and academic courses emphasizing the environment; (2) cooperative research dealing with significant environmental issues and problems; (3) service programs designed to improve the environment; and (4) campus operations such as energy and resource conservation to effectively improve the environment of the ACS campuses and their adjoining community. In each of these areas, the consortium aims to change how people think and act.

Courses are expected to convey information vital to a clear understanding of the environment and the related theme of sustainable development. As students and faculty absorb new information and increase their understanding, it is hoped that they will be more acutely sensitive to the broad range and complexity of environmental questions. Equipped with heightened understanding of what can and should be done, the individuals influenced by this program will be positioned to play important roles in preserving, protecting and advancing the environment while addressing other needs of the society.

Collaborative research is viewed as a mechanism through which ACS faculty and students can decipher and explain complicated and pressing environmental issues and illuminate ways of resolving those issues. The research projects provide opportunities for faculty and students to work together, each teaching and learning in the process.

The third facet of the proposed environmental structure is service to the broader community. The consortium is able to direct the energy and resources of the 15 members and focus them on specific opportunities to render an environmental service. The task is not to uncover new areas of need, but to take critical areas already identified and direct the talents from 15 institutions toward meeting those needs. The impact of such a combined endeavor will justify the time and effort expended in setting the priorities for action and acting collaboratively to assemble the necessary resources and execute those actions.

The impact of this service is broad. It ranges throughout the region and beyond, encompassing urban, inter-city areas coping with an embarrassment of threatening circumstances, to rural sections needing cleaner streams and managed forests. Moreover, the influence extends to the nation and the world, with lessons to be shared. The immediate impact is on local areas served by the ACS institutions, but the long-term influence will extend throughout the region and beyond, as institutions share their lessons and experiences on a widespread basis.

The fourth feature applies the environmental emphasis to the daily operations of each college and university. Through this effort, ACS can ensure that the institutions themselves will embody the environmental values they are working assiduously to extend beyond the campuses. The institutions share information and stimulate each other to carry out recycling projects, protection of green areas on campus, the avoidance of waste and waste products frequently generated, conservation of energy and thrusting sustainable development in front of everyone on an everyday basis.

The following are specific examples of programs and activities either completed, ongoing or in the development phase as well as the overall philosophy contributing to project development. Because the emphasis is on collaboration, initial activities focused on building these relationships to enhance long-term collaboration within the consortium.

Environmental Education. *The challenge: environmental education has not been a top priority in higher education in general and particularly at the undergraduate level.* To respond to this challenge, ACS has sought to increase environmental literacy among the campuses through expanded environmental course offerings, experiential learning, and faculty development. It encourages collaborative interdisciplinary studies between faculty across fields, programs, departments and institutional boundaries. Actions are being taken to provide enhanced career preparation and planning services consistent with their educational preparation.

Several aspects of environmental education were originally proposed as part of the ACS environmental initiative: new course development, enhancement of existing courses, experiential learning, faculty development, and career planning and placement. One of the difficulties in justifying and creating new courses in Environmental Studies is defining a need for such courses, and need is often based on student demand and the appropriate fit into existing majors. Only a few ACS institutions have a designated "Environmental Studies" major or minor, and only a single institution, Rollins College, has a designated Environmental Studies Department. Therefore an initial emphasis has been placed on curriculum review toward the development of Environmental Studies majors and minors. Faculty interest appears to be high throughout the ACS. As an example, a recent poll of University of Richmond faculty from 13 different academic departments indicated a high interest in Environmental Studies.

In June 1998, the University of Richmond convened a workshop of the 15 ACS schools to discuss the growing interest in Environmental Studies on the ACS campuses, and guide them in the development of their curricula including the development of concentrations, minors, and majors. Specific topics of discussion included the purposes of environmental education for undergraduates, the content of environmental education, organization, administration, and staffing and the establishment and maintenance of such academic programs. Eight ACS schools have subsequently established formal committees to explore the development of environmental programs and review the existing curriculum. In this regard the ACS institutions appear to be following a national trend toward an increase in the number of environmental studies and science programs on the undergraduate level (Strauss 1996). Although it is unclear at this point whether the ACS institutions exploring curriculum change will emphasize environmental studies - natural sciences within the context of the humanities and social science - or environmental sciences - a much stronger emphasis in the natural sciences.

Several new courses have been developed for ACS students, emphasizing interdisciplinary approaches and drawing upon the expertise of ACS faculty. The ACS program "Sustainable Development in Costa Rica", a five-week summer interdisciplinary study abroad program that is open to all ACS students is an initial collaboration between faculty from the university of the South, Rollins College and Birmingham-Southern College. The concept of sustainable development is explored through study of the relationship between living standards and natural resource use (Allen 1997). Students spend considerable time in the forest examining rain forest destruction and preservation, as well as living in the local communities, and examining projects to improve the lives of these people.

Faculty from Millsaps College initiated an additional pilot course "Living in the Yucatan" in the spring and summer of 1998. The course focused on the rise and fall of Maya civilization, the colonial adaptation to a tropical environment, and the study of the contemporary ecological issues in the Yucatan peninsula. This program serves as the cornerstone for a proposed program for environmental citizenship, creating a network of academic and ecological connections necessary for the program's overall success, and the development of services for research opportunities to be used by ACS faculty and students in the future. Initial partners included SEMARNAP (The Mexican national Institute of Ecology), several private non-profits: the Akumal Research Station, the Amigos de Sian Kian, Protnatura, INAH (The Mexican National Institute of Anthropology and History), and UADY (Autonomous University of Yucatan). These institutes provided valuable support in the form of lecturers and guides, as well as overall support for the development of an interdisciplinary research program for the environmental issues in the Yucatan Peninsula. A unique part of the course was the examination of the social structure of the tourist city of Cancun and its impact on the surrounding tropical ecosystem. In cooperation with the Amigos de Sian Kian, the issue was explored; the collection of materials and resulting discussion were in actuality the first detailed examination of the issue. These materials have since been incorporated as an important part of the Amigos program. Plans are now being made to continue the course in 1999, expanding research opportunities for ACS students and faculty.

The development of new courses is essential; however, ways must be sought to enhance current course offerings by adding environmental dimensions. For non-environmental courses, there is a need to identify environmental concerns, factors, studies or examples that can be incorporated to enrich course content and encourage students to confront environmental questions. For example, faculty at Rhodes College teaching a course on U.S. public policy, have introduced a discussion on public policy and the environment, discussing such issues as the state of the environment, historical development of U.S. environmental policy, and the clean water and air acts. This is an example where the faculty member in consultation with the ACS environmental program was able to discuss this interest and be directed to other faculty among the ACS institutions that could provide syllabus and teaching support.

Concomitant with curriculum development, is the need for faculty development, oriented toward expanding understanding of the environment and helping faculty develop their skills in teaching environmental subjects and engaging student interest. The ACS environmental fellows, who have a special interest and training in various aspects of the environment, are available to assist other faculty and staff in becoming more environmentally aware and capable. They are proactive in mentoring individual faculty members and inspiring them to make a difference in the lives of their students. The consortium currently offers an intense one-week summer teaching and learning workshop, dealing with general pedagogical issues. It consists principally of a microteaching experience through which faculty participants teach one another. Future workshops may focus on the environment.

ACS sponsored workshops provide faculty and staff with the opportunity to enhance their knowledge of various environmental subjects, and overall provide a stimulating environment in which to increase their environmental awareness. Specifically, these workshops engage faculty and staff in interdisciplinary discussions with their peers from throughout ACS, creating future opportunities for collaborative teaching, research, and program development. In 1998 five workshops were held focusing on a variety of environmental issues. Each sought to discuss issues relevant to the environment and higher education. Both the Hendrix College and Birmingham-Southern College workshops provided a unique opportunity for faculty and staff to directly interact, promoting integrated program development. Career planning and service directors attended the Hendrix workshop, and operational staff attended the Birmingham-Southern College workshop. As a result, the ÁCS career service directors are working directly with the faculty to develop an environmental internship program, providing unique opportunities for students to gain environmental experience in a variety of disciplines. Faculty, staff and operations staff are actively working together to conduct campus environmental audits on several ACS campuses and more are being planned as campus community projects. This integrated approach provides increased environmental awareness and simultaneously creates a sense of responsibility and ownership on the part of the institution. The ACS environmental fellows are instrumental in developing these relationships, providing a direct link to campus professional offices and identifying the needs of both staff and faculty.

In addition to program workshops, ACS regularly convenes meetings of key administrative, faculty, and staff groups from ACS institutions for purposes of sharing information, examining issues, and/or problem solving. Examples of such groups specific to the environmental initiative include the ACS Academic Vice Presidents and Deans, Directors of Career Planning and Placement, Physical Plant Directors, Purchasing Directors and Chief Business Officers. The career planning and service directors have utilized such meetings to develop and implement a joint ACS jobs and internships board on the web.

Research Program. *The challenge: nationally, environmental research has failed some of the same tests failed by the education program, by being at times too limited, too narrow or specialized, or too prone to fixate on the latest environmental fads or topics.* ACS has responded to meet this challenge by fostering research programs that emphasize collaborative interdisciplinary research pertaining to environmental subjects. Ongoing and planned research attempts to deal with immediate and local concerns of the southeast U.S., but also focuses on long-term critical topics that are regional, national and international in scope. Researchers are encouraged to link their projects to the environmental courses and the services being offered or contemplated within the ACS community, and to conduct research and implement innovative ideas to enhance the environmental quality on their campuses and the surrounding community. Undergraduate research efforts on ACS campuses should bring together faculty and students, involving students from the inception and including them in post-research activities - discussion, presentation and publication of results.

Promoting interdisciplinary research has historically been difficult; development of interdisciplinary collaborative research programs across institutions is an even greater challenge. Specifically, environmental research has sometimes lacked the interdisciplinary approaches required to clarify important environmental problems. Lacking collaboration, opportunities are missed to provide a more exhaustive analysis of the data critical to successful problem solving. Collaborative research efforts are promoted through the ACS consortium wide grant program.

The ACS program director and environmental fellows actively seek to promote such collaborations by disseminating information and linking faculty across institutions. Current efforts to aid this process include an inventory of past and current ACS faculty environmental research, establishment of an ACS bulletin board and appropriate list-servers linking various faculty groups. Upon completion of the research inventory, the information will be placed on the web in the form of a browseable database to include all relevant literature and associated faculty research interests.

Initial examples of collaborative research are linked to previously described environmental education efforts. Living in the Yucatan project utilizes field-based studies to do basic research in coastal ecology, Mayan culture, and old growth forest ecology. Mayan archeological research at Ek Balam, located in the northeast part of the Yucatan, has been the focus of ongoing research since 1984 (Bey and Ringle 1995). Ek Balam was untouched in 1984 when research efforts began, thus all change in the natural and cultural environment related to archeology and tourism is a recent development and well documented. The Ek Balam site with its long history - occupied from 600 B.C. through 1610 A.D. - and its massive monumental architecture, led to its being declared one of the 10 most important archeological sites in the Yucatan. Present research will combine student research opportunities with ongoing ACS faculty research as well as with efforts of the Mexican government. Related research is planned for Rancho Kiuic - located in the southwest Yucatan - in the summer of 1999. This relatively undisturbed area is rich in biological, archeological, colonial and ethnographic resources. This multidisciplinary research is being coordinated between ACS faculty and members of the INAH and University of Yucatan. ACS offers numerous venues to promote research results of this project and allow development of future collaboration including ACS student seminars, lecture series, workshops, ACS newsletter, and the annual Latin American Studies Symposium hosted by the ACS member school Birmingham-Southern College. Long-term plans include development of a research center as a platform for creating research collaborations in the ACS and bringing together both ACS faculty and students with Yucatecan institutions and their faculty and students.

A recently initiated research program at the University of the South, "The Effects of Economic Growth in the Rural South", focuses on environmental problems of interest to the southeast. Specifically, this collaborative investigation examines the effects of economic growth in the rural South, and provides a synthetic examination of how growth affects biodiversity.[43] Faculty from across disciplines and from throughout the ACS will investigate issues specific to: (1) private landowner incentives to protect biodiversity in rural Tennessee, (2) land use policy, and (3) housing development and bird conservation, collecting data on how bird populations respond to changes in forest structure and composition, and housing development on the Cumberland Plateau.

---

[43] Growth: Boon or Bane? An In-depth Analysis of the Prospective Effects of Economic and Population Growth on Franklin County, Tennessee." With Dutch Horchem. Presented at the Seventh International Symposium on Society and Resource Management, University of Missouri-Columbia, May 29, 1998.

The Efficacy of TN's Forest Greenbelt Program as an Incentive for Protecting Biodiversity: A Case Study of Franklin County." With Madelaine Haddican. Presented at the Seventh International Symposium on Society and Resource Management, University of Missouri-Columbia, May 29, 1998.

Other recently initiated projects designed to foster collaborative research are in the areas of sustainable development, campus-based archeology, and campus operations business processes. It is the desire of ACS to link all research projects to environmental courses and service-learning activities, providing a forum to enhance all aspects of the initiative. Utilizing the existing ACS environmental program committee members and environmental fellows, enhanced mechanisms are also being considered to promote collaborative research. ACS continues to develop its communication network and foster an enhanced ACS community whereby faculty consciously seeks out collaborations beyond their own institution.

Service Activities. *The challenges in rendering environmental service are staggering in terms of the sheer number and enormity of the problems demanding remedy.* In meeting this challenge, ACS must seek to better inform and educate the members of the campus community as well as the constituencies outside the campus community. ACS actions in environmental service share the same basic features as in environmental education and research: (1) an assessment of current service activities and projects and the availability of ACS expertise to service the community; (2) a focus on collaborative ventures; and (3) formation of new partnerships which may include communities, organizations, government, business and industry local to the ACS campuses, as well as similar groups regionally, nationally, and internationally.

Initial service based activities are tied directly to ongoing educational and research projects as described previously. These are field courses, which introduce service elements to promote environmental awareness. Both the Yucatan and Costa Rica projects described previously have introduced service-learning elements to complement the educational and research aspects of these courses. In Costa Rica, students live in local communities directly participating in sustainable community projects and gain first hand knowledge of relevant issues in an applied context. Students may also elect to stay in Costa Rica upon completion of the formal course and directly participate in service internships.

The initial success of both the Yucatan and Costa Rican projects, and a preliminary trip to the Dominica to explore opportunities, persuaded ACS faculty to meet and discuss future joint projects particularly as they related to research and service opportunities. ACS service projects are now being planned in the Dominica Republic, Honduras, South Africa, Guyana, and rural Tennessee. Another exciting opportunity exists through Birmingham-Southern College's Environmental Center. The Environmental Center staff provides both on-campus and community-based educational programs. Over 12,000 school children and teachers (K-12) visit the center and the outdoor ecoscape each year.[44] The Center staff has developed community-based ecoscapes in the neighborhoods of Birmingham further promoting environmental education and providing the area residents with an enhanced sense of community pride. Center staff is now providing outreach to other ACS schools exploring similar service and education opportunities.

Campus Operations. *The challenge: in their own operations, institutions must live up to their ideals of responsible environmental citizenship.* This means that ACS institutional policies and practices regarding their operations, programs, physical plant, purchasing, and their activities

---

[44] Personal communication, Roald Hazelhoff, Director of the Southern Environmental Center, Birmingham-Southern College, Birmingham, Alabama.

must be environmentally sensitive, defensible, and sustainable. To respond to this challenge, the individual ACS institutions are seeking to develop and promote practices that reduce the negative impacts of campus operations and maximize the potentially beneficial effects of sustainable campus operations. Faculty, staff, and students are instrumental in the process, using the institution as their personal "learning laboratory", in which all concerned can learn to analyze complex environmental problems and engineer practical solutions to campus operational problems.

The ACS colleges and universities acknowledge that as microcosms of the larger community, they exert significant influence on the outside world. As a result, the example of their commitment to environmentally responsible living has far-reaching ramifications to the institution and surrounding communities. Institutional desire and commitment to be good stewards of their immediate environs has allowed the ACS campus communities to come together and act cooperatively in seeking solutions and acting responsibly. Students are encouraged to work in cooperation with faculty and staff and are providing the energy and enthusiasm as each campus begins to evaluate its operations. ACS students have started new recycling programs and are reevaluating and reforming older programs. Recycling initiatives at Rollins and Hendrix Colleges are providing models to other ACS schools.

In addition, campus environmental audits have been initiated by the students either as independent studies, capstone courses, or as independent projects through the student campus organizations. Between 1998 and 1999 audits were initiated at Centenary College, Hendrix College, Rhodes College University of Richmond, Birmingham-Southern College, and Southwestern University, with an audit planned in 2000 for Rollins College. The primary goal of these audits is to provide a forum to educate the campus community about associated environmental problems and the need to act with environmental responsibility. Only then can appropriate environmental measures be successfully implemented. A unique component of these audits is the ongoing creation of an online ACS database for purposes of research and classroom learning to all ACS institutions. ACS has provided leadership in this process through the environmental faculty fellows who are able to act as advisors and provide initial contacts with the appropriate campus staff. The ACS student interns, working with the faculty fellows, provide the required student leadership and help to coordinate all aspects of these projects. In all instances, these efforts are coordinated with faculty, staff and the administration. It is clearly recognized that change can only be accomplished through cooperation and not criticism; a positive focus and cooperation are driving these efforts.

Other operational initiatives are being put forth in the areas of purchasing and energy efficiency. The Rollins College energy audit and outreach efforts have been described previously. The ACS Purchasing Directors with the assistance of Emory University (Atlanta, GA) are exploring joint purchasing options including potential "green" purchasing in several areas. Helping these efforts is an ongoing joint research effort at Millsaps College and Birmingham-Southern College to systematically analyze campus paper usage. The primary goal of this project is to reduce costs associated with a college's usage of office paper through the application of information technology. Data is being collected on campus business processes, and an attempt is being made to better understand how paper is used as a communication medium. Identification of specific business processes and associated paper trails can assist in attempts to eliminate waste and reduce costs. Davidson College hosted a meeting of several ACS schools and other schools from around the country in February of 1999, to examine sustainable campus development. The workshop cosponsored by ACS and the National Wildlife Federation's Campus Ecology Program, is unique in that it used a multidisciplinary team approach. Each participating institution was asked to send a team comprised of faculty, staff, administrators and students, an appropriate cross-section of the campus community. The workshop focused on three aspects of sustainable campus design: architecture, landscaping, and transportation, and provided lessons in environmental responsibility and cost-efficient opportunities. The ACS teams were able to return to their individual campuses with specific strategies for action, and provide outreach to other campuses that were unable to participate.

Future Issues and Challenges

Throughout this chapter, references have been made to ongoing and proposed projects. Requests to the ACS institutions for collaborative project proposals are sought twice a year, and other projects are developed in cooperation with the program director and individual faculty. An ACS environmental lecture series has been established and schools are cooperating to develop critical topics and coordinate scheduled appearances for speakers. The program director in cooperation with the academic fellows has also initiated a series of "environmental forums" on each campus to explore the topic of environmental sustainability and literacy and promote and enhance the environmental initiative on each ACS campus. These forums invite the campus community, including the faculty, staff, students, and administration, and representatives from the neighboring communities. Initial forums have been successful in enhancing campus awareness of the initiative as well as increasing the overall number of participants actively engaged in activities designed to educate and reform aspects of higher education. Additional resources are provided to ACS campuses through faculty consultants providing critical expertise to others in the consortium who might otherwise lack the resources or knowledge on their campus. The ultimate goal of this program is to lay the groundwork for a network of inter-institutional peer support in each of the program priority areas.

This concept is being extended further through the development of regional "Centers of Excellence." The intent of center development is to reform environmental studies learning through the establishment of educational centers providing opportunities for teaching, research and training. Initial proposals for specific centers have been developed at three ACS campuses and steps are being taken to develop and implement these centers. Further coordination is required, however, and mechanisms including funding and staffing must be resolved. Preliminary goals of the center are to:

- Use regional centers as the foci to build and maintain coalitions of faculty who will implement and sustain reform in undergraduate education throughout ACS.
- Prepare faculty at these regional centers to eventually become ACS interdisciplinary consultants or advisors of faculty and students with a particular emphasis on new faculty development.

- Enable ACS faculty to gain experience in interdisciplinary environmental studies through teaching and learning through team-taught classes, workshops, and seminars that model this kind of approach and through interdisciplinary research.
- Enhance both faculty and student opportunities to gain a broad-based understanding of the environment through direct experience with methods and processes of inquiry in the field and in undergraduate interdisciplinary courses.
- Facilitate collaboration and communication among faculty about their reforms in teaching about the environment.

The rationale behind the inclusion of centers of excellence as part of the ACS environmental initiative is to bring together certain educational, research, service and operational projects into a cooperative effort related to a common theme. By linking all of the efforts together, it is felt that the impact can be maximized for faculty, students and staff participating in the projects as well as for the environment and the society at large.

Despite the early successes of the ACS environmental initiative, many challenges remain. ACS must continue to encourage and foster collaboration, and be creative in seeking ways to extend collaboration among the member institutions. The development of a program framework, which outlines measures and steps toward a successful initiative has provided initial guidance, but the completion of a consortium based comprehensive strategic environmental plan is required to provide strong program guidance and reinforce the commitment on the part of ACS and its member institutions. Efforts must continue to build a strong campus constituency that will promote program activities and heighten awareness about the importance and need for improved environmental literacy in higher education. Finally, steps must be taken to institutionalize the program. Ultimately through the actions taken and planned, ACS must continue to encourage and develop projects and resources that directly emanate from within the respective institutions, as well as prepare the necessary leadership to ensure long-term program success.

Ultimately, initiative outcomes - as identified here - can significantly advance the cause of sustainable development for the immediate and long-term future of ACS as well as higher education in general. In sheer numbers, this project will affect thousands of people - students, faculty, and staff on each ACS campus; the surrounding neighborhoods and communities; potentially entire regions of the U.S. and other countries. And, it will spark a process that will extend well beyond the initial four-year period of the ACS environmental initiative.

Such outcomes are likely because of the collaborative action implemented by the consortium. The institutions of ACS have pledged to make this a joint effort model of such cooperation, maximizing the impact on the environment and bringing credit to all involved.

References

Allen, B. (1997) Teaching sustainable development in Costa Rica. In Abrmas, R. (ed.) Weaving connections: cultures and environment, environmental education and the people of the world. *Selected papers from the 26th annual conference of the North American Association for Environmental Education.*

Bey, G. and W. R. (1995) Proyecto Ek Balam: Preliminary Report on the 1994 Field Season. *Report submitted to the National Science Foundation in Partial Fulfillment of Research Grant SBR-9321603 and to the Instituto Nacional de Antropología e Historia Mexico, D.F. and Mérida, Mexico.*

Creighton, S. H. 1998. *Greening the Ivory Tower: Improving the Environmental Track Record of Colleges and Universities.* Cambridge, MA: MIT Press.

Eagan, D.J. and Keniry, J. (1998) *Green Investment, Green Return: How Practical Conservation Projects Save Millions on America's Campuses.* Washington, DC: National Wildlife Federation.

Keniry, J. (1995) *Ecodemia: Campus Environmental Stewardship at the Turn of the 21st Century.* Washington, DC: National Wildlife Federation.

Rollins College, Environmental Studies Department (1998) *Winter Springs Town Center Greenspace Plan* (Executive Summary). Michael Design Associates, Inc., Dover, Kohl and Partners.

Strauss, B. H. (1996) *The Class of 2000 Report: Environmental Education, Practices and Activism on Campus.* New York, NY: Nathans Cummings Foundation.

Chapter 13

The Dutch Sustainability Award for Higher Education 1998

Hanno Lans

Abstract

Do universities teach their students to handle environmental and sustainability aspects? All studies and all Faculties ought to do that to achieve a sustainable society. Such a society needs people who act according to the challenges of sustainable development. In companies, government, arts and science. Everywhere. The Dutch Ministry of Education and the Ministry of Environment are encouraging higher education institutions to integrate environmental and sustainability aspects in the curricula. To put inspiring initiatives in the spotlight, the Departments awarded an attractive prize in 1998: The Dutch Sustainability Award for Higher Education 1998. This article describes the nominations, the organisation and the criteria.

Introduction

The "Dutch Sustainability Award for Higher Education" is a practical example of stimulating the greening of education at universities. The award both stimulated new initiatives to integrate sustainable development in curricula as well as highlighting existing initiatives. As a result of the Award there is now more clarity about criteria for sustainable development in curricula. Because of the effectiveness of the Award, the government will continue to award the prize, in addition to its existing funds for greening higher education (US$ 500.000 annually).

The award consisted of two prizes of US$ 50.000 as well as two small stimulating prizes. The two prizes were meant for two categories of higher education systems in the Netherlands: universities and 'hogescholen' (universities for professional education).

Note of the editor: in this chapter, as elsewhere in the book, there are occasions when the term "Faculty" do not refer to academic staff (as in North America) , but to units within a university.

The aim of the award was to stimulate and to promote initiatives for greening curricula in all disciplines. The award was meant for non-environmental programs. Environmental studies or environmental care projects could only participate when they led to the greening of other education programs. The jury asked all Faculties, studies and clusters of studies, which had started to integrate environment and sustainability, to send in their initiatives. The jury nominated seven initiatives, which are described below. Award winners were the Technical University of Delft and the Van Hall Institute.

The nominations

Stoas APH Dronten - Stoas APH is an agricultural teacher institution   (Agricultural College). Stoas aims to help students to develop capacities for a just and sustainable world. This means an emphasis on personal vision, ethics and attitudes. The project was initiated by one teacher and has been extended to the whole institution. A close connection exists between the environmental care system, natural environment and the education program.

Faculty of Engineering, University for Professional Education Ijsselland, Deventer - The Faculty runs the project 'sustainable Faculty'. This Faculty presents a clear example of a metamorphosis towards an environmental and sustainability approach. Sustainable development is seen as a challenge for the disciplines town and country planning, technical management and material technology. Step by step other faculties have become involved, such as teacher training, business and health. Environment is an aspect of most courses and the teaching methods are interactive. The university building is a national example of energy saving building methods.

Faculty of Engineering, University of Twente - The discipline of engineering demands more than ever, knowledge of other disciplines. Engineering should be based on environmental aspects. This initiative stimulates environmental awareness and life cycle analysis by engineering students. Energy-analysis, flow sheeting, diffusion, transport and risks analysis are part of the program. Students work together in a course to analyse the energy cycle of products based on a special software database. Besides this, it is possible to specialize in green technology.

Animal farming, Agricultural University Wageningen - The section zootechnology of the Agricultural University Wageningen integrated the systems approach into the program of animal farming. The environmental problems of animal farming are discussed in many countries. Social and ethical aspects are taken into account. The impact on international students and co-operation with developing countries is seen as positive.

Technical University Eindhoven - The Technical University Eindhoven gives students of all disciplines the opportunity to obtain the certificate 'technology for sustainable development'. A one-year study in the field of sustainable technology is required. Students are able to show the labor market their green capacities. Although this is an optional certification, this initiative led to the situation that all faculties started up green courses. The next step will be a compulsory green introductory course for all disciplines.

Faculty of Architecture, Technical University Delft - This university is the Award winner of the Dutch universities. For the past 20 years the working group SOM at the Faculty of Architecture has been responding to the environmental challenges and needs for sustainable architecture. Sustainability is presented as a challenge towards all students of architecture in a special environmental course IMAGO. In other courses the environmental aspects are part of the course. The faculty plays a leading role in developing models and ideas for sustainable architecture. Use of materials, solar energy, energy saving, renovation and urban environment are taken into account.

Van Hall Institute Leeuwarden - The Van Hall Institute in Leeuwarden is the Award winner in the category higher professional education. The project 'the green university' involves all departments and the institutional co-ordination is very strong. Besides, ethics is an important aspect in the curricula and the university is situated in a sustainable building. Management, business centre, teaching and technical staff are all involved. Regional co-operation, such as software development, advising and training is part of the project. Teaching staff evaluate the green aspects of the curricula on a regular basis.

Stimulating prizes

The project 'Environment in Business Management' is a consortium of three business Faculties (Hanzehogeschool Groningen, Fontys University of Eindhoven and Van Hall Institute Leeuwarden). This new project aims to integrate sustainable business courses into the programs, to set up green specialisation possibilities and to start training programs for business people. The jury loved this initiative in this important field.

The integration of sustainability at the Faculty of Literature at the University of Groningen is remarkable.The project 'sustainable living with the natural environment' is an initiative of the section history and archaeology. Courses are given on the history of man and environment in specific regions, and are suited to students of history, archaeology and literature. These courses are optional, but in the near future some of them will be part of the core curricula. In the opinion of the jury, this initiative demonstrated perfectly the ways in which it is possible for humanities and liberal arts to incorporate sustainability into their programs.

The organisation

The idea of the Award started during a congress in 1996 organised by the student network for sustainable development, LHUMP. The former Minister of Education, Mr Ritzen, stated that higher education institutions should be forerunners for sustainability, and promised to set up an award. The integration of sustainable development in higher education was insufficient, despite governmental policy and the signing of the Copernicus-charter by the universities. After lobbying of LHUMP, the Minister indeed initiated the prize and both the Ministry of Education and the Ministry of Environment set aside a sum of money.

At the end of 1997 both Ministries instructed the Institute for Environmental Education, SME, to co-ordinate the Award. In January 1998 a mailing was send out to the Rectors of all higher education institutions. Besides this mailing, an electronic message was also distributed by the association of universities to contacts of the student network LHUMP. A submission form was included for the registration of initiatives.   This form was also downloadable at the website of the Ministry of Education. On four pages, a Faculty or university had to describe their initiative. It was difficult for the organisation to define the questions. Some research was done to find out indicators for green higher education. There was hardly any literature about indicators for sustainable curricula; most literature was focused on environmental studies, primary/secondary education or on environmental management. Nevertheless, the questionnaire   (form)   worked well.

The response was overwhelming. Before the deadline we knew nothing about the number or quality level of the initiatives. Of course we also made an overview in advance of interesting initiatives and asked them to participate. No less than 30 entries were received, from a broad range of studies: law, agriculture, history, industrial design, architecture, teacher education, science, management and tourism.

A jury was appointed. The jury members were former Minister of Environment and former UNEP director Mr Alders, Mr Van Gelder, provincial governor, Mr Van der Plas, former rector of Wageningen and one of the initiators of the Copernicus-charter, Ms Olijdam as representative of the Student Union and LHUMP and Ms Hommes, former professor.

The jury developed criteria during their meetings and in agreement with the secretary. The chosen seven entries were asked to work out a longer description as well as a presentation.

On April 15th 1998 the Minister of Environment, Mrs. de Boer, and a representative of the Minister of Education, presented the Award in The Hague. Policy-makers and key persons of the universities were invited. More than a hundred persons were present. The presentation of each nomination took 10 minutes and was supported by computer animated projections. Nominees were also asked to make a poster presentation that could be looked at during the break.

Participants of the meeting were enthusiastic to start up a network afterwards. The evaluation showed that the participants were satisfied too. They were very positive about the Award as an instrument to green higher education and show progress in this field. The Award handled sustainable development in higher education in a very positive way, and gave teachers the opportunity to get attention and appreciation in their own institution.

It was suggested that the nominees should also be given a prize because of the time invested, that more work be invested in the PR at the end, and that the Award be repeated on a regular base.

Afterwards a book was published which has since been distributed to all institutions. The content of the book includes background information on the scheme, the jury report, a description of all the initiatives and a list of useful addresses and literature. The Ministries also saw the results in a very positive light and decided to continue the Award.

The criteria

The focus of the Award was on how programs teach their students to handle environmental and sustainability aspects. So, the criteria should be primarily based on the students' curriculum. Secondly, the integration process is important for the continuity of the initiative. And finally, institutional commitment ensures a positive image, impact and consistency of the initiative.

Institutional commitment

The jury tried to get an idea about the impact of the initiative on society. They examined the activities for the local community and developing countries. According to Agenda 21, research and education institutions should work closely together with the local community for sustainable development and start international co-operation with developing countries.

An environmental care system on the part of the institution is important for green consistency towards students. This was not a crucial criterion because most of the initiatives did not have the authority to influence the environmental care on a central institutional level.

Integration process

An important question is if the initiative itself is based within a Faculty or curriculum which is already defined as 'Environmental Studies'. Integrating sustainable development in environmental studies can be seen as quality improvement or actualisation of the curriculum, not as a real integration process. The jury skipped some entries that are focussed on environmental studies and and thus did not extend their influence to non-environmental studies. Other entries succeeded in reaching other studies, for example by offering environmental courses.

If it is real integration, what about the maturity of the initiative? Is the initiative already fully embedded in the curriculum or still in process? The Award is not aimed at new, unproven initiatives. Because of this, some new promising initiatives (especially in humanities and business education) could not be nominated.

Training of teachers is important to green all the courses of the program. Only some initiatives really succeeded in motivating the teaching staff to regularly deepen and to focus on sustainable development. The jury also took into account the effects on the higher education institution. Are other faculties or programs stimulated to join or start an integration initiative?

Students' curriculum

Most important is the students' curriculum itself. The students' curriculum consists of all the courses a student should attend to graduate in his or her discipline. The jury discussed both the quality as well as the quantity of the sustainability aspects.

The jury looked at the position of environment and sustainability in the curriculum, both the spread over the years, the compulsory character and the weight of the courses. Is there, for example, only a green course in the preliminary examination or is sustainability repeated in courses up until the thesis? Is environment and sustainability offered in optional courses or also as part of the compulsory courses? The jury was also interested in the number of credits students could get with sustainability. It became clear that it is unimportant whether integration began with one compulsory green course focusing on sustainable development or whether students attended several courses in which the aspect of sustainability was interwoven. The result should be a consequent green focus on the discipline throughout the entire course. Optional courses are seen as important for students and teachers specialising in environmental aspects, although they are no solution for a real green program. Sustainable development is too important to be omitted.

Every discipline seems to have its own buzzwords (e.g. life-cycle analysis, organic agriculture, social responsibility), and perspective towards sustainable development. This is important to keep in mind when defining the 'green' courses. Engineering and science courses have many opportunities to focus on the environmental impact of the discipline. Other disciplines focus on sustainable development as an important ethical and social issue (for example, cases in business education or politics), or as a way to understand the history of human nature (nature-culture relation in arts, psychology and history).

One of the challenges of sustainable development is the need for interdisciplinary co-operation, problem-solving capacities and ethical reflection. This can be seen as the quality of integration.

Table 1 - Indicators for the integration of sustainable development in higher education programs
Institutional commitment ❑   Co-operation with the local community ❑   Co-operation with developing countries ❑   Environmental care system
Integration process ❑   Is it a non-environmental study program ❑   Policy for training and motivation of teachers ❑   Maturity of the integration process ❑   Impact towards the greening of other curricula

Students curriculum (most important aspect)
❑   Compulsory courses with aspects of sustainability in each year
❑   Optional courses with aspects of sustainability in each year
❑   Spreading of the courses
❑   Quality of the cluster of these courses:
          - participation of students in working groups
          - working with students from other disciplines
          - broadness of sustainability subjects
          - ethics and personal reflection

The jury preferred initiatives with green courses where students are confronted with the environment in an active and problem oriented way, especially where there were groups with students and teachers from both science and humanities programmes. Sustainable development is complex and needs interdisciplinary perspectives.

Summing up, the jury took into account the students' curriculum, the process of integration and institutional commitment, with the main focus on the students' curriculum. As far as the curriculum is concerned, the prime need is to define the green courses in each year and afterwards focus on the quality. In Table 1 all indicators are listed.

Problems in the selection process

The initiatives nominated were all from agricultural and engineering courses. Their longer tradition of integrating environmental aspects into their curriculum is due to environmental regulations and public debates in these sectors. Initiatives from other disciplines were in an early stage of development. The jury hoped to nominate a broader range of disciplines. An improvement might be to make some categories of disciplines.

Another point to be made is about the 'translation' of the concept of sustainable development in the various disciplines. Engineers talk about life-cycle analysis in product development, teacher training works on nature experiences and justice. Management education works on environment, labor and quality. It is important to keep this aspect in mind when comparing the initiatives.

Another difficulty was the range of initiatives. Most were focused on curriculum level, but surprisingly, some universities sent in initiatives to integrate sustainability in all their programs. The nominations of Delft and Eindhoven differed in this respect. How to choose between these initiatives, between a little green in all curricula or a lot of green in one curriculum?

Institutions pro-active with sustainable development argue that they listen to the labour market and societal needs. Some others highlight their own mission and relation with the community. Sustainable development is even the key mission for some institutions.

Some institutions noticed a lack of interest in environmental issues on the part of the students. But, this mostly depends on the way it is taught. Multi-disciplinary education, problem oriented education, discussions about ethics are integrated in the regular curriculum. Afterwards, students are enthusiastic and become aware of their discipline and the environment. A side effect of multi-disciplinary education is that teachers form teams, and discussions take place between teachers about their disciplines.

Evaluation

When talking about integration of sustainable development, it is important to focus on the course from a student's point of view: the curriculum. When and how does a student get sustainability in his/her curriculum. From that perspective it is also important to focus on the compulsory, core his/her curriculum. From that perspective it is also important to focus on the compulsory, core curriculum. Optional courses are relevant and necessary for interested, environmentally aware students. But they are not sufficient to educate all students to be environmentally aware. There are two important distinctions to consider regarding the core curriculum: you can analyse the quantity of sustainable development elements, and you can have a look at the quality of the sustainable development aspects. Both are important. Some curricula pay only a few hours´ attention to the environmental effects. Other curricula pay a lot of attention to technical solutions, but fail to mention the social and ethical aspects.

The evaluation showed that teachers, government and students were enthusiastic about the Award as an instrument to green higher education and show good examples. The government shows its awareness for the importance of sustainable higher education. The result has been potential networks, an overview of projects and an impulse for new initiatives. It seems that such an Award can be a powerful instrument for governments to motivate universities.

References

CRE (1994) *Copernicus-Charter*. Geneva: CRE.

Lans, H., Vos, J.P. (eds) (1998) *Duurzame ontwikkeling en hoger onderwijs*. Gravenhage: Elsevier bedrijfsinformatie.

LHUMP (1998) web pages: *www.studentssupport.nl/lhump*.

Chapter 14

Transformation or Irrelevance:
The Challenge of Academic Planning for Environmental Education in the 21ST Century[45]

David W. Orr

Abstract

This chapter contains some consideration on the subject matter of academic planning and sustainability, as well as a description of the sustainability principles behind the Environmental Studies Centre at Oberlin College.

Preface

The subject of this paper this is academic planning. The challenge of equipping students to participate in the building of a sustainable and decent society is the fundamental challenge to educational institutions at all levels. What would it mean for colleges and universities to get serious about „the underlying intellectual issues and moral imperatives of having responsibility for the earth, and to do so with an intensity and ingenuity matching that shown by previous generations in obeying the command to have dominion over the planet"? (Pelikan, 1992). In exploring that question, I will organize my remarks in three parts beginning with the factors that may explain, in part, why colleges and universities have been so slow to respond to environmental issues. In the second part I will describe a project on my campus that required a radically different approach to planning. In the third section I will offer some reflections about how we might improve environmental planning.

---

[45] *Note of the editor: This paper, which has been slightly edited, was initially published in „Academic Planning in College and University Environmental Programs: Proceedings of the 1998 Sanibel Symposium", edited by Peter Blaze Corcoran, James L. Elder and Richard Tchen. Many thanks to the author and editors for the permission to reproduce it.*

Part I

It is increasingly obvious that within the lifetimes of students now attending college, world population is expected to rise to a number between 9-12 billion people, human actions will drive perhaps 20% of the species now on the earth into extinction, and the emission of heat trapping gases will force global climate into a less stable and probably far less desirable state. Surveying these and other global trends, 102 Nobel laureates in science and 1600 other scientists from 70 countries signed the *World Scientists' Warning to Humanity* (1992) which read in part:

> "Human beings and the natural world are on a collision course. . . . If not checked, many of our current practices put at serious risk the future that we wish for human society and . . . may so alter the living world that it will be unable to sustain life in the manner that we know. Fundamental changes are urgent if we are to avoid the collision our present course will bring about.
>
> We the undersigned, senior members of the world's scientific community, hereby warn all humanity of what lies ahead. A great change in our stewardship of the earth and the life on it is required, if vast human misery is to be avoided and our global home on this planet is not to be irretrievably mutilated."

A substantial and growing body of scientific evidence, in fact, confirms the view that humans are at or near critical thresholds of planetary stability and ecological carrying capacity. Evidence that we are crossing these thresholds will become apparent in increasing disease, famine, species extinction, habitat destruction, ecological instability, increasing number and severity of storms, drought, heat waves, technological accidents caused by a growing willingness to do things we would otherwise not want to do, and growing violence over the control of water and resources. Humankind, in other words, is now in the first truly global crisis that concerns our survival as a species, the terms by which we might do so, and what it means to be human. Since mutual dependence on a common global environment is the one thing all of us share, global change is not just another issue on a long list, but the lens through which all other issues must be seen.

All of us here today have heard such things many times before. Most of you have uttered similar warnings. And all of you have labored long and hard to change the curriculum and operational directions of your own institutions. But relative to the magnitude of the challenges ahead, the inescapable fact is that 20-25 years of dedicated and often visionary work to build environment into the curriculum have not dented the problem. Higher education goes on much as it has for a century or more, but now with computers. In the face of impending problems and potential catastrophes described in the World Scientists Warning, the response of colleges and universities is generally lethargic. As a result, despite the growth in numbers of environmental studies programs, most college and university graduates are fundamentally ignorant about ecology, global environmental change, and why these things ought to matter to them. Why have institutions of higher education - of all organizations - been so complacent in the face of mounting evidence that humanity is in real jeopardy of mutilating its earthly home. This is not, on the surface at least, what one might expect of institutions dedicated to advancing knowledge and presumably to the health of the world their students will inherit. Yet virtually everywhere there is a pattern of denial, evidence of what Thomas Berry calls "a deep cultural pathology." Why is this so?

The answers, I think, lie at different levels. First, at an organizational level denial is embedded in the very fabric of bureaucracy, management, and committee structure characteristic of higher education in the post World War II era. Colleges and universities have become over managed and under-led institutions operating more and more like businesses with customers. College presidents increasingly regard themselves as CEOs whose chief mission is fundraising. Few think of themselves as intellectual and moral leaders and will not often involve themselves in controversies that jeopardize their upward mobility. The result is a poverty of wisdom in high places reinforced by a fundamental ignorance of ecology and the basics of global change. If administrators (and trustees) are aware of the reality of global change, that awareness is seldom allowed to influence institutional priorities. Institutions of higher education are, accordingly, governed on the assumption that business will continue more or less as usual for as long as the mind can imagine. Blindness, and sometimes outright ignorance, is reinforced by the financial and ideological dependence of colleges and universities that tends to make them reluctant, unimaginative, and mostly toothless critics of everything from free trade and the electronic global economy to the efforts underway to re-engineer the fabric of life.

At the faculty level, denial takes the form of excuses that we simply do not have the time or expertise to worry about issues beyond our particular specialization, especially those that make us feel uncomfortable in polite circumstances. It simply does not pay for scholars to question the anthropocentrism or "pre-analytic" assumptions buried in their disciplines to say nothing about questioning those of other disciplines. Those who do, are mostly either safely tenured or short-timers who go on to careers outside the academy. For all of the talk about freedom of inquiry, the fact is that all-too-often disciplinary standards, professional loyalties, and words like "rigor" are used to suppress debate about fundamental assumptions and paradigms. Colleges and universities, often regarded as places of radicalism, are seldom very radical about issues having to do with the environment. In this regard, the striking fact about faculty life is not so much the conversations that we have as those we do not have. I am thinking of the urgent need for biologists to converse with economists or ethicists to talk with genetic engineers. When such conversations do occur, the results can be provocative and fundamentally important

There is more to be said, however. Denial is not just a way of avoiding the future, it is also a way to avoid discussing our own complicity in the larger problems of our time. In his time, George Orwell noted that:

> "we all live by robbing Asiatic coolies and those of us who are 'enlightened' all maintain that those coolies ought to be set free; but our standard of living and hence our 'enlightenment,' demands that the robbery shall continue."

Not much has changed. In an ecological perspective, we continue to live comfortably by robbing the poor and diminishing the prospects of our children. In the words of Catholic theologian Thomas Berry:

"The university, as now functioning, prepares students for their role in extending human dominion over the natural world, not for intimate presence to the natural world. Use of this power in a deleterious manner has devastated the planet. We suddenly discover that we are losing some of our most exalted human experiences that come to us through our participation in the natural world about us. So awesome is the devastation we are bringing about that we can only conclude that we are caught in a deep cultural pathology, a pathology that is sustained intellectually by the university, economically by the corporation, legally by the constitution, religiously by the church."

All of us here tonight are part of this system. We are well paid. We have sabbaticals and time off to do research. We fly to exotic places to discuss how to save the world thereby adding to the problem of climatic change. Relative to the vast majority of people, we have a good thing going. And our standard of living and our enlightenment, too, demands that the theft continue.

As for our students, despite the rise in interest in environmental problems in the past 20 years, most will graduate knowing little about the environment and see scant reason to care. An annual survey of entering freshman indicates that 74.9% of incoming first-year students prefer being "well-off" to developing a philosophy of life or improving their minds (New York Times, January 1, 1998). Interest in causes such as environment or racial justice has apparently declined sharply. Twenty years earlier the percentages were reversed. The study concludes that this is the most apathetic and apolitical generation surveyed since the poll began.

The practical effect of denial at all levels becomes evident when colleges and universities develop "Strategic Plans" to chart their future. The results are seldom very strategic nor are they often useful as plans. Mostly, they are full of self-congratulation and empty posturing intending to improve their "market share" of students and raise money. And none that I have seen acknowledges that environmental change on a global scale has anything to do with the educational mission of the particular institution or that it might radically alter the lives and career prospects of their students. Most institutional planning reflects old and worn out assumptions that Homo sapiens is an insignificant force in nature. Planning documents are accordingly filled with undefined phrases about diversity, multiculturalism, and social empathy without saying what these words have to do with the preservation of biological and real cultural diversity. Only a few colleges have made knowledge of how the physical world works a high priority for their students or an operational priority for the institution. But many have made student "wellness" a major priority by building campus fitness centers and putting salad bars in dining centers without apparent awareness that human wellness in a sick environment is temporary at best. In short, planning in higher education seldom reflects the central fact of our existence—that aware of it or not, we are part of an ecological community and that community is coming undone in no small measure because of the choices and actions of highly educated people. What can be done?

Part II

Most of what little I know at first hand about academic planning I have learned in the past three years in an effort to design and build an Environmental Studies Center on the Oberlin College campus. My official role was to raise the necessary funds from "sources not otherwise likely to give to the college." Less officially, I was heavily involved in the selection of the architect, development of the building program, and building design. My experience, described below, may or may not be entirely typical of planning on other campuses. In broad outline, however, I think the case may shed light on how campus planning relative to environmental issues might be improved.

In June of 1995 with the leadership and active support of a new President, Nancy Dye, the Trustees of Oberlin College granted approval to raise funds and design an Environmental Studies Center that would meet advanced standards for ecological design. My role in the project entailed both fund-raising and facilitating the design process. The project was not done as part of a major capital campaign because doing so would have delayed the project indefinitely, and the likelihood of the Environmental Studies Center being included in any such campaign would have been small in any event. In short, to be done at all, the project would have to occur outside the normal planning and fund-raising activities of the college. Moreover, opportunity presented itself in the arrival of a new President sympathetic to environmental studies and to curricular innovation generally.

The project had a history that extended back to the mid-1980s with faculty discussions about creating an environmental center. Those discussions, however, resulted in no action. In 1992-1993 a year-long class on ecological design rekindled the idea and developed a pre-program for an Environmental Studies Center at Oberlin College. Twenty-five students and a dozen architects met over two semesters to discuss ecological design and to develop the core ideas for the project. We began by questioning why we ought to do anything at all. Once the need for facilities was established, participants questioned whether we ought to build new facilities or renovate an existing building. After careful analysis students and faculty settled on the necessity for new construction. The basic program that emerged from the year-long effort called for a ~14,000 square ft building that:

- discharged no wastewater, i.e. "drinking water in, drinking water out";

- generated from sunlight more electricity than it used over the course of a year;

- used no materials known to be carcinogenic, mutagenic, or endocrine disrupters;

- used energy and materials with great efficiency;

- promoted competence with environmental technologies;

- used products and materials grown or manufactured sustainably;

- was landscaped to promote biological diversity;

- promoted analytical skill in assessing full costs over the lifetime of the building;

- promoted ecological competence and mindfulness of place;

- became in its design and operations, genuinely pedagogical; and

- met rigorous requirements for full-cost accounting.

We intended, in other words, a building that caused no ugliness, human or ecological, somewhere else or at some later time.

When finally allowed to proceed in June, 1995 the terms of the approval set stringent boundaries on the risks the college was willing to accept. Funds could not be solicited from any source connected with the college and from none expected to give in the future. I was given two years in which to raise funds and complete the basic design work. Both requirements influenced the pace and character of the project. The fact that we could not solicit funds from donors affiliated in one way or another with the College required that the building be designed to be as widely appealing as possible. But no other kind of building would be worth doing anyway. The short timetable required that we move quickly to select an architect and design team and get on with the job at hand.

To help coordinate the design of the project and to engage students, faculty, and the wider community in the design process, I hired two graduates from the Class of 1993. I also engaged California Polytechnic University architect, John Lyle, to help conduct the major design charettes or planning sessions that began in the fall of 1995. Some 250 students, faculty, and community members participated in the thirteen charettes in which the goals for the Center were developed and refined. This was the first time in anyone's recollection that students were engaged in the actual design of a college building. Our intent was to make the design experience as educational as possible. Overall, it worked quite well.

In the same period we advertised the project nationally and eventually received 26 applications from architectural firms with interests in the emerging field of "green architecture." We selected five for interview and in January of 1996 selected William McDonough & Partners in Charlottesville, Virginia as the lead design firm. With their help we also assembled a design team of engineers, landscape architects, and others that would meet throughout the process. To fulfill the requirement that the building generate more electricity than it used, we engaged Amory Lovins and Bill Browning from the Rocky Mountain Institute as well as scientists from NASA's Lewis Space Center. In order to meet the standard of zero discharge we engaged the services of John Todd and Michael Shaw - the leading figures in the field of ecological engineering. For landscaping we brought in John Lyle and the firm of Andropogen, Inc. from Philadelphia. To this team we added a structural and mechanical engineering firm from New York City, a firm to model energy performance, and a local contractor. During the programming and schematic design phase this team and representatives from the College met by conference call weekly and in regular face-to-face sessions.

The team approach to architectural design was new for the College. Typically, the architects do their work alone, passing finished blueprints along to the structural and mechanical engineers who are told to heat and cool it and hand the project off to the landscape architects to prettify the results. By engaging the full design team from the beginning we intended to maximize the integration of building systems and technologies and that between the building and its landscape. Early on, we decided that the standard for technology in the building was to be state-of-the-shelf, but that for the overall design of the building and its various systems was to be state-of-the-art. In other words, we did not want the risk of untried technologies, but we did want the overall product to be at the frontier of what it is now possible to do with ecologically smart design.

The building program called for major changes, not only in the design process but also in the selection of materials, relationship to manufacturers, and in the way we counted the costs of the project. We intended to use materials that did not compromise the dignity or health of people somewhere else. We also wanted to use materials that had as little embodied fossil energy as possible, hence giving preference to those locally manufactured or grown. In the process we discovered how little is generally known about the ecological and human effects of materials use and how little the present tax and pricing system supports standards upholding ecological or human integrity. Unsurprisingly, we also discovered that the present system of building codes and permitting does little to encourage innovation leading to greater resource efficiency and environmental quality.

Typical buildings are a snapshot of the state of technology at the time they were designed and obsolesce quickly thereafter. In this case, however, we intended for the building to remain technologically dynamic over a long period of time. In effect, we proposed that the building adapt or learn as the state of technology changed and as our understanding of design became more sophisticated. This meant that we did not want to own particular components of the building such as the power system (photovoltaics and fuel cells) which would become obsolete as technology advanced. We are exploring other arrangements, including leasing materials and technologies that will change markedly over the lifetime of the building.

The same strategy applied to materials. William McDonough & Partners regarded the building as a union of two different metabolisms, one industrial, the other ecological. Materials that might eventually decompose into soil were considered part of an ecological metabolism. Otherwise they were part of an industrial metabolism and might be leased from the manufacturer as a "product of service" and eventually returned as a feedstock to be remanufactured into new products. Interface Corporation in Atlanta, for example, is leasing the carpet and raised flooring for the center for $1/year and will exchange it at the end of its useful lifetime.

Further, standard cost accounting includes only costs of design and construction. As a consequence, institutions tend to ignore operating costs that buildings incur over their expected lifetimes as well as all of those other costs to environment and human health that are not included in the prices of energy, materials, and waste disposal. In this project we plan to account for the full costs of the project including those to the environment. Overall, the budget for the Center ($6.1 million) is higher than a typical building of the same size because we included:

- students, faculty, and community members in the design process;

- research into materials and technologies to meet program goals;

- higher performance standards, eg. zero discharge and net energy export;

- more sophisticated technologies;

- greater efforts to integrate technologies and systems;

- a building maintenance fund in the project budget.

In addition, we plan to do a materials audit of the building, including an estimate of the amount of CO_2 released because of the project along with a proposal of ways to offset these costs.

Finally, when all of the systems are operational the building will produce its own electricity, saving ~$21,000/year. The college has agreed to contribute the saved costs for five years into a building endowment fund to be matched 1:1.5 by the Heinz foundation. In other words, we will use savings from energy efficiency and renewables to fund building maintenance over the longer term.

The project is on schedule for a summer, 1998 groundbreaking with a tentative completion date in mid-1999. The basic energy, lighting, and fluid dynamics models have been completed and we now know that the goals described in the building program can be met. The anticipated energy performance of the building (figure one) will be half or less of what is now considered to be the "green" standard.

HEATING, VENTILATION, AC, & LIGHTING COSTS *(PER FT²/YEAR)*			
	ESCTR	„GREEN"	AVERAGE
BTU's/FT²/YR	10,500-15,000	30-50,000	70,000
$/FT²/YR	.20-.29	.80	1.00-1.50
SAVINGS/YR: (w/o pv's)	xxx	$6,783	$16,093
TOTAL ENERGY BUDGET: 39,000-58,500 kwh/yr			

Figure 1: The anticipated energy performance of the building

Moreover, when all of the systems are completed, the building will generate the electricity it will use from a combination of photovoltaics and fuel cell designed by NASA. It will purify wastewater on site. It will minimize or eliminate the use of toxic materials. It will be designed to remain technologically dynamic well into the future. It will be instrumented to display energy and significant ecological data in a central atrium. We intend for the wood and other materials used in the building to be purchased from forests that meet the highest standards for ecological management. The story of the building will be prominently displayed throughout the structure. It will be landscaped to include a small wetland and forest as well as gardens, orchards, and greenhouse. In short, it is being designed and built to instruct future students in the arts of ecological competence and the possibilities of ecological design applied to buildings, energy systems, wastewater, agriculture, landscapes, and technology. As important as the building and its landscape are, the more important effects of the project have been its impact on those who participated in the project. Some of the students who devoted time and energy to the project began to describe it as „our legacy" to the College. Because of their work on the project many of them learned about ecological design and how to solve real problems by doing it with some of the best practitioners in the world. Some of the faculty who participated in the effort and who were skeptical about the possibility of changing the institution, came to see change as sometimes possible.

Part III

What would required for colleges and universities to respond to the challenges and opportunities ahead with energy and imagination? I would like to offer seven suggestions based on the experience described above.

1. Develop Leadership. The essential factor in the Oberlin project was the support of the President. Without it the project would not have been possible. Generally, however, I think it is fair to say that relative to issues having to do with the long-term sustainability of the human enterprise there is a leadership vacuum in higher education. This vacuum is evidence of a general ignorance of the dynamics and substance of environmental problems in high places. The large majority of college administrators simply have not thought very deeply about long-term ecological and population trends or how their institution might respond to them. In this regard colleges are a bit like ships at sea with storm clouds ahead and no one scanning the horizon from the crow's nest. Accordingly, colleges and universities need a new generation of leadership dedicated to overcoming the complacency, self-congratulation, and busyness that often pervades higher education.

Therefore, serious efforts to improve both the substance and process of environmental planning in higher education must begin with efforts to remedy the ecological illiteracy of those who commission, conduct, and evaluate plans. The solution, admittedly easier said than done, is to implement efforts to improve ecological literacy of administrators and trustees in the same way that Second Nature is doing through faculty workshops.

2. Institutional Policy. After detailed analysis of the energy performance of buildings on the Stanford University campus one engineering student wrote that „Stanford's buildings may not be illegal, but they are irresponsible" (Selmon and Schneider, 1997, p.28). The same could be said of all but a handful of buildings on college campuses and most campus operations for that matter. But it is possible to design buildings and entire campuses that are energy efficient, powered by current sunlight, discharge no waste, and demonstrate ecological competence (Lyle, 1994). And through better design we can teach our students that our ecological problems are solvable and that doing so would help to solve other problems as well.

The creation of the Oberlin environmental studies center was more difficult than it should have been because the college, like most others, has no energy or environmental policy for new construction and none for operations, purchasing, investment, or curriculum. Yet on most campuses there are good models in the form of policy guidelines and administrative procedures that guide efforts to develop and upgrade computer literacy, and improve fairness between people of different gender, sexual orientation, and race. There is also a small, but growing, number of institutions implementing rigorous standards for energy efficiency, recycling, water, and waste. The important planning questions have to do with how all colleges might be energized to rethink what the various measures of institutional success paraded in annual surveys of colleges and universities mean at a time when the entire human enterprise is in jeopardy.

Any such policy ought to begin with a benchmark audit of inputs and outputs and set targets that steadily improve energy and resource efficiency, reduce CO_2 emissions, close waste loops, and minimize environmental impacts over a period of years as if evolution, ecology, thermodynamics, and the long-term future really mattered. That policy ought to set upper levels for acceptable paybacks for the increased costs sometimes incurred by improved efficiency and environmental performance at, say, ten years, equivalent to an annual rate of return of 7%. Further, an environmental policy ought to include practical steps to use institutional buying and investments to help leverage the emergence of sustainable communities in the surrounding region. For example, buying locally from manufacturers and farmers who do their work with care for the environment ought to become a central part of institutional policy.

3. Promote Innovation. Colleges are often risk-averse institutions in which the cardinal rule for administrators and faculty alike seems to be: do not make a mistake. The penalties for taking chances are generally high enough that few are willing to risk much. As a result, institutions of higher education innovate slowly and painfully. In the words of one study:

> "Colleges and universities are indeed insulated from many competitive pressures; they have no stockholders, and their governing boards have few ready measures to judge performance . . . Thus top university administrators often operate reactively. Their agendas are molded by whoever is sufficiently motivated to demand their attention. Short-run problem solving erodes the time available to focus on the 'big picture'" (Siegfried, Getz, Anderson, 1995).

Institutional conservatism in the case described above occurred as constant pressure to eliminate all financial risk to the college, regardless of longer term benefits in the form of educational opportunities for students, improved admissions yield, and favorable publicity. Being on budget became more important than achieving the larger vision. The project came perilously close to being shelved after one year because estimated costs were thought to be rising faster than pledges. In such circumstances, the reaction of the institution was to reduce the scope of the program or, perhaps, to terminate the project altogether.

Ironically, the „make no mistake" strategy can create costs and risks of a different sort. Indecisiveness, in the guise of fiscal conservatism, added perhaps 10-15% to the overall costs of the project described above and caused significant delays that increased costs further. But the greater risk is that higher education will simply fail to respond with vigor and imagination to the largest issues on the human agenda which indirectly and directly have to do with population growth, resources, climate stability, soil loss, and biotic impoverishment. The contrast between colleges and corporations in this regard is striking. No viable business could long survive the kind of complacency and inertia characteristic of most institutions of higher education.

There are many good reasons for Colleges and universities to encourage staff, faculty, and administrators to take initiative for good cause without fear of penalty if things do not work out. The question is how, not whether, to encourage the spirit of innovation throughout the institution. Beyond removing the penalties for failure, institutions can encourage innovation through a variety of measures beginning with simple recognition of those who do it. Further, innovators ought to be rewarded financially. Savings or avoided costs from improved efficiency, for example, ought to be reinvested into a fund to finance ongoing innovation and reward personal initiative.

4. Integrated Planning. The Oberlin project program required us to design not just a building, but a whole system integrating technology, energy use, life cycle costs of materials, structure, the landscape, environmental impacts, and the larger educational purposes. This, in turn, required an unusual level of creativity, flexibility, collegiality, and a high tolerance for risk. Operationally, the project required a high level of integration across departments and operational divisions of the college including the office of construction, college operations, finance and development, various faculty departments, the architects, and members of the design team. This level of integration proved to be difficult to achieve and the project came close to collapse again late in the second year. It was saved only when the President brought in an outside facilitator to mediate between the design team and college officials.

For a variety of reasons having to do with turf protection, division of labor, and the low priority assigned to the environment, college planning tends to be fragmentary and short term. There are few incentives to do system-wide planning which requires transcending administrative departments or administrative-academic boundaries even when there are good financial or intellectual reasons to do so. Budgetary planning tends to be short term precluding life-cycle costing. The alternative, which Peter Senge calls the „learning organization," is a more fluid, open, adaptable, farsighted, and forgiving kind of organization (Senge, 1990). It would be ironic indeed if academic institutions had to learn how to learn from the more progressive part of the business world.

5. Planning begins with the Educational Mission. The planning for the this project began not by projecting the trajectory of one discipline or another but rather by asking what students would need to know in order to help make a sustainable and sustaining world in the 21st century. The answer students themselves gave included such things as knowledge of solar technologies, ecological design, full-cost accounting, and practical skills of restoration ecology, gardening, horticulture, and forestry. The fact is that most disciplines need criticism that can only come from outside the discipline where the „pre-analytic" assumptions are open to review and criticism. Taking long-term global change seriously would require us to think more carefully about what liberal education means in our time and what our students will need to know to be relevant to the large issues of their times.

To extend this point further, campus planning ought to begin with questions about what students will need to know to help in the effort to build a sustainable world rather than questions about disciplinary priorities and abstractions about the „advancement of knowledge." The design of new science facilities, for example, might begin with an acknowledgement that we are living through a century in which scientific knowledge has often been used promiscuously. The evidence is found in nuclear weapons, holes in the ozone layer, thousands of toxic waste dumps, and even in the 300-500 chemicals inscribed in our fatty tissues that do not belong there. Could we rethink how we conduct scientific education. Could we teach chemistry, for example, as nature does it—what is being called „biomimicry"? When nature creates hazardous chemicals it does so in small amounts that are contained and are always biodegradable. Why not teach students to do chemistry similarly and to be utterly circumspect about making chemicals for which there is no evolutionary experience.

By some reckoning we are about to enter a period of promiscuous biology in which some will reengineer the fabric of life on earth more to their liking. Humankind will survive the twentieth century, but with less margin for error than we might have wanted. We are not likely, however, to survive a century of promiscuous biology in a way that enhances our humanity. To protect and enhance life in the century ahead, students will need to know many things including how to discriminate between knowledge that advances life and that which places it in jeopardy or diminishes it. Planning, accordingly, should begin with questions about values and goals then reason back to curriculum and finally to architectural design and operations.

All of this implies the need to rethink what the liberal arts mean in an ecological perspective. It means exploring the unexamined assumptions implicit in our technological fundamentalism, the controlling assumptions hidden in a curriculum organized by departments and disciplines, and the anthropocentrism that limits our willingness to see ourselves as only a part of a larger ecological community on a long evolutionary journey. Our students will need to think in patterns and systems yet, rhetoric to the contrary, we still tend to emphasize disciplinary specialization. They will need a kind of lateral rigor to combine knowledge from different fields, yet we still educate them as if rigor was exclusively vertical and meant going deeper and deeper into a particular discipline. They will need a larger sense of beauty that insists on causing no ugliness, human or ecological, somewhere else or at some later time. Yet we still educate them as if art, science, morality, and the long-term human future were unrelated. The relevant planning questions have to do with how we might create the resources, time, and intellectual tolerance to question the reductionism and anthropocentrism buried both in institutional operations and in the organization of our academic life.

6. The Importance of Vision. The Oberlin project was financially possible in large part because the building program and the fund-raising strategy were one and same. Since trustees, alumni, and others with any likelihood of giving to the college could not be asked for funds, we could not raise money by playing the card of institutional loyalty. Accordingly, I did not attempt to sell a building so much as a set of ideas about the human role in the natural world crystallized in the form of a building. As a fund-raising project, in other words, the right building in an ecologically constrained world and the smart building converged around a project that aimed to advance the dialogue about the relationship between architecture and pedagogy and about the human role in the natural world. But college planners, who regard themselves as utterly practical people, are often uncomfortable by anything remotely visionary. Those who have to raise funds, on the other hand, know that vision is ultimately the only thing they have to offer to prospective donors.

But there is far more at issue than self-interest narrowly defined. Most institutions began with a vision of how peoples' lives and the world might be improved. Oberlin College, for example, is a distinctive institution in large measure because its founders and early leaders were willing to risk the very existence of the college for the ideal of human equality. We have drawn on the moral capital they created ever since. In our own time it is fair to ask of any of our institutions what we are willing to risk and what moral capital we will leave behind. Many of our predecessors risked it all for human equality. That struggle continues, but it is now subsumed in a far larger struggle to ensure a habitable planet for coming generations so that all the other struggles might go on. Future generations, the presumed beneficiaries of our strategic planning, will care not a lick for how we stacked up against the conventional indicators of institutional success. They will measure us, rather, by our foresight and for what we were willing to risk on their behalf.

7. Institutional Learning. Finally, the real test for any innovation is the extent to which it changes the default settings and becomes part of the routine behavior of the institution. There is a tendency for institutions to seal off innovations rather like the body encases alien viruses. Some on my campus still regard the Environmental Studies Center as an interesting, but isolated experiment having no relation to other buildings now in the planning stage or to campus landscaping or resource management. The pedagogically challenged will see no further possibilities for rethinking the process, substance, and goals of education relative to the challenges of the 21st century. If these attitudes persist, the Environmental Studies Center will exist as an island on a campus that simply mirrors the larger culture. On the other hand, the project offers a model that might inform curriculum, architectural standards for all new construction and renovation, decisions about landscape management, financial decisions about payback times and full-cost accounting, and creative ways to engage the wider community.

	Environmental Studies Center	Typical planning
Starting Point	curriculum	architecture
Paradigm	ecological	industrial
Time Horizon	long term	short/medium
Scope of planning	large	limited
Student/community participation	encouraged	excluded
Planning structure	integrated	serial/linear
Technological innovation	high	moderate/low
Materials selection	embodied energy	initial cost
Energy accounting	yes	no
Environmental accounting	yes	no
Project accounting	least-cost/end-use	conventional
Life-cycle costs	low	high
Building obsolesence	slow	rapid
Riskiness	moderate to high	low
Planning style	collegial	adversarial

Figure 2: Planning Models Compared

Part IV

More than any other institution in modern society, colleges and universities have a moral stake in the health, beauty, and integrity of the world their students will inherit. We have an obligation to provide our students with tangible models that calibrate our highest values with our best capabilities; models that they can see, touch, and experience. We have an obligation to create grounds for hope in our students some of whom see themselves as the „X generation." But hope is different from wishful thinking so we have a corollary obligation to equip our students with the analytical skills and practical competence necessary to do the hard work ahead of reweaving the human presence in the world. When the pedagogical abstractions, words, and whole courses do not fit the way the academic campus in fact works, they learn that hope is just wishful thinking or worse, rank hypocrisy.

We have, therefore, a moral interest in making certain that campus purchasing, investments, and operations of the physical plant do not undermine the integrity, beauty, and stability of the world students will inherit. With that obligation in mind, could farsighted colleges take the lead to declare, say, a ten year goal to power themselves by a combination of greater efficiency, emerging solar technologies, and hydrogen? Why not? The limits are no longer technological or even economic, but those of imagination and commitment. Could some declare a similar goal to become zero-discharge campuses and eliminate waste in all of its forms? Again, why not? Through the imaginative use of our buying and investment power could they help the emergence of a genuinely sustainable economy in their surrounding communities? And could they incorporate such things into the curriculum in ways that cross disciplinary boundaries while having a practical effect on the world? Why not? The important planning questions have to do with how institutions of higher education might imaginatively calibrate their moral interest in the long-term future with their actual institutional behavior and do so as part of a larger effort to teach the next generation that the world is indeed rich in good possibilities.

References

Cohen, J. (1995) *How Many People Can the Earth Support*. New York: Norton.

Daily, G. (1997) *Nature's Services: Societal Dependence on Natural Ecosystems*. Washington: Island Press.

Lyle, J. (1994) *Regenerative Design for Sustainable Development*. New York: John Wiley.

Pelikan, J. (1992) *The Idea of the University*. New Haven: Yale University Press.

Science (25 July, 1997), Special issue on „Human Dominated Ecosystems"

Senge, P. (1990) The Fifth Discipline: The Art & Practice of the Learning Organization. New York: Doubleday.

Selmon, E., Schneider, S. (1997) *Energy/Environment Curriculum Enhancement: 'Real World' Projects Confronting Obstacles to Energy Efficiency Implementation in Local Institutions.* (unpublished).

Wacknernagel, M., and Rees, W (1996) *Our Ecological Footprint: Reducing Human Impact on the Earth.* Philadelphia: New Society Publishers.

World Scientists Warning to Humanity, Union of Concerned Scientists (1992).

Chapter 15

Greening Campuses: An overview of student activism and progressive administration

Scott Cole

Abstract

The following are case studies of both student-activism and progressive administrations whose goal is increasing the procurement of recycled paper on university campuses in the United States. By no means an exhaustive list, this article hopes to highlight issues that both students and administrations face in the quest to 'green' their campuses. These case studies have been collected as part of an effort by students at Duke University to convince their own administration to (1) follow their own recommendations mabe by the Paper Task Force, an Industry-Academic partnership, which summarized the availability and need to buy recycled and (2) to follow the lead of publicly-funded universities which are mandated to purchase paper with specified post-consumer content. The findings prove that there is variable success in the procurement of recycled paper.

Introduction

If environmental semantics of the 1990's were dominated by the buzzword, *sustainability*, it is likely that the future will see the rhetoric become dominated by the following phrase: „*Closing the Loop.*" Paul Hawken's book, The Ecology of Commerce, makes a distinction between *linear growth* - the rapid process of exploitation, utilization, and creation of residuals - and *cyclical growth* - where resources enter the stream of production and remain without forming large quantities of residuals. Hawken's restorative economy is one in which the loop is closed and resources are not only used more efficiently, but also continually re-used and recycled throughout the economic system. The restorative economy is based on Mother Nature's model of an ecological system where energy is derived from by-products of other organisms. Hawken describes the goal of the human economic system, „The task ... is to create an economy that lives off of current income, not capital resources," (p. 181).

Though Hawken questions "the notion that we can 'save' the environment by recycling our coke cans," (p.202) he underscores the importance of buying materials previously seen as residuals. In other words, Hawken concentrates not on what recycling can do for our local landfill, but on what it can accomplish vis-à-vis our resources. In terms of a renewable resource such as paper, this means addressing not only the production, but also the consumption of paper across industries and high-volume users. The Paper Task Force examined both of these aspects.

Why is buying recycled paper an especially important recommendation? To begin with, recycling is only environmentally effective if there is a market for the material. Because paper represents such a large percentage of the waste stream, it stands to be especially important to collectors because it represents a significant quantity of inputs for the producers of recycled paper. An in-house study of the EPA's waste stream from their 11 buildings in the Washington D.C. area showed that 39% of the solid waste discarded was paper and paper products. A 1994 estimate by the EPA states that paper represents 36% of the waste stream nationally. Prioritizing a recycling strategy suggests that paper would be an important item to scrutinize. The Paper Task Force was also designed to create such a strategy.

The Paper Task Force - a coalition made up of Duke University, Johnson & Johnson, McDonald's Corporation, NationsBank, Environmental Defense Fund, Prudential Insurance Company of America, and Time Inc. - was established in 1995. From Hawken's perspective, these economic agents were taking the first steps toward closing the loop by identifying the impacts, crafting strategies to reduce paper use and to use the resource more efficiently. Though a far cry from implementing Hawken's restorative economy, these economic interests had recognized that exploiting the paper resource in a linear pattern was not sustainable.

The recommendations of the Paper Task Force are aimed at paper purchasers in North America with an aim of "crafting a voluntary, cost-effective initiative for environmental improvement." Their final recommendations (August 1995) encompassed four main areas: source reduction, forest management, pulp and paper manufacturing, and recycling and buying recycled paper. The latter area is pertinent to this paper and will be examined through case studies on university campuses.

Examining case studies can prove useful to both reluctant universities and progressive administrations. Those universities which are (1) disinclined to switch over from traditional paper suppliers or (2) unaware or unwilling to utilize their power as consumers to wrought environmental change, can benefit from a review of their colleagues' experience. Exposing success on university campuses across the country can prove to be a powerful tool in the pocket of student activists. This is my hope with the Duke Administration who fears that making the switch prematurely may cause an unwanted financial burden or a backlash against an inferior product.

Case Studies can prove just as useful to the "leaders of the pack." Given the multitude of strategies available to 'green' your campus, it is highly likely that a school will benefit from learning additional innovative techniques. The Colleges and Universities Recycling Coalition (CURC) - a division of the National Recycling Coalition, a nonprofit organization dedicated to the advancement and improvement of recycling - has designed a mechanism to share experiences. The Campus Recycling Conferences "provide recycling professionals with an on-going source of training, peer networking and opportunities geared specifically to education needs." These conferences help them to accomplish their mission: "Facilitating information exchange between institutions of higher education regarding integrated waste management practices ... by creating linkages with our academic resources." The 1999 second annual series has included stops at Stanford University, Northeastern University, and Miami University of Ohio. (More information can be found at www.earthsystems.org/curc/curc)

PURCHASING RECYCLED PAPER: CASE STUDIES

The following case studies are in no particular order. They are designed to give an overview of the issues faced by schools that (1) wish to switch, (2) are in the transition to switching, or (3) have successfully made the switch to recycled paper.

UNIVERSITY OF COLORADO, BOULDER

Jack Debell, Director of Colorado's Recycling Services, runs "an aggressive closed-loop procurement program." Colorado has successfully made the switch to Eureka Brand Paper, which is processed by Fort James Paper Company in Oregon - the same paper company that buys their recycled paper stock. Debell is putting into practice what most academics only talk about: closing the loop with the purchase of recycled materials. In fact, due to a student "pro-cot," (A pro-active technique that demonstrates that students will only buy recycled products, rather than refusing to buy virgin) the university bookstore has devoted an entire aisle to "Green Products" which contains recycled notepads, paper, and envelopes. The bookstore carries large amounts of both the 35% PC and the 100% PC Eureka paper in order to assuage the fears of university departments who complain about the lack of availability of recycled paper.

Colorado is a stellar program because of Jack's myriad responsibilities. He sits on the University's Solid Waste Advisory Board and also helps to run the Buy Recycled Business Alliance - a group within the NRC. In addition, Jack has spoken at the Campus Recycling Conferences put on by the CURC. Last fall his talk was entitled, "Buy Recycled Toolkit Workshop."

Jack has had an obvious influence on the procurement of recycled goods, despite the fact that his job is focused on the collection of recyclables. One reason he remains credible across the university bureaucracy is that he advocates a P-Q-A approach to the purchasing of recycled alternatives: Price, Quality, and Availability. While price and availability are no-brainers for comparison shopping techniques, the issue of quality proves to be critical. "Recycled Paper products started off on the wrong foot about 10 years ago by introducing an inferior product and expecting rational people to buy it," says Jack. Therefore, Colorado depends heavily on independent testing to critique recycled alternatives. They made use of California's progressive legislation by applying the "Accepted Brands List" of paper suppliers to their purchasing options. To gain access to this list, a paper supplier must be independently tested by the State of California for such characteristics as brightness, smoothness, functionality in zero-graphic (hi-speed) copiers, thickness, and durability in dry climates (lack of humidity wreaks havoc on a paper's lifetime). Over a dozen criteria are tested before the state can declare a paper within "acceptable performance" standard.

In addition to independent testing, Jack has promoted a high-profile and pragmatic test on Colorado's campus: He solicits departments who are willing to participate in a recycled paper demonstration and anonymously places (1) a ream of virgin and (2) the brightest sample of recycled paper he can find and asks them if they can tell the difference. He said the results turn out to be surprising and are helpful in dispelling the stigma of 'dirty' recycled paper.

It is important to note that no university can practically utilize recycled paper for all of their needs (nor should they, as will be discussed below). In fact, the University of Colorado spends only 60% of their budget on recycled paper. Presumably, the virgin stock is zero-graphic paper, which is utilized in the most demanding environment: high speed, high quality copiers, which cannot tolerate dust (a common side effect of recycled paper). Dual Use paper, on the other hand, can be used in copiers or printers and is not scrutinized to the extent of zero-graphic paper. The purchasing of recycled paper tends to increase with the proportion of dual use paper utilized by a university and tends to decrease with the proportion of zero-graphic paper utilized.

STANFORD LAW SCHOOL

This private institution was able to make use of state regulations and a fortuitous pricing schedule to purchase recycled paper products. Two years ago the school hired a recycling consultant to examine the budget and discovered that recycled letterhead was cheaper than virgin. The consultant deftly made use of these savings by cross-subsidizing the purchase of recycled copy paper, which was at a premium. Prices change continuously, which prevents Stanford from simply passing this 'recipe of success' on to other schools. Nonetheless, a few lessons emerge: Research prices; be willing to sacrifice the 'bright white' look in one paper use in order to afford the premium for purchasing recycled paper for other uses; and be creative with a limited budget.

In addition, the State of California has required that court submissions be on recycled paper. This regulation has a much broader result than simply mandating public agencies to purchase and use recycled paper. In fact, second year law student Brian Shimdt, made a good point when he said, "Getting courts - especially federal courts - to require recycled submissions would be a great goal for a national campaign." It would have a domino-like effect by causing law firms, business, and 'friends of the courts' throughout the country to re-think their purchasing habits. Of course, enforcement of such a provision is likely to be awkward ("The court refuses to hear the defendant ... until he returns with the required 40% recycled paper").

UNIVERSITY OF MIAMI OF OHIO

Dick Keebler, director of procurement, has faced an all too common problem in his failed attempt to switch to recycled paper: increased cost. The departments simply cannot, or will not, pay the additional price for recycled paper when their university contract stipulates a far greater quantity of virgin paper for the same price. The University of Ohio does utilize bathroom paper products with high-post consumer content, though according to Keebler, "This has become the norm in the industry."

As mentioned above, a university should not aim to purchase recycled paper for all their paper needs. Why? The answer forms the paradox of closed-loop paper recycling. High post-consumer content paper demands large amounts of high quality virgin paper stock as input. Though this input can be recycled paper, the truth is that recycled paper can only be recycled a finite number of times (Dick Keebler estimates 3-4 cycles). Thus, closed-loop paper recycling is not literally closed - it has an input in the form of virgin paper and it has a leak in the form of recycled paper that has reached its maximum lifetime within the loop. Therefore, universities can actually justify limited use of virgin paper on environmental grounds: They are supporting the 'paper loop' by perpetuating its viability.

UNIVERSITY OF NORTH CAROLINA- CHAPEL HILL

UNC-Chapel Hill is already under contract to purchase 30% recycled paper, but is in the transition to upgrade to 50% recycled content, if student activists have their way.

UNC-CH is an example of a school that benefits from a governmental mandate to purchase paper with specified post-consumer content. UNC-CH is one of sixteen state-run schools whose purchasing is centralized into a "State Term Contract."

This contract stipulates the brand of paper (and non-paper supplies) to be purchased by state-run universities and all state agencies. While bulk orders of this magnitude have obvious financial benefits, it also presents a greater challenge to activists who wish to re-direct the inertia of historical purchasing habits (On the flip side, large challenges offer large rewards!) The Students Environmental Action Committee (SEAC) chapter at UNC-CH soon found themselves at the forefront of a movement, which quickly became larger than they had imagined. Linda Chupkowski, a sophomore activist, told me, "We (SEAC) started out as a group with an agenda of increasing recycled paper on campus. Before long, we realized that if we wanted to make progress, we were going to have to change all 16 schools in the system."

Their goal is to change the State Term contract to require 50% post-consumer content in everyday paper use and to make 100% post-consumer paper available to students, faculty, and departments who wish to use it. Currently, the state contract is required by law to spend 50% of its paper expenditures on recycled paper (defined as paper with at least 30% PC).

On top of this, Governor Hunt has signed an Executive Order (EO#8) which mandates that all North Carolina universities and state agencies spend 65% of their budget on recycled paper (Because the EO is not binding by law, the expenditures often slide back to the minimum 50% requirement). The students at UNC-CH are pushing for Gov. Hunt to follow the lead of President Clinton who signed a Federal Executive Order in June of 1998, which required that 100% of the paper budgets for federal agencies be put toward recycled paper (also defined as 30% PC). This move was intended to end the use of virgin paper in the Federal Government.

The bottom-up strategy taken by UNC-CH started with a petition-signing drive. They collected over 3,000 signatures from students who supported the purchasing of high PC content paper. They used the petition to persuade professors, alumni, department heads, and Don Sykes, the overseer of the State Term Contract. Grass roots support played a strong role by providing a foundation of support and applying pressure to decision-makers.

In leading the pack of 16 schools, UNC-CH has arranged for a conference between the student activists on other campuses, including UNC-Ashville, Appalachian State, UNC-Greensboro, UNC-Wilmington, North Carolina State University, Winsten-Salem University, and North Carolina A&T. The hope is to create linkages between schools and to bring additional pressure upon the State Term Contract. Despite its status as a private institution which lacks public (exterior) pressure to buy recycled paper, Duke was also invited to attend the conference.

One caveat of the public 'purchasing mandates' is that the sixteen state institutions are eligible to apply for government grants to cover the premium for recycled paper. In other words, the government mandates the purchasing of more expensive materials, but then provides the money - to those who apply - to cover the cost of their regulation. UNC-CH applied for and received a $13,000 grant last year, which they put toward the purchase of 30% post-consumer paper. Jeff Fischer estimated that this subsidy covers less than one cent per page, but was a financial free-fall to public institutions which private institutions cannot utilize. It is probable that if SEAC's goal of purchasing 50% PC paper is reached, UNC-CH will apply for a larger grant to cover the premium - as will the other 15 schools. It will be interesting to see whether the state will consider the availability of funds for recycled paper grants when deciding on whether to ratchet-up the regulations on paper purchasing.

SHIPPENSBURG UNIVERSITY, Pennsylvania

The Student Environmental Action Coalition members at Shippensburg University (a private institution with approximately 5400 undergraduates, 3500 graduates) are in transition and hope to bring a unique paper to their campus.

SEAC members have taken on the crusade to procure paper with high post consumer content and without the Chlorine bleaching process. NEW LIFE! Paper (80% recycled) is made by Roland Paper mill of Canada (one of only a handful of paper mills that produces chlorine-free paper) and distributed locally by Green Line Paper Co. in York, Pennsylvania. Chlorine is the traditional chemical used in the bleaching process, but recent advances in technology have made it possible to use alternatives. Chlorine forms dioxin - a known human carcinogen - and also bonds with other chemicals to form fatal compounds.
The alternatives to bleach, such as hydrogen peroxide, have only recently been utilized in large-scale operations - as is evident by the fact that only 3 mills carry alternative-bleached paper.

Like the University of Chapel Hill, the impetus for changing purchasing habits at Shippensburg has come from the students in a bottom-up strategy. However, it differs because it is derived first and foremost from a desire to switch to a non-chlorine-bleached paper. Shippensburg's SEAC members started by approaching the university president and soliciting her support before approaching individual paper users (departments) or even paper purchasers. They were inspired by the success of a local township government that had been saving money by using NEW LIFE! paper. The students at Shippensburg decided to mimic the success of this local government and, with the support of the university president, have facilitated contact between their director of procurement services and the local paper distributor. The students' hope is to bring NEW LIFE! paper under contract with the university when the current contract expires in July of 1999.

DUKE

I am a member of a student task force that hopes to make headway in changing Duke's paper purchasing habits. Currently, Duke utilizes a majority of virgin paper, with small amounts of recycled paper available at the University's Copy Center - for a premium. As mentioned in the introduction, Duke was a member of the Paper Task Force, but has only been able to live up to a few of its own recommendations for reducing paper use. I have had a chance to speak to a few key players at Duke: Paul Brummet, an author of the PTF and formerly the director of procurement services; Della Adkins, manager of the Copy Center which represents over 10% of paper consumption on campus; Jay Senerchia, the current director of procurement services; and Grahm Butler, director of Duke Recycles. These four have helped me to get a hold of the issues surrounding paper use on a campus of nearly 6,000 undergraduates and 10,000 students in all.

The Supply Network

Duke's uses two paper suppliers - Corporate Express and Xerox Paper. Duke has used Corporate Express as a convenience - low volume users can purchase their paper from the same place they buy their other office supplies; albeit with an additional handling fee. Dillard Paper Company based in Raleigh supplies the bulk of the paper and delivers it straight to the departments on demand. During Brummet's tenure, the traditional technique of buying in tremendous bulk and storing in a warehouse was eliminated. Brummet recognized that the cost saving from bulk purchasing was not covering the cost of storing the paper on campus, and therefore closed down Duke's warehouses.

The intricacies of supplier relationships are likely to play a large role in persuading Duke to change its purchasing habits. Having eliminated its warehouses, Duke is dependent upon a local distributor for its paper and therefore favors 'shopping locally.' In addition, Duke has been able to secure very low prices from suppliers based on solid long-term relationships. This poses a challenge for student activists: we must work within the framework of local suppliers to find recycled paper of acceptable quality and price.

In addition, Duke's campus is a sprawling and decentralized organism. The result is that centralized paper purchasing through a Duke contract is atypical. While Jay Senerchia, a director of procurement services, negotiates a contract for all departments, this does not stipulate a minimum volume of purchasing in order to qualify for the low price. Instead, individual departments are free to buy 'outside the contract' if they choose. Given that a new contract is in the works as of March of 1999, the student activists hope to discover exactly which departments use the most paper and to wean them off virgin and onto a recycled paper called Great White Shark.

Before Paul retired, he thought he had a solution to buying recycled. Union Camp Paper Mill, based in Franklin, Virginia, sells 35% post consumer paper called Great White Shark. It has been successfully tested on Duke copy machines, was readily available, but had failed the price test. It was initially 15% higher than comparable virgin paper, but Paul was able to talk them down to 5%. However, five percent represents a large financial loss - especially when department budgets continually shrink.

My student task force hopes to re-start this campaign and to move Duke toward the path already taken by the University of Colorado: closing the loop. Duke Recycles, directed by Grahm Butler, has continually increased its collection of recycled paper stock since its creation in 1990. They sell their paper to Paper Stock of Durham, NC, which then sells it to the Union Camp Mill in Franklin, VA, as an input to their Great White Shark recycled paper. If we can persuade Union Camp to sell their Great White Shark (likely through a local distributor) to Duke at a price comparable to the virgin that is used now ... we might have a deal.

The incentives that are stimulated by such an agreement demonstrate the logistics of 'closing the loop.' If Union Camp Mill can broker a $5 million contract (hypothetical number) with Duke, then Duke can turn around and demand that Paper Stock of Durham guarantee a higher price for our paper collections around campus. If Paper Stock refuses, it will be in Union Camp's interest to cover the increase themselves in order to facilitate their $5 million deal. Thus, while Duke may pay a slightly higher price for the recycled paper - vis-à-vis virgin paper - it is unlikely they will lose out financially because they will have price floors for their recycled paper stock collection.
Just like Stanford, Duke could deftly balance funds and cross-subsidize in the name of a greener and more sustainable campus.

Conclusions

November 15, 1998, was America Recycles Day sponsored by the Environmental Protection Agency and the Environmental Defense Fund. Their slogan was, "If you're not buying recycled, you're not recycling." Persuading university campuses across the country to contribute to the ever-expanding recycling movement is crucial to its success. This paper was designed to share the challenges and success of switching to recycled paper. Government agencies - both state and federal - have mandated the switch to recycled paper. These mandates carry over to state-run campuses across the country, but leave private institutions to make their own decisions. As is evident by Stanford Law School and the potential for success at Shippensburg University, private institutions do not preclude the switch. The students at Duke University hope to utilize the success stories of college campuses around the country and prove that buying recycled is the prudent step to take in greening our campus.

Chapter 16

Sustainable agriculture and land management in the liberal arts: A case study

Eugene B. Bakko

Abstract

St. Olaf College has embarked on a program in sustainable agriculture and natural habitat restoration on college owned farmland to enhance our learning environment and to engage in a more active environmental stewardship of the land. In addition to a 250 acre (115 hectares) campus, the college owns approximately 600 acres (270 hectares) of cultivated farmland. A sustainable agriculture project was started in 1993 on 48 acres (22 hectares). In addition, approximately 140 acres (64 hectares) have been restored to prairie, woodland or wetland over the past decade. These projects have provided unique opportunities for research, class field trips and recreational activities as well as exposing students to environmental experiences in sustainability that could not be conducted in the classroom.

Introduction

If one looks at the history of planet Earth in the context of one year, with the physical formation of the planet occurring on January 1, then first life appeared sometime during June. The dinosaurs ruled the earth during mid-December with the Rocky Mountains in America forming shortly after. Early *Homo sapiens* arrived on the scene about 10:30 p.m. on December 31 and the first agriculture was introduced at 11:59:20 PM. At 11:59:59.9 p.m. the Renaissance, with its introduction of science, started in Europe. The onslaught of industrial agriculture has therefore happened in the very last part of the last second before the present moment. Yet, the impact of this agriculture has been profound. Advanced machinery, new seed varieties and chemicals have allowed more people to be fed by fewer farmers. Wendell Berry (1977) described this in terms of reducing the ratio of eyes to acres (hectares). He stated that the care and management of agricultural systems requires an overseeing of the land that cannot be minimized below a certain point and yet remain sustainable. Ironically, most people enjoy the freedom from the land, but at the same time are becoming increasingly dependent on the expertise of others and affected by their actions.

Sustainable agriculture is a concept that arose out of concern for this development in culture and agriculture. Knowledge of the detrimental effects of soil erosion has been growing since the invention of the plow. However, it was not until Rachel Carson's Silent Spring (1962), that the general public became concerned with the potential detrimental effects of agricultural chemicals and, in turn, started to become concerned with the overall effects of industrial agriculture. Although Rachel Carson's writings were widely read, changes in mainstream agriculture were slow to come. However, increased concern in recent years has resulted in an acceleration of changes in agriculture (Bourne 1999).

"Sustainable", "alternative", "organic" and "low-input" are terms to describe agriculture that is oriented toward no exhaustion of natural resources, less pollution, and lower energy consumption - both in farming practices and in people's lives. "Sustainable" agriculture is the term that seems to be prevalent today.

Theologist Dean Freudenberger (1995) listed four elements essential for a responsible agriculture: 1) Species are preserved; 2) the health and fertility of the land is improved from generation to generation; 3) ecological integrity and justice in personal and community relationships are enhanced; and 4) agricultural technologies for the production of food and fiber are self-reliant and regenerative from generation to generation. The idea of environmentally responsible (sustainable) actions for future generations has become eminent among environmentalists and proponents of sustainable development. However, it requires a strong ethic for farmers to consider the future when their low profit margins seem to demand the movement toward factory oriented farms and their children often have little or no interest in taking over the family farm.

The dilemma described above is one that affects most living creatures on this planet in some way or another. However, aside from "agricultural" colleges and universities, most students in higher education do not have the opportunity for academic exposure to agriculture. And, in many of the agricultural universities, exposure has historically been primarily to the industrial approach of agriculture. This presents unique challenges as well as opportunities for non-agricultural institutions of higher education to accept the responsibility to provoke thought, instill knowledge, and if possible, provide opportunities for experiential learning on this controversial topic. Teaching courses is the obvious method to provide learning experiences for students. However, many colleges and universities have rural land holdings that provide opportunity for thoughtful land management decisions that can involve the academic sector of the institution. In addition, these land holdings can also provide excellent non-classroom learning experiences for students.

Over the past two decades, St. Olaf College has offered a variety of courses, some within disciplines and some interdisciplinary, focusing on societal and environmental impacts of industrial vs. sustainable agriculture. The college is also endowed with approximately 600 acres (270 hectares) of farmland adjacent to the 250 acre (115 hectares) campus. This land is rented to local farmers to provide income for the college. Within the past decade the college has embarked on a plan to convert a small portion of this farmland from conventional to sustainable agriculture involving student research. In that same time, other areas of our college farmland have been restored to natural habitats, providing opportunity for much student involvement and learning experiences. Because many educational institutions own or have access to rural land holdings, this chapter will focus on the "non-classroom" learning experiences provided on St. Olaf College land.

Sustainable Agriculture

Historically, all St. Olaf College farmland has been farmed "conventionally" using a corn-corn-soybean (C-C-S) crop rotation. Because all college farmland is cash-rented by farmers, any change in farming practices away from "conventional" methods has to be profitable for the farmer. Thus, in 1992, two Environmental Studies students (one majoring in Physics, the other in Economics) conducted a feasibility study. They interviewed the conventional farmer already renting college land and the potential sustainable farmer by collecting information from them on inputs, costs, labor time in the field, crop prices, yields, chemical use, energy consumption, etc. Their findings indicated that profit margins for a more sustainable farming system involving increased crop diversity would be comparable to that of a conventional system. They also concluded that it would reduce use of agri-chemicals and increase fossil fuel energy efficiency.

In 1993, 48 acres were converted to a five-year corn-soybeans-oats/alfalfa-alfalfa-alfalfa (C-S-O/A A-A) crop rotation. An arrangement for this was made with a local farmer who included alfalfa in his rotation and was willing to rent the parcel of land from the college. This type of rotation is thought to be more sustainable for several reasons. The use of a perennial cover-crop (alfalfa) reduces erosion rates. Alfalfa is a legume that incorporates nitrogen into the soil by the process of nitrogen fixation involving symbiotic bacteria, thus decreasing the dependence on commercial fertilizer, which is a product of fossil fuel. Finally, this rotation helps to reduce the use of commercial pesticides because the increased crop diversity provides some natural insect and weed control by interrupting the life cycles of these undesirable organisms in the corn or soybean monocultures.

Funding from the Minnesota Department of Agriculture's Energy and Sustainable Agriculture Program enabled summer field research to get started. Students worked throughout the summer for three years conducting field studies on soil erosion, soil organisms, soil organic matter and weed growth. They also obtained data from the farmers on fuel and chemical inputs, overall costs, yields, labor, and energy efficiency.

Soil erosion was calculated using the U. S. Department of Agriculture Universal Soil Loss Equation (Halsey 1980). This incorporated data from soil type, degree and length of slope, rainfall, crop planted, and the methods as well as the timing of tilling. We found that soil erosion was reduced by 60% in the sustainable (C-S-O/A-A-A) crop rotation. This was due primarily to the fact that the soil had continuous plant cover for three years out of the five-year crop rotation.

Use of commercial fertilizer and pesticides (herbicides and insecticides) was monitored for both farming operations. Total use of these chemicals was reduced by 65% in the sustainable operation. There were several reasons for this: 1) Although alfalfa required some potassium, it required no nitrogen fertilizer or pesticide during three years of the five-year crop rotation; 2) Nitrogen fertilizer input for corn was reduced because of the nitrogen "fixed" in the soil by the alfalfa and symbiotic bacteria; 3) Application of insecticide on the corn was not necessary because the corn was not grown two years in a row as it was in the conventional system.

Energy consumption was determined by comparing energy content (kcal) of fuel (gasoline and diesel) as well as of agri-chemicals (fertilizer and pesticides) consumed in each operation (Pimentel 1980). While agri-chemicals were reduced by 65% in the sustainable operation, fuel consumption for running machinery approximately doubled. This was because the sustainable farmer had to make more trips over the fields for cultivation as well as the repeated cutting and baling of alfalfa. However, total energy content of all fossil-based farm chemicals (fuel and agri-chemicals) was reduced by 20% for the sustainable operation because of reduced use of agri-chemicals.

Crop production and net income/acre were slightly higher for the sustainable crop rotation but there was no significant difference between these and the conventional system. However, time spent in farm labor was nearly three times greater for the sustainable operation. This meant that fewer acres could be farmed sustainably.

Wendell Berry (1977) defines sustainable agriculture as "supporting both the land and the people". Our study demonstrated that adding a cover-crop to the rotation increased sustainability in an environmental sense, thus being good for the land. However, market prices for commodity products will have to change before farmers can survive economically on such a diverse rotation. In America, government price support for corn is a major reason why that crop is grown so extensively. This is environmentally damaging because corn is a row crop, thus allowing for significant erosion during heavy rains. Also, current corn hybrids demand high fertilizer and herbicide inputs, and insecticides usually have to be applied when corn is grown two or more years consecutively. Thus, either a change in government policy toward more equitable support for diverse crops or a change in the marketplace where a larger diversity of crops receive better prices will have to occur before significant numbers of farmers can convert from present conventional agriculture to a more sustainable system.

This study provided our students with the opportunity to learn first-hand about two different farming operations. Not only did they collect biological data in the field, they interacted directly with the farmers to learn about the actual costs, time, and general problems that occur in this important sector of our society. While many young idealistic students may be critical of farmers who do not practice "sustainable" agriculture, this study demonstrated that the answers are not as easy as just changing farming methods. Market factors dictate the economic conditions under which farmers have to operate and these forces are generally beyond the farmer's control. Thus, it becomes much more of a societal problem that requires knowledge and intelligent decisions by the business and political sector as well as the consuming and voting public.

Natural Habitat Restoration

The expansion of agriculture over the past century has resulted in the clearing of many natural habitats, both terrestrial and aquatic. This has been especially pronounced in areas containing fertile soils. Resulting from this have been problems in soil erosion, surface water pollution from runoff, ground water pollution through seepage, as well as the reduction or elimination of native plant and animal species. As the rate of species extinction continues to increase, we are becoming more and more aware of the importance, the value and the necessity of developing a land ethic

(Leopold 1966). To do this, we need to preserve native genetic stock, help it to propagate naturally and learn how to live within the laws of nature rather than continually try to change and control her. In addition to working to preserve and protect what remains of natural ecosystems, there is a relatively new and exciting activity developing, the restoration of natural habitats.

At St. Olaf College we have been restoring natural habitats on agricultural land for the past decade. The college is located in a region that was originally occupied by a mixture of tall grass prairie, hardwood forests, shallow wetlands and lakes. In 1988 the college enrolled 22 acres (10 hectares) of farmland into the Conservation Reserve Program (CRP) administered by the U. S. Department of Agriculture. This was planted with native hardwood trees and became the first of many habitat restoration projects that have also included wetlands and prairies.

Prairies: Native prairie, particularly native tall grass prairie, has historically been one of the most diminished habitats in North America because of its fertile soils and the ease with which the land could be cleared for agriculture. Due to awareness and the resurgence of interest in this habitat, the restoration of prairies has increased substantially within the past 20 years in this part of the country where it originally occurred (Murry 1996, Shirley 1994).

To date, we have planted forty-five acres (20 hectares) of native prairie grasses and forbs since 1989. Native seed is acquired locally within a 100 mile (160 km) radius from commercial prairie restoration businesses that have started in response to public interest in this activity. We have also collected wildflower seed from native prairies in the region to start potted plants in the college greenhouse. These were subsequently transplanted to prairie sites in the spring and early summer.

Our first planting was a small two acre (0.9 hectare) prairie planted by hand. Subsequent prairie lands were planted with machinery. We typically plant 5-8 species of grasses and 20-30 species of forbs. It is best to establish as much diversity as possible with the original planting because it is more difficult to add species later, as they do not compete well once the grasses have become well established.

Woodlands: Approximately 100 acres (45 hectares) have been planted with over 25,000 tree seedlings or nursery stock trees. Most of our tree plantings have occurred on agricultural land that was taken out of production and enrolled into the CRP. Small seedlings (10 – 50 cm) were planted in these areas. Seedlings are inexpensive to purchase and can be planted efficiently, either by hand or by machine.

In addition, we have planted about 10 acres (4.5 hectares) of trees on "mowed lawn". This has been in an effort to reduce mowing and provide more natural habitat in close proximity to the campus buildings. When planting on campus lawn, we typically plant nursery stock trees that range in size from one to three meters in height. This is more costly and time-consuming but results in a small "forest look" after the first year of planting.

Wetlands: The draining of shallow wetlands has been very extensive in areas suitable for farming. This has resulted in a variety of problems including flooding, loss of ground water recharge, pollution of surface waters, the diminishing of aquatic plant and animal species, etc. To counteract this trend, the U. S. Fish and Wildlife Service has embarked on an aggressive wetland restoration program. We have taken advantage of this program and, since 1993, have restored six wetlands ranging in size from 1/4 acre (0.2 hectare) to nine acres (4 hectares) of surface water. Wetland sites that were drained years ago were identified by surveying and from maps. All restored wetlands are surrounded by other natural areas we have restored (prairie and woodland) to buffer them from agricultural and development runoff.

Actual wetland restoration was conducted by the governmental agency. This was usually done in the late summer or fall season. The restored areas filled with water during the first spring season with the snowmelt and spring rains. Wetland restoration is a relatively easy process accomplished within 1 - 3 days, sometimes in a single day, by constructing a small earthen dike or by destroying agriculture drain tiles, or by a combination of both. Because all restored sites are located in low-lying areas that once contained water, extensive digging is not necessary. The ideal depth for productive wetlands is 10 – 100 cm. Wetlands deeper than that are less beneficial because they will be too deep for emergent vegetation and waterfowl cannot feed as well.

Over 400 waterfowl have been observed on the largest wetland at one time during spring migrations. Nesting waterfowl were observed on all restored wetlands during the first spring and summer. Ten to fifteen broods of nesting ducks have been present on the wetlands each breeding season.

Educational Value

The educational value of the above projects to the St. Olaf College community has exceeded our best expectations. Agriculture experience and learning has been a large void in liberal arts education (Orr 1991). Our sustainable agriculture project provided excellent experiential learning opportunities for the students involved to become familiar with this universal problem and understand it in a way that learning in the classroom would not have achieved. They wrote extensive papers, gave presentations to faculty and fellow students as well as presenting their findings at regional science meetings. Information from these studies has been incorporated into biology and environmental classes at St. Olaf to help enlighten the larger campus community about problems and controversy concerning agriculture. These classes can actually visit the farm site conveniently. The fact that the information used to illustrate agricultural problems comes from our own campus helps to heighten student interest.

Students in our first-year general biology courses take field trips to the natural areas and are required to conduct a short-term study/observation with subsequent write-up as a partial requirement for the course. Numerous advanced field biology classes use our natural lands for field trips and independent study. In addition to Biology, other departments that have involved the natural and agricultural lands in their education include Art, Chemistry, Environmental Studies, Philosophy, Physical Education, Psychology and Religion.

We have established a student naturalist position. This person manages an environmental bulletin board, organizes student volunteers for outdoor projects such as tree plantings, writes environmental articles for student publications and gives educational field trips.

With support from the Blandin Foundation, we have established The School Nature Area Project (SNAP). Qualified administrators and teachers in SNAP educate and instruct public schools in the restoration of natural lands on school-owned property. This has grown statewide with approximately 200 public schools participating and over 2400 acres (1100 hectares) of land affected to date. SNAP uses St. Olaf College natural lands for teacher workshops to instruct and provide examples of natural land restoration. They also employ St. Olaf students to help in this endeavor.

In addition to agriculture research, there have been numerous independent student and faculty research projects conducted on the natural areas. These projects include studies on plant diversity, restoration techniques and procedures, survival and growth of tree plantings, waterfowl migrations and nesting success, animal population studies, weed control in natural areas, population genetics of duckweed, and reproductive/nesting studies on a bluebird trail of 70 nest boxes (Palahniuk and Bakko 1995).

Besides "formal learning" activities for students, maintenance work on the land requires much student involvement from which considerable learning can result. These experiences include periodic burning of prairie grasses, tree planting, trail construction and maintenance, weed documentation and control, seed gathering from other areas with subsequent propagation, etc.

Because of the established trail system, much recreation and personal enjoyment takes place on these lands as well. The trails allow people to explore the restoration projects and the agriculture project. The St. Olaf College Athletic Department hosts several cross-country running events every year using the trail system. And finally, the area provides opportunity for walking, jogging, bird watching, cross-country skiing, and general "escape" from daily routine.

Future Plans

Continued expansion of sustainable agriculture practices and natural habitat restoration will occur on most college farmland not planned for future building development. Plans are under way to establish a food composting facility to handle all college cafeteria food wastes. The organic product of this facility will be used on college land as fertilizer. Continued research and studies on a wide variety of projects will enable us to monitor these systems over long term and provide continued experiential learning opportunities for our students.

Conclusion

Colleges and universities that own or have access to rural land holdings have opportunities and options to provide experiential learning for their students. This can involve planning, decision making, observation and active projects. Work in sustainable agriculture offers unique possibilities to gain knowledge and understanding of a critically important aspect of our society that would be difficult to learn or appreciate in the more traditional classroom setting. Restoration of natural habitats offers our students opportunity for practical field experience, better understanding of the complexities of ecosystems and instills in them an appreciation for a land ethic.

References

Berry, W. (1977) *The Unsettling of America: Culture and Agriculture*. San Francisco: Sierra Club Books.

Bourne, J. (1999) Special Report: The Organic Revolution. Audubon 101: 64-70.

Carson, R. (1962) *Silent Spring*. Boston: Houghton Mifflin Company.

Freudenberger, D. (1995) *The Elements of a Responsible Agriculture: A Glimpse at Issues Facing Rural American Communities and The Shape of a Post-Petroleum Agriculture*. The Agriculture Seminar for Clergy. Univ. of Minnesota Southern Experiment Station, Waseca, MN, USA.

Halsey, C. (1980) *The Universal Soil Loss Equation and Its Use in Agriculture*. Univ. of Minnesota Agriculture Extension Service, Extension folder546.

Leopold, A. (1966) "Land Ethic" in: *A Sand County Almanac: With Essays on Conservation from Round River*. New York and Oxford: Oxford University Press.

Murry, M. F. (1996) *Prairie Restoration for Schools: A Guide to Restoration from Site Analysis to Management*. Univ. of Wisc. – Madison, Arboretum.

Orr, D. (1991) Biological diversity, agriculture, and the liberal arts. *Conservation Biology* 5: 268-270.

Palahniuk, D. and Bakko, E. (1995) Nesting activity on a box-paired trail. *Sialia* 17:3-6.

Pimentel, D. (1980) *Handbook of Energy Utilization in Agriculture*. Boca Raton, Florida: CRC Press Inc.

Shirley, S. (1994) *Restoring Tallgrass Prairie: An Illustrated Manual for Iowa and the Upper Midwest*. Iowa City, IA: U. of Iowa Press.

Acknowledgments

I wish to thank Cherie Wieber and Derek Fisher for their work on the agriculture feasibility study. I thank Jan Nicholls, Erica Wetzler and Ketil Rogn for their field research on the agriculture project. I also thank farmers Ray Larson and David Sorem for their cooperation and for taking time to share information with students. We are grateful to the Minnesota Department of Agriculture, the Blandin Foundation and the Howard Hughes Medical Institute for financial support.

Appendix 1

University and Sustainability: an African perspective

Samson Katikiti

Introduction

The role of Universities as major players in the move to attain sustainability the world over is an agreed fact. Also in Africa. Their role is especially important in developing countries where most Universities do not possess the human resources and the capacity to provide solutions to the problems of environmental degradation and economic development. However, the ability of the Universities to take this leading role is under threat due to the absence, in some cases, of qualified personnel and reduced funding for projects on sustainable development as well as lack of training of University staff on issues of sustainable development. Lack of capacity and generally low salaries has led academics to move to other sectors and - often- to other countries. This has a great impact on both the organisational capacity within the University as well as the capacity to come up with solutions, since most of the staff that leave are mainly those in senior positions at the Universities.

Dealing with a real problem

One of the major obstacles towards implementing sustainability at universities in this part of the world is a real understanding of the meaning of sustainable development. This is a very serious problem as it is difficult for both lecturers and students to start working towards something they do not even understand. Agenda 21, the blue-print document on sustainable development, is not readily available to either students or teaching staff. This is a pity since a basic step such as acquiring such a document may open up various possibilities for real work.

Despite their constraints, the quality of students and lecturers within most African universities is good enough to enable them to perform concrete work towards sustainable development. There is, however, a need for the training and encouragement of many of the present lecturers to understand what sustainable development is, and to appreciate how it applies in their field of specialisation. This is especially important when it is considered that local people should aim at the solution of local problems. Although there is a lot of information which can be accessed using modern communication systems like the internet, such facilities are not available for use by most of the members of the African university community. Access to both internet and e-mail facilities has been very low. Those who do have access to the facilities generally need more knowledge of how best to use them so as to gain maximum benefit from them. Things like newsgroups, discussion groups and information networks on some of the most important web sites are necessary since, in most cases, time for use of computers is limited.

Most of the lecturers at the Universities offer consultancy services to many companies and organisations. Whilst these are of great importance, I have a feeling that these solution-based approaches to sustainable development only result in short-term benefits as opposed to the long-term benefits of real fact finding. This culture of short-term solutions is bound to trickle down to the students and finally end up as a culture within the universities. Although this is understood on the grounds of lecturers supplementing their incomes, it has huge detrimental effects on the outputs from the universities in the long run. This culture results in a lack of an integrated approach to problem solving.

As things stand in most African universities, there are clear-cut boundaries between most departments, with many departments operating independently of the others and only cooperating on logistical issues. Due to the exodus of lecturers, there is a large increase in part-time lecturers and -similarly- some full-time lecturers acting as part-time lecturers due to many external (i.e. out of the university) assignments. In cases like this, it is highly unlikely or more or less impossible for lecturers to come up with initiatives for working with other departments on collaborative education and research programs. Most of the cases in which there is collaborative research among departments involve courses which are inevitable in the recipient department. The challenge then is to come up with collaborative research and teaching programs and especially in the case of programs related to sustainable development.

The prime role of universities in society is becoming increasingly important, especially in developing countries where there is a greater challenge involved in fostering economic needs whilst ensuring environmental protection. In order to fulfill this responsibility, there is a need for better funding of universities to carry out projects and programs which help solve the challenges of society. In most cases in developing countries however, the funds received by each university are very limited. Most of the work done by university staff as consultancy work is personal work and not for the benefit of the community. Since this is most of the work they do, it reduces their role of providing information to their students (or the public) and their ability to raise the awareness of the public on environmental issues. Taking into account the fact that they get their income from projects they do for these companies, it becomes increasingly difficult for them to criticise the hand that feeds them.

A result of this state of affairs is that a significant amount of the work meant for professionals and qualified staff is done by students. Most of these initiatives are only presented to the members of the University community during final presentations on completion of a course. Since students come and go, there is then little effort to publish the often valuable results of such works for the whole community. There is also a slower response to the promotion of networks of experts on the national or regional level and this is due to lack of funding for these networks.

At the University of Zimbabwe, there is the Institute of Environmental Studies whose mission is to contribute to the development and sustained well-being of the people of Zimbabwe and

Southern Africa through education, research, information and consultancy services on the environment. The Institute was established in 1994 as an independent unit within the University of Zimbabwe in response to national concerns about the ecological, social and economic consequences of environmental change. It operates as a partnership between Departments within the University of Zimbabwe and other institutions. Its chief role, though, is as a facilitator, as a front door to harnessing the wide range of resources available throughout the University. The main objectives of the Institute are:

- to improve the scientific basis for the management of urban and rural environments in Southern Africa;

- to strengthen the capacities of the institutions to tackle national, regional and global problems and plan and implement environmentally sustainable development policies, programs and activities;

- to contribute to policy development so as to ensure sound use and management of the environment.

The Institute also aims to contribute to better informed and more effective public participation in decision-making on environmental and sustainable development issues, to improve communication among scientists, and to foster inter-disciplinary collaboration.

This is a positive move towards raising awareness on sustainable development both within the university and in the country. Its role of fostering inter-disciplinary collaboration within the University community is a positive step in the direction of enhancing the role of universities in coming out with better solutions to sustainable development issues. But this can only be achieved by fostering cooperation between the university (as one body) and the community (as another). Such an integration has yet to be achieved.

The way ahead

Due to the global effects of environmental problems, there is increased cooperation among nations and institutions of Higher Education in finding lasting solutions. The Southern African Network for Training on the Environment, whose mission is to enhance natural resources management and environmental protection through co-ordinated training programs in Southern Africa, is an example of how such cooperation may be achieved.

Formed in 1995, this network aims to bring together universities and other institutions in the Southern African region in a program on environmental training. It also has an initiative to improve training courses on the environment and natural resource protection, and to support efforts towards sustainable development. The network comprises individuals drawn from a host of institutions in southern Africa. It was initiated largely by persons in the earth sciences dealing with remote sensing, geographical information systems and the "brown" environmental issues (pollution and waste management). It was created in a manner that allows additional sub-groupings to form, so the issues covered expanded into the "green" environmental issues and now include many other disciplines(e.g natural resource management, land use and water management).

The network now has about 200 members in about a dozen projects. Each project is aiming to establish a short course program which is founded on cost-recovery and sustainable principles. The materials for the training workshops are being produced by network groups. The networks organise a number of training courses for their members in the area of management, cost recovery principles, market survey and information management. A highly successful course on Environmental Impact Assessment has been launched by one of the network members, based on the lessons learnt in the network.

In a region where there is a chronic lack of resources, but abundant manpower, networking may provide a solution for the problems outlined in this chapter, combining the use of resources, sharing them and trying to address needs that would otherwise remain untackled.

Conclusions

The main problems of funding and exodus of staff are still the key problems affecting institutions in Southern Africa and in Zimbabwe, in particular. This does not only affect the quality of staff within the university but it also deters continuity. Although these problems occur, the universities still remain the most important partners in the move towards establishing sustainable development. All that is needed is, in addition to a lot of good will to deal with the day-to-day constraints, general acceptance of the need to raise awareness within the university community on the issues of sustainable development as well as the need for training in this area.

Consulted Literature

AAU (1997) *Declaration and Action Plan on Higher Education in Africa* (Dakar, Senegal, 1-4 April 1997).

Institute of Environmental Studies(University of Zimbabwe) and Southern African Network for Training on the Environment. *Fact Sheets* (1997).

International Association of Universities (1998) Kyoto Declaration. IAU: Paris.

UNESCO (1997) *Transdisciplinary Project "Educating for a Sustainable Future"*. International Conference on "Environment and Society: Education and Public Awareness for Sustainability" (Thessaloniki, 8-12 December 1997).

UNESCO (1998) *Thematic Debate: Preparing for a Sustainable Future: Higher Education and Sustainable Human Development* (UNESCO World Conference on Higher Education, Paris 1998).

Appendix 2

The Need for Student Inputs: oikos - International Student Organization for Sustainable Economics and Management

Alexander Barkawi

Introduction

The NGO oikos was founded in 1987 at the University of St. Gallen, Switzerland. In that year, a core group of doctoral students had joined forces to promote the integration of environmental aspects into Management and Economics. Convinced that long-term economic success is closely related to ecological responsibility, they embarked on a journey to merge ecological and economic interests. By establishing oikos as a local student organisation they hoped to make a lasting contribution towards achieving this goal. They also aimed to lay a strong foundation for future students to target this objective and to build on the achievements of their predecessors.

Activities

'oikos' is the greek root syllable of the words ecology and economy. In choosing this name, the founders emphasized their conviction that these domains belong together. They stressed a firm belief that only a constructive and open-minded dialogue could bring about the cooperative spirit needed for innovative solutions. Students were predestinate to offer a platform for this dialogue, and oikos took its chance. In 1988, the group organised its first conference, bringing together 150 participants from business, academia, politics and NGOs to discuss the integration of environmental concerns into economic thinking. The outcome surpassed the group's highest expectations. On the last conference day, various business representatives declared their interest in creating a Swiss network of companies to promote environmental awareness within the economy. It only took them a couple of months to round up support of 50 other executives and to establish the Swiss Association for Environmentally Conscious Management. Ten years later, more than 300 companies had joined them.

The success of the first oikos conference motivated the group to organize a second convention in 1989. And again, their efforts lead to concrete results by bringing together five companies to establish the oikos Foundation. This institution was set up to finance research and, eventually, to fund the start-up phase of a fully operational research institute in the field of ecology and economy. Since its establishment the oikos Foundation has channeled more than one million Swiss Francs into research projects in the field of environmental economics and management. The bulk of this sum went to the Institute for Economy and the Environment which was established at the University of St. Gallen in 1993. Today, this institute is home base to 22 researchers.

Within two years after its establishment, oikos had set up a business association for environmental management, a foundation to finance research in this field and, thus, the seeds for a new university institute for economy and environment. The oikos students knew that they were on the right track and they continued to follow it. They equally knew that there was still a long way ahead of them to reach their objective. During the following years, oikos organized a yearly conference, workshops, panel discussions, simulation games, and other events to give insights into environmental challenges and ways to face them. They integrated ecological considerations into lectures on Marketing, Human Resources, International Trade and other subjects. They offered workshops on Environmental Consulting, Eco-Banking, Sustainable Tourism, and other fields of industry. And in 1997, they departed for new waters and started doing all this on an international scale.

In that year, the group's tenth anniversary had given reason to reflect on past achievements and future ambitions. Its track record was motivating. More than a hundred students had been active in the group, more than a thousand participants had taken part in its events, and an uncountable number of persons had learnt about oikos activities from the press and its publications. Why should it not be possible to reach these milestones in other countries? Globalisation was bringing along great potentials to target oikos objectives not only at the University of St. Gallen, but at faculties for Management and Economics throughout the world. Building up an international network of students to promote environmental issues within teaching and research was a striking vision. Knowing that such a network would eventually create a worldwide network of oikos alumni only increased excitement about it.

In January 1998, a core group of two people started working full-time on the establishment of further oikos groups and the founding of a new umbrella organisation, oikos International. Within twelve months, they had established further oikos locations in Germany, Austria, Sweden and the Czech Republic. In December 1998, representatives of all local groups came together at the University of St. Gallen and officially founded oikos International.

The founding conference of oikos International was attended by 60 students from 15 European countries. They had come to St. Gallen to work out an agenda for the integration of sustainability issues into economics and management. For the past decades this integration has taken place mostly outside mainstream departments, journals and classes. Ecological and social issues are - if at all - addressed in a world of their own; in a world of specialised institutes, supplementary courses and niche journals. It is time to change this. Today, we need to target full integration of sustainability issues into mainstream curricula of Management and Economics. If we want to move the economy towards sustainability, we have to change the way we are being prepared and educated for our future work. We must be aware of the ecological and social challenges we are facing. We must be aware of the huge opportunities which exist to meet these challenges. And we have to make academics aware that we require their support, regardless of whether they focus their activities on accounting, human resources, public finance or other subjects. Sustainable development must stand as a vision for all of us.

The founding conference of oikos International was a starting point to achieve this goal. Its participants defined important sustainability objectives, strategies and actors of change with regard to six different subjects: innovation and entrepreneurship, accounting and controlling, human resources, marketing, public finance, and international trade. They discussed major arguments why the chosen objectives are important, why the selected strategies are realistic, why the specified actors of change are influential, and thus, why we should seek to integrate these issues into teaching and research on a worldwide scale.

With regard to sustainability objectives, the participants aimed to operationalize the Brundtland definition of sustainable development to reach concrete ecological and social targets with regard to the subject in question. Incorporating the social dimension of sustainability into this task was a major concern of the event. For a long time, social aspects of sustainable development were mostly referred to in prefaces and introductions as well as overall sustainability guidelines. The more concrete research and teaching became with regard to these guidelines, the less they included social needs. In view of 18 million unemployed fellow Europeans, fragile pension systems and rising economic inequities, oikos wanted to reinforce a holistic approach to sustainability. A sustainable Europe will not come true without jobs, functioning care for the elder generation, and overall social peace. A sustainable Europe will only come true if we aim for social and ecological objectives at the same time. Thus, lectures in innovation need to address the issue of job creation, textbooks in accounting must consider the need for social and ecological measures, professors for Human Resources need to think about happiness at the workplace, Marketing students should discuss the creation of unsustainable needs through advertisements, Public Finance courses should point out the necessity to maintain basic public services, and International Trade researchers should give some thought to reaching a more equitable distribution of the gains from world trade.

Targeting these objectives requires realistic strategies and concrete action. During the conference, participants discussed the most promising ones. They searched for arguments why researchers, teachers and students need to integrate these strategies into their academic activities, to analyze various ways for their implementation and to take leadership to enact them. Enforcing global environmental standards, integrating ecological costs into transportation prices, reforming the tax system, including social aspects in financial statements, and creating new lifestyles were among the issues that were identified in this context.

To enact these strategies, winning over actors of change is crucial. The conference therefore emphasized the need for knowledge about objectives and internal mechanisms of key institutions. Participants defined the most important organisations for which we must develop a better understanding, if we want to forge the alliances we need for a sustainable future. If we want to move the economy towards the guiding principles of sustainable development, we must understand the inner workings of the World Trade Organization (WTO), the International Monetary Fund (IMF), the World Bank, the Federal Accounting and Standards Board (FASB), and many other institutions. We must also develop an understanding for abilities and constraints of various managerial roles. Can CEOs turn a company around towards sustainability? What are their personal traits, if they can? What are the roles of environmental managers? Do they have an impact if they are located outside the business lines?

These and other issues are part of an agenda that oikos will seek to bring to faculties for Economics and Management on a worldwide scale. Upon leaving the founding conference, some of the participants were already convinced that they wanted to join forces with oikos to achieve this goal. They pledged to establish a local oikos group at their university and thereby build up a strong institutional foundation to integrate sustainability issues into their faculty. Building up an oikos group is easy. All one has to do is to bring together three enthusiastic and motivated students who want to make an impact at their university. The rest will come by itself. Writing down statutes, organising first events, putting together a circle of sponsors, getting an office, and establishing an advisory council are easy tasks, if the spirit is right, if the core group wants to make an impact.

The Executive Board of oikos International is there to support them making this difference. Support is given by working together with local promoters in the start-up phase, permanently providing the groups with organizational know-how, organizing skill seminars, helping them to establish contacts with key decision-makers in their country, providing them with PR-material as well as coordinating common projects, communication and encounters between local chapters. oikos International is also responsible for sustaining an international network of oikos alumni. With the oikos Manual the group has published a booklet that aims to give useful hints for founding an oikos group, organizing oikos activities and sustaining the professional platform that makes these activities possible. Members of the Executive Board visit local oikos groups at their university and support them on the spot. They also organize an annual meeting of all local oikos chapters and other interested students. This forum gives oikos the opportunity to come together each year, evaluate success of the past and define priorities for the future. It is a constant point of reflection within a long process that seeks to push Economics and Management towards the guidelines of sustainability; a process that gives students the tools they need to build the world they want.

About the authors

Reflecting the diversity of higher eduction institutions and the range of actors which play a key role in university life, this book contains inputs from senior researchers, professors, members of staff and students, as well as NGOs working on the topic. The rationale behind this approach, especially in terms of inputs from students, is the need to involve more and more of them, since these future professionals will be well placed -and hopefully motivated- to bring about elements of sustainability as part of their new activities and as part of their careers. A short description of the authors follows.

Aaron S. Allen received his B.Sc. (Ecological Studies) and B.A. (Music History) degrees from Tulane University in New Orleans, LA, in 1999. He served as the president Tulane's student environmental service and education organisation, the Green Club, for three years. Aaron has been recognised for his on-campus achievements at Tulane with his selection on the All-USA College Academic Team, and he is a two-time recipient of the Morris K. Udall Award for National Environmental Excellence.

Contact:
Aaron Allen
Environmental Studies Program
201 Alcee Fortier Hall
Tulane University
New Orleans, LA 70118
USA
e-mail: greenclb@mailhost.tcs.tulane.edu

Alberto Arenas is a Ph.D. candidate from the Graduate School of Education at the University of California, Berkeley, specialising in environmental education and sustainable development. He has done extensive research in the United States and Colombia in the area of school-based enterprises with a social and ecological focus. He currently teaches organic agriculture to students of different ages.

Contact:
Alberto Arenas
Social and Cultural Studies
Graduate School of Education
4501 Tolman Hall
University of California, Berkeley
USA
e-mail: arenas@socrates.berkeley.edu

Alexander Barkawi is a doctoral student at the University of St. Gallen, Switzerland, and President of oikos International. Before joining the founding team of oikos International in 1998 he had worked for the local oikos chapter in St. Gallen for five years.

Contact:
　　Alexander Barkawi
　　oikos International
　　Bodanstr. 2, 9000 St. Gallen
　　Switzerland
　　e-mail: barkawi@oikosinternational.org

Prof. **Steve Breyman**, a political scientist, teaches Environmental Atudies and International Relations in the Department of Science and Technology Studies at Rensselaer Polytechnic Institute in Troy, New York, where he is Director of the Ecological Economics, Values and Policy program. He is on the Executive Committee of the Board of Directors of Environmental Advocates, and is Secretary of the Governing Board of Common Cause/New York. Breyman is author of Why Movements Matter: The West German Peace Movement and the End of the Cold War (State University of New York Press, 1999).

Contact:
　　Prof. Steve Breyman, Ph.D.
　　Department of STS
　　Rensselaer
　　Troy, NY 12180-3590
　　USA
　　e-mail: breyms@rpi.edu

Wynn Calder is Coordinator of outreach and membership at ULSF and CRLE, editor of the ULSF publication, The Declaration, and currently coordinating ULSF's Higher Education Sustainabiliy Indicators Project. Prior to this, Mr. Calder studied and worked at Harvard University in Cambridge, Massachusetts, USA. He has been a teacher of history and philosophy at Milton Academy in Milton, Massachusetts. He was also a mental health specialist and researcher in adolescent psychology at McLean Hospital near Boston. Mr. Calder has edited articles on adolescent psychology and a textbook.

Contact:
　　Wynn Calder
　　ULSF
　　2100 L Street, NW
　　Washington, DC 20037
　　USA
　　e-mail: wynncalder@aol.com

Scott Cole is a senior at Duke University majoring in Environmental Science and Policy, with a minor in Economics. Mr. Cole attended the University of Tasmania, for a Semester where he studied the environmental politics of that region of Australia. He will soon take a position as Research Analyst with Industrial Economics Incorporated of Cambridge, Massachusetts where he shall look at reviews of „Natural Resource Damage Assessments" upon public land.

Contact:
Scott Cole
Duke University
PO Box 96903
Durham, NC 27708
USA
e-mail: sgc2@acpub.duke.edu

Dr. **Richard Clugston** is Executive Director of the Association of University Leaders for a Sustainable Future (ULSF) and the Center for Respect of Life and Environment (CRLE), based in Washington, DC, USA, as well as publisher and editor of Earth Ethics. Prior to this he was a faculty member with the College of Human Ecology at the University of Minnesota, and later a strategic planner in Academic Affairs, Continuing Education and the Office of the President. Dr. Clugston has taught and published on human development, strategic planning, educational reform, and most recently on environmental ethics, spirituality and sustainability.

Contact:
Richard M. Clugston, Ph.D.
ULSF
2100 L St., NW
Washington, DC 20037
USA
e-mail: rmclugston@aol.com

Dr. **Andy Davey** and Dr. **Graham Earl** were, when writing their chapters, members of the Centre for Environmental Strategy (CES), University of Surrey, registered on the Brunel University/University of Surrey Engineering Doctorate programme in Environmental Technology. **Professor Roland Clift** is Professor of Environmental Technology, the Founding Director of CES and was previously Head of the Department of Chemical and Process Engineering at the University of Surrey. He is a member of the Royal Commission on Environmental Pollution, of the UK Ecolabelling Board, of the Technical Opportunities Panel of EPSRC, of the SETAC-Europe LCA Steering Committee, and of the "Groupe des Sages" which advises DGXI of the European Commission on the application of LCA to Ecolabelling. He has published extensively in the fields of powder technology, life-cycle assessment and industrial ecology.

Contact:
Professor Roland Clift, Ph.D.
Director Centre for Environmental Strategy
Centre for Environmental Strategy
School of Engineering in the Environment
University of Surrey
Guildford
Surrey GU2 5XH
UK
e-mail: R.Clift@surrey.ac.uk

Nan Jenks-Jay is the Director of Environmental Affairs & Planning at Middlebury College, in Vermont (USA). This is a senior administrative position, where the vision for the College regarding one of four areas that the President and Trustees of the College have designated as "peaks of excellence", is created. The environmental peak, which is one of the four peaks of excellence, includes both the academic program and the sustainabile campus and development initiative. In addition to teaching a number of courses, Nan´s responsibilities entail the design and development of the leadership required to support the environment peak of excellence.

Contact
Nan Jenks-Jay
Director
Environmental Affairs & Planning
Middlebury College
Farrell House
Middlebury VT 05753
USA
e-mail: nan.jenks-jay@middlebury.edu

Samson Katikiti is a third year engineering student at the University of Zimbabwe. He is a member of the Global Organisation of Students for Environmental Action, the Students for Environmental Action (Zimbabwe), the Unitwin Student Network (an international organisation working on the role of students in the various university structures) and editor of the newsletters issued by the Institute of Environmental Studies and the SANTREN. He took part on the thematic debate on sustainable development at the UNESCO´s World Conference on Higher Education.

Contact:
5 Abel Road, Athlone
Greendale
Harare
Zimbabwe
e-mail: katikiti@compcentre.uz.ac.zw

Hanno Lans, is an environmental sociology student involved in LHUMP, the Dutch member organisation of the Global Organisation of Students for Environmental Action. He is working at present on a project to green marketing education at SME, Institute for Environmental Communication.

Contact:
SME MilieuAdviseurs
Postbus 13030, 3507 LA Utrecht
The Netherlands
e-mail: sme@sme.nl

Prof. **Walter Leal Filho** coordinates various European projects on environmental communication and teaches environmental communication and education issues at universities in Europe, Africa and Asia. He is the editor of the journal "Environmental Management and Health", the "European Environmental Education Newsletter" and the series "Environmental Education, Communication and Sustainability", with publications in English and German. He has published over 20 books and in excess of one hundred scientific papers, conference papers and articles dealing with environmental education, communication and sustainable development issues.

Contact:
Prof. Walter Leal Filho, Ph.D., DSc.
TUHH/TU-TECH
Environmental Technology
Schellerdamm 4, D-21079, Hamburg
Germany
e-mail: leal@tu-harburg.de

Dr. **Andreas Megerle** works at the Chair of Applied Geography at the university of Tuebingen (Germany). He teaches different spatial planning issues. His publications and projects focus on themes such as nature conservation, environmental planning and sustainable tourism planning.

Contact:
Dr. Andreas Megerle
Applied Geography, university of Tuebingen
Hoelderlinstrasse 12
D-72074 Tuebingen
e-mail: Andreas.Megerle@uni-tuebingen.de

Heidi Megerle studied Geography, Geology and Botanics at the universities of Tuebingen and Aix-en-Provence (France). Today she is working as a freelancer in the fields of environmental impact assessments, sustainable development and sustainable tourism.

Contact:
   Heidi Megerle
   Silcherstr. 3
   D-72667 Schlaitdorf
   e-mail: Megerle.Schlaitdorf@t-online.de; Heidi.Megerle@uni-tuebingen.de

Dr.ir Karel F. Mulder is a member of the section Technology Assessment of the Faculty of Technology, Policy and Management. Since 1994, he presides the Department of Technology & Society of the Dutch Royal Society of Engineers (KIvI). Since September 1998, he has been the leader of the DUT project Educating Engineers for Sustainable Development.

Contact:
   Dr.ir. Karel F.Mulder
   Delft University of Technology
   Faculty of Technology & Society
   De Vries van Heystplantsoen 2
   NL 2628 RZ Delft
   The Netherlands
   e-mail: mulder@wtm.tudelft.nl

Prof. David Orr is currently Professor and chair of the Environmental Studies Programme at Oberlin College. He is perhaps best known as an environmental educator and for his pioneering work on environmental literacy and campus ecology. His present work is focused on ecological design. During the past three years he spearheaded the effort to design and build a $7 million environmental Studies Center at Oberlin College. He is the author of Earth in Mind (1994) and Ecological Literacy (1992) and over 100 published articles.

Contact:
   Prof. David Orr, Ph.D.
   Environmental Studies Program
   Oberlin College
   10 N. Professor Street, Rice Hall
   Oberlin, OH 44074
   USA
   e-mail: David.Orr@oberlin.edu

Jacob Park is a Washington D.C.-based policy analyst who specializes in environmental business and political issues in Japan and the Asia-Pacific region. His recent publications include "Governing US Climate Change Policy: From Scientific Obscurity to Foreign Policy Prominence" in Paul Harris (ed), Environmental Change and US Foreign Policy (Forthcoming), "Globalization and Environment: Political Economy of Natural Resources in Indonesia" in Dimitris Stevis and Valerie Assetto (eds), Political Economy of the Global Environment (Lynne Riener, 2000) and "Politics and Business of Sustainable Development in Japan", Working Paper Series (1999), JIMT Program - IC2 Institute, University of Texas, Austin, among others.

Contact:
Jacob Park
1616 16th St. NW Apt: 306
Washington DC 20009
USA
e-mail: jpark@bss2.umd.edu

Prof. **Jacques Roturier** is based at the Nuclear Physics Laboratory at the University of Bordeaux 1 (France) where his teaching activity is mainly devoted to giving lectures on Energy Efficiency studies. He also leads the R-D Energy Efficiency group. In that field, he has held the chairmanship of several EC (DG-XVII) working groups.

Contact:
Prof. Jacques Roturier, Ph.D.
CENBG-IN2P3
Université Bordeaux 1
BP 120 - 33175
GRADIGNAN-Cedex
France
e-mail: roturier@cenbg.in2p3.fr

Ted Tschang is a research associate at the United Nations University's Institute of Advanced Studies in Tokyo. He completed his doctorate in Public Policy and Management from Carnegie Mellon University, with particular reference to industry ecology. His research has focused on the analysis of trends in virtual education, applications of knowledge management to development, sustainable development in China, and industrial ecology. He recently co-edited a manuscript on new trends in information technology and the emergence of virtual universities.

Contact:
Ted Tschang
United Nations University/Institute of Advanced Studies
53-67 Jingumae, 5-Chome
Shibuya-ku
Tokyo 150
Japan
e-mail: tschang@ias.unu.edu

Prof. **Robert Whyte** is the Director of Environmental Programs for the Associated Colleges of the South in Atlanta, Georgia (USA), where he directs collaborative and interdisciplinary environmental activities and programs among the 15 member colleges and universities. He is also adjunct faculty for selected ACS schools teaching environmentally related courses. He has an earned doctorate in Botany and has worked for several natural resource management agencies on the local, state and federal levels. In addition to promoting sustainability and environmental citizenship, related research and management interests include wetland and lake management and water resource issues, with a particular interest in the Laurentian Great Lakes of North America.

Contact:

Prof. Robert S. Whyte, Ph.D.
Director of Environmental Programs
Associated Colleges of the South.
1975 Century Blvd., NE Suite 10
Atlanta, GA 30345
E-mail: rswhyte@acs.colleges.org

Thematic index

Academic planning (Chapter 5, 7, 9, 12, 14, 15)

Africa (Appendix 1)

Agenda 21 (Chapters 1, 10)

Association of European Universities (Chapters 1, 3)

Case studies (Chapters 3, 4, 5, 6, 8, 9, 10)

Copernicus (Chapters 1, 3, 8)

Environmental management (Chapters 5, 7, 8, 15, 16)

Ethics (Chapters 2, 6, 9)

European trends (Chapters 1, 8)

France (Chapters 1, 8)

Germany (Chapters 1, 10)

Guidance (Chapters 2, 3, 6, 10, 12)

Information exchange (Chapter 1, 2, 7, 9, 10, 11, 2, 13, 15, Appendix 2)

Institutional committment (Chapters 1, 2, 3, 5, 6, 7, 9, 13, 14, Appendix 1)

Leardership (Chapters 2, 3)

Netherlands (Chapters 1, 13)

North America (Chapters 2, 5, 6, 7, 9, 12, 14, 15, 16)

Oikos (Appendix 2)

Participation (Chapters 1, 2, 3, 4, 5, 6, 7, 10, 12, 13, 14, 15, 16, Appendix 2)

Policies (Chapters 1, 2, 3, 4, 5, 6, 9, 11, 12, 15)

Stakeholders (Chapter 3)

Umweltbildung, Umweltkommunikation und Nachhaltigkeit
Environmental Education, Communication and Sustainability

Herausgegeben von/Edited by Walter Leal Filho